SOUTH AFRICA'S CONSTITUTION AND THE LAW OF THE TOWNSHIP

Law, Justice and Society in Africa

ISSN 3050-2829 (Print)
ISSN 3050-2837 (Online)

This new series welcomes interdisciplinary monographs and edited collections that rethink conventional approaches to contemporary legal issues in Africa. Innovative and scholarly books that challenge Eurocentric normative assumptions in the fields of law and society and socio-legal studies are of particular interest. Topics might include African-centred critical approaches to constitutionalism, property law, legal theory, law and humanities, human rights, transitional justice, environmental law, or law and development.

Series Editors

Professor Ambreena Manji, Professor of Land Law and Development and Africa Dean at Cardiff University, ManjiA1@cardiff.ac.uk

Professor Joel M. Modiri, Associate Professor and Head of the Department of Jurisprudence at the University of Pretoria, joel.modiri@up.ac.za

Preliminary enquiries and proposals from prospective authors are welcome. Please contact the Series Editors with an outline or download the proposal form at www.jamescurrey.com.

Previous Volumes

Transformative Constitutionalism and Kenya: Law-making, Political Process, and the State (2010–2025), Guatam Bhatia

SOUTH AFRICA'S CONSTITUTION AND THE LAW OF THE TOWNSHIP

LOOTING FROM BELOW

David Dickinson

James Currey

First published 2025

James Currey

ISBN 978-1-84701-426-9

James Currey
is an imprint of
Boydell & Brewer Ltd
PO Box 9, Woodbridge
Suffolk IP12 3DF (GB)
www.jamescurrey.com
and of
Boydell & Brewer Inc.
668 Mt Hope Avenue
Rochester, NY 14620-2731 (US)
www.boydellandbrewer.com

Our Authorised Representative for product safety in the EU is Easy Access System Europe – Mustamäe tee 50, 10621 Tallinn, Estonia, *gpsr.requests@easproject.com*

British Library Cataloguing in Publication Data

A CIP record for this book is available from the British Library

CONTENTS

PREFACE

THIS BOOK draws on my long-term involvement with South African townships. Townships are from the perspective of the suburb, which I use as shorthand for the wealthiest fraction of the country's population, the "other" South Africa. Getting to know the lives of township residents has meant crossing boundaries. I am not alone in crossing from suburb to township, but, tellingly in a deeply divided country, we are few.

I started to visit townships after arriving in South Africa in January 1994. I wanted to know what life was like for people there. Curiosity is an important academic attribute, and without it I would not have collected much of the material in this book. But it does not explain why my engagement with townships now stretches to decades. This has been sustained not only by curiosity, but also by political belief and moral conviction, and because the township has become a home and people within it friends.

The book only partially answers what life is like in townships. The *menyetla* or opportunities described and analysed are only one facet of township life, but an important one. It illustrates the *lex lokasi*, or law of the township, that is the book's focus. It is, however, an uncomfortable topic to be delving into; mud raking in the lives of township residents, most of whom are poor. Reviewers of the manuscript have stressed the need for contextualisation. Paraphrasing, their concern is that describing how people hustle to make ends meet creates a picture of township residents as law breakers. In turn, this produces a racialised narrative that obscures the larger framework of South Africa's structural violence, historical and current. The comment is valid. However, read in its entirety, the book provides appropriate context, without blurring the analytical lens of *menyetla* used to develop the socio-legal, and political, arguments presented.

The best way to find out what it is like to live in a township is to live in a township. This I have done in a fragmented way alongside another, far more privileged, life in the suburb. The book draws on my long-term involvement in two South African townships: Katlehong, southeast of Johannesburg in the Gauteng metropolis, and Mashaeng, in the rural Eastern Free State. The bulk of the material presented is drawn from visits to Katlehong that began in 1997. This is, however, supplemented by my part-time residency in Mashaeng since 2007; Sehlajaneng, in Qwaqwa, where I lived for six months in 2016;

and other townships, informal settlements, and farm villages visited for one reason or another.

As I describe later, it is not possible to clearly separate my research in the township from my presence in the township. Consequently, over the years many friends and acquaintances in Katlehong, Mashaeng, Sehlajaneng, and elsewhere have contributed directly and indirectly to this book. They know who they are, and I thank them. Thanks also to Jon Klaaren and Jared McDonald, who looked and commented on early outlines of the book, as well as anonymous readers of the manuscript. Finally, a shout out to *GroundUp,* the South African not-for-profit news agency that uniquely provides extensive and reliable coverage of township life.

David Dickinson
Johannesburg
April 2025

ABBREVIATIONS

ANC:	African National Congress
ATM:	Automatic Telling Machine
BLA:	Black Local Authority
CBD:	Central Business District
CEO:	Chief Executive Officer
COVID-19:	COronaVIrus Disease of 2019
CPF:	Community Policing Forum
DEPACU:	Democratic Postal and Communications Union
DNA:	Department of Native Affairs
DTI:	Department of Trade and Industry
ESTA:	Extension of Security of Tenure Act 62 of 1997
FWA:	Fraud, Waste, and Abuse
GDP:	Gross Domestic Product
GEMS:	Government Employees Medical Scheme
ICU:	Intensive Care Unit
ID:	Identity (book/card)
IDP:	Integrated Development Plan
LHR:	Lawyers for Human Rights
LED:	Local Economic Development
MEDiPOS:	A medical aid scheme for SAPO employees
MCP:	Mail Collection Point
NGO:	Non-Governmental Organisation
NSB:	National Sorghum Breweries
NSFAS:	National Student Financial Aid Scheme
PAC:	Pan African Congress
PRASA:	Passenger Rail Authority of South Africa
PWV:	Pretoria, Witwatersrand, and Vaal (now Gauteng)

RDP:	Reconstruction and Development Plan
SAB:	South African Breweries
SACP:	South African Communist Party
SAPO:	South African Post Office
SAPS:	South African Police Service
SASSA:	South African Social Security Agency
SCOPA:	Standing Committee on Public Accounts
SOE:	State owned enterprise
SRD:	Social Relief of Distress grant
T&D:	Transmission & Distribution network for electricity
UBC:	Urban Bantu Council
UIF:	Unemployment Insurance Fund
WHO:	World Health Organisation

RACIAL CATEGORIES

The racial categories used in this book are those used in South Africa's employment equity legislation:

- African: of African descent.
- Black: African, coloured or Indian. (Though in context it may refer only to Africans.)
- Coloured: of mixed-race descent.
- Indian: of Indian descent.
- White: of European descent.

Introduction: Looting from below

Introduction

THIS BOOK explores the agency of those residing in South African townships within the context of the country's failing attempt at social and economic transformation. This transformation was to replace apartheid with democracy, social justice, and a human-rights infused rule of law. The country's constitution, the supreme law of the land, was to, *inter alia*, "Improve the quality of life of all citizens and free the potential of each person …".[1] These hopes are fast fading.

Agency creates social order as much as social order determines agency. A key argument developed in this book is that two forms of order exist in contemporary South Africa. With township and suburb juxtaposed, the argument is that the law *operating* in each are different: the *lex lokasi* in the township and the *lex constitutional* in the suburb. In theory, the *lex constitutional*, the constitutionally defined legal system, is the law of the land and therefore of both suburb and township. The analytical point of departure is to challenge this assertion by contrasting the *de facto* social orders of township and suburb and behaviour within them.

Shortly, I describe the socio-geographic binary of township and suburb and their respective socio-legal orders: the *lex lokasi* and *lex constitutional*. This is a bold contrast. South Africa's actual social geography is far more complex than this binary division allows. Even if we accept this two-fold division as usefully illustrating a divided country, aligning divisions of race and class, we must account for how, within the country, the line of division is shifting. Increasingly, the *lex lokasi* is overtaking the *lex constitutional*; the law of the township penetrating, unevenly, into the suburb. Nevertheless, I persist with these binaries, as I do with other introduced dualities, for heuristic reasons, until the concluding chapter.

The agency I explore is that of township residents who grasp, either individually or in loose confederations, *menyetla*, or opportunities to gain some advantage. South Africa is being looted from above in what in shorthand is

1 Constitution of South Africa (1996). Preamble.

described as state capture,[2] but the focus here is on looting from below. The taking up of these *menyetla*, on the scale that is occurring, are a reaction to the country's failed transformation, yet they also accelerate that failure. Collective, long-term strategies of social and economic development are undermined by individual action focused on short-term advantage.

In this chapter, I engage with key concepts: *menyetla*; corruption and the relationship between looting from above and below; the division between township and suburb; and that between the *lex lokasi* and *lex constitutional*. The different *menyetla* described in subsequent chapters are flagged along with key points they contribute to a wider thesis being pursued: that the agency of township residents is driving social change far more powerfully than constitutional transformation.

The book is based on my "township life." The core of this has been in Katlehong, a large urban township in Gauteng which I have been visiting since 1997, and Mashaeng, a small township in the rural Free State province where I have lived part time since 2007. Later, I describe how the book was researched and written.

In concluding the chapter, I summarise the context for the book's arguments: that apartheid's social order has not been replaced by the *lex constitutional* and the hoped-for transformation, but increasingly by an entropic trajectory in which individuals are in a constant struggle that undermines collective provision.

Menyetla

Many speak for the poor, but few do so without explaining what the poor should do. The messages vary: that education is the key to success, or that the poor must put in an honest day's work for an honest day's pay, or accept that half a loaf is better than none, or manage their money wisely, or vote for party X, or join a union, or petition the authorities, or return to the traditions of their ancestors, or have faith in God, and so on *waya-waya*. What I describe is how the poor think and act for themselves by seizing *menyetla*. By *menyetla*, I refer to opportunities taken underhand which are to different degrees, in terms of the *lex constitutional*, illicit or illegal. All too often we overlook the agency of those scrabbling to survive, even as we dither between condemning and excusing their failure to follow our advice.

2 About which there is a substantial and growing literature. In addition to the five reports of the Zondo Commission and daily media reports on corruption, scholarly and in-depth accounts include: Myburg (2017); Chipkin and Swilling (2018); February (2019); Pauw (2022); Haffajee and Chipkin (2022); Jansen (2023); and De Ruyter (2023).

In Sesotho, an indigenous South African language, a *monyetla*, plural *menyetla,*[3] is a narrow alley or passage.[4] Used figuratively, it is an opportunity. An opportunity in the English language may be legal or illegal, legitimate or illegitimate, moral or immoral, but it generally suggests something laudable. An opportunity to study, an opportunity for promotion, an opportunity to relax, and so on. In Sesotho, *monyetla* carries greater neutrality.

At an early point in my Sesotho language journey, I asked my friend and language teacher, Maja Mokhutsoane, to differentiate between *monyetla* (opportunity) and *leqheka* (trick or scam). After we had wrestled with these and related words, Maja said he needed to smoke. It was a request for a cigarette. The sale of untaxed cigarettes is illegal. So too in South Africa is selling single cigarettes, or *loose draw*.[5] We were in Katlehong and, in line with a central point made in this book, these laws do not apply. At least not usually. However, at the time, the price of township cigarettes was oscillating wildly. There had been a national crackdown on untaxed cigarettes and the black market was volatile. Some supply chains had been closed while others remained open. *Loose draw* could cost anything between 50 cents and R2, depending on where you bought. I asked Maja how much they were at the nearby *spaza* shop. He said he thought they were *ponto*, or R2, apiece and I handed over a two-rand coin. When he came back with four cigarettes, I was annoyed. Two rand is not a lot, but I had given him money for a smoke, not to stock up. He had, I said, pulled a *leqheka* on me. He laughed good-naturedly and, drawing on our lesson, told me it wasn't a *leqheka* but a *monyetla*. So, I learnt.

In this book, I use the term opportunity and *monyetla* interchangeably, but I do so with the emphasis on the Sesotho neutrality: that *menyetla* may involve deceit, crime, or other malfeasance is unimportant beyond the risk attached. Risk is an ever-present companion to opportunity in the township. But since in the township everything is contested, chances must be taken if you are to survive or succeed.

Looting from above: looting from below

The Public Protector's 2017 report *State of Capture* exposed how three Indian businessmen, the Gupta brothers, influenced the appointment of South African ministers and government officials to benefit from state contracts. The report introduced the concept of state capture. The Zondo Commission of Inquiry subsequently provided detail of how politicians, government

[3] The noun classes of Sesotho are distinguished by their prefixes that also indicate number: for Class 2 nouns, the prefix "mo" indicates the singular and "me" indicates plural.

[4] The isiZulu equivalent being *ithuba*.

[5] Under the *Tobacco Products Control Amendments Act* 63 of 2008.

officials, tenderpreneurs,[6] and middlemen[7] milked state-owned enterprises and government spending through corrupt means for private gain: state capture or looting from above.

Corruption, present in every society, is a central concern of development scholars, practitioners, and aid agencies. The predominant view is that it is bad for development. More nuanced perspectives suggest that corruption is destructive only in certain forms and beyond a certain scale. These nuances need not overly concern us. David Bruce outlines how in South Africa "corruption has run away with itself" to the point that it threatens the elite's ability to credibly put itself forward as acting in the national interest.[8] Since then, things have only got worse. Quite patently, it has undermined the developmental dreams of the new democracy. As Karl von Holdt (2019) points out, funds syphoned from the public purse are not productively invested but spent on conspicuous consumption and financing patronage networks.

The idea that *the* state was captured is misleading since it implies that one entity gained control over the other. There are manifold networks of corruption. These patronage networks, competing against each other for influence, stretch from the apex of the ruling party and the state executive down to ward councillors and ward committees and are linked to partners in the private sector. Ferial Haffajee and Ivor Chipkin explain that state capture consists of many networks operating as a "matrix."[9] These networks, while without any central coordination, amount to a "system [that] has percolated all the way to the level at which ordinary life is lived. At each level, the mechanism of extraction operates to ruin South Africa…".

Joseph Nye's (1967) classic definition of corruption is the misuse of public office for private gain. This definition is widely applied, but it is narrow. South Africa's statutory definition of corruption, in the *Prevention and Combatting of Corrupt Activities Act*, defines corruption as a crime in which power, whether public or private, is misused for financial gain. This extends beyond state actors to employment, public and private tenders, commercial contracts, auctions, sporting events, and gambling.

Olivier De Sardan (1999) provides a wider definition with the idea of a corruption complex – a constellation of practices that are *seen* as corrupt but

6 Tenderpreneur is a portmanteau of "tendering" and "entrepreneur." A tenderpreneur is a person who obtains tenders and contracts from public or private entities. They may then be passed on several times before the final recipient of the skimmed contract carries out the work. Tenderpreneurship is often accomplished by overpricing and/or shoddy workmanship and/or excessive "under the table" advances termed commissions. (Wikipedia NDa).

7 And women.

8 Bruce (2014:58).

9 Haffajee and Chipkin (2022:93).

don't necessarily fall into Nye's or statutory definitions of corruption. These practices include nepotism, abuse of power, embezzlement, misappropriation, and influence-peddling. De Sardan's constellation of corruption relies on there being consensus over what is *seen* to be corrupt. Yet, what may be defined as corruption can be framed by those involved as legitimate. If this is true for those looting from above, as Haffajee and Chipkin (2022) outline, then it is also true for those looting from below, since they can justify their actions by referencing poverty or disadvantage.

Morally, we may distinguish between stealing to eat and the theft of public money to fund lavish lifestyles. In practice, the division is not always so clear. However, what is clear is that looting from above and below are, if carried out at scale, corrosive of social fabric. They result in the older meaning of corruption: decay and putrification. The social body of the new South Africa is increasingly necrotic. The proverb that a fish rots from the head is to be heeded. Nevertheless, an important aspect of South Africa's corroding social order is how looting from above legitimises looting from below, and that looting from below protects those looting from above.

The following chapter introduces the various dimensions of South Africa's increasingly violent, interwoven economic and political crises and maps out responses to increasing social instability.

Township and suburb

The division between township and suburb, a central dichotomy in this book, is based on very real geographies that testify to a still starkly divided country thirty years since the end of apartheid. However, used here they are also Weberian ideal types that simplify a complex reality. Racial segregation began under colonialism, but the township in contemporary South Africa remains an enduring legacy of apartheid's racialised, spatial planning. Under apartheid, there were separate townships for Africans, coloureds, and Indians – the racial categorisations for those deemed "non-white."[10]

Township in this book refers to African townships that form clearly demarcated physical locations which remain racially homogenous long after the repeal of legislation restricting where races could reside. Specifically, it draws on African townships in Gauteng and the Free State provinces with which I am familiar. However, I also use the term township in the broader sense

[10] The term non-white is now regarded as derogatory. In this book, I use the current statutory definitions of race used in the *Employment Equity Act* of 1998. African refers to the indigenous inhabitants of the country, though in popular use this is often interchangeable with "black." White refers to those of European origin, Indian to those of Asian origin, and coloured those with mixed decent. Within this statutory definition, "black" refers to African, Indian, and coloured collectively.

of being one part of an unequal society. Included in this wider understanding of township are all those in the lower rungs of South African society, even if they do not physically reside in a township. This includes the unemployed, informal workers, precarious workers, permanently employed manual and lower-level administrative workers, the township petty bourgeoisie and entrepreneurs, and the African lower middle-class occupations of nurses, teachers, police, and so on. With this wider meaning I divide South Africa's geography into the binary of township and suburb.

The suburb is the rest of South Africa. Narrowly defined, suburbs are the wealthy, tree-lined neighbourhoods of cities and town, ranging from the opulent to the down at heel but still relatively comfortable. As with township, I also use a wider conception; this suburb includes not only tree-lined neighbourhoods but also townhouse complexes and gated estates, the universities, corporate offices, professionals, and the courts. Unlike the townships as narrowly defined, this suburban world is slowly and unevenly becoming racially heterogeneous. Despite the diversity under the wider concept of suburb, it remains a small fraction of the country's population. Perhaps 10 per cent. An important, and obvious, difference between suburb and township, narrowly or broadly conceptualised, is economic privilege, whether long established or newly acquired.

There are clear parallels between township and suburb as widely defined and Partha Chatterjee's (2004) concepts of civil and governed society. In *The Politics of the Governed* Chatterjee differentiates between Western (former colonisers) and postcolonial societies. The former developed popular sovereignty, that is democracy, along with citizens' equal rights within their nation states, or "republican citizenship." By contrast, the subaltern population of colonised territories were subject to administration by colonial authorities. This division, Chatterjee argues, transitioned into the postcolonial society with former liberation movements implementing developmental policies, through government agencies, for the population that, "promised to end poverty and backwardness by adopting appropriate policies of economic growth and social reform."[11] The result has been a division between an organised elite, what Chatterjee terms civil society, and an unorganised subaltern domain or political society, the governed. Chatterjee's civil society is "… the closed association of modern elite groups, sequestered from the wider popular life of the communities, walled up within enclaves of civic freedom and rational law."[12]

This can be mapped onto South Africa. The colonial power handed over the administration of Africans to white settlers. The end of apartheid brought the ANC to power promising "a better life for all!" with development policies nested within the legal framework of constitutional transformation. Chatterjee's civil society corresponds to the suburb broadly defined, and the governed

[11] Chatterjee (2004:37).

[12] Chatterjee (2004:4).

corresponds to the township broadly defined. Except, as this book outlines, governance of the township by the suburb is largely illusory.

Chatterjee focuses on the relationship between civil society and the governed as that between state agencies and associations of the governed. Associations of the governed in South African townships certainly exist; however, for the most part they are either ephemeral or hollow or both, with their leaders representing, as the joke goes, little more than their own jackets. Frequently, they are dependent on state patronage. As Chatterjee puts it, they provide "convenient instruments for the administration of welfare to marginal and underprivileged population groups."[13] They may be lauded as organs of civil society but in practice are little more than conduits for welfare or information in a mutual process of state–association legitimation.

Chatterjee outlines that subaltern populations "operate the levers of the governmental system, to apply pressure at the right places or negotiate for better terms."[14] What Eldin describes as "political mobilisation."[15] However, the analysis presented in this book, focusing on South African townships, diverges from Chatterjee's framework in an important way. Collective mobilisation around illegitimate opportunities does occur, and Chapter 10 provides such an example: how neighbourhoods in Katlehong Township blocked the Metrorail line in support of their demand against the state electricity company. However, what a focus on community, collectives, or associations does not take into account is that in South African townships illegitimate opportunities are for the most part taken not collectively, but individually, or by temporarily aligned syndicates of confederates pursuing *menyetla*.[16] Indeed, the Metrorail example illustrates how collective action by one section of the township was criticised in other sections for being *dom* (stupid), not only because it disrupted their lives, but because the organisers of the blockade failed to see the superiority of quiet individual electricity theft over open defiance and demand.

13 Chatterjee (2004:40)

14 Chatterjee (2008:60).

15 Eldin (2005:141).

16 An arguable exception is land invasions or occupations which are widespread in South African urban areas. These are far more likely to succeed if done at scale. This activity is not covered in this book. However, it's not clear cut that land invasions represent collective action. Such invasions may well be coordinated in that they are initiated by one or more groups, often for political reasons, but cohesion of occupiers is another matter; see Dickinson (2020a) and Levenson (2022). Certainly, illicit infrastructure on occupied land is, as illustrated in Chapter 5, installed and maintained on an individual, informal market basis.

The *lex constitutional* and *lex lokasi*

The difference between township and suburb that I focus on is their distinct, *de facto*, legal systems; the *lex lokasi* in the township, the *lex constitutional* in the suburb. Chapter 4 examines this legal binary in detail. But first a caveat. The physical and cultural division between township and suburb is clear, but their legal apartness less so.

The law of the land, the *lex constitutional*, operates in its most complete form in the suburb. Of course, this writ is never complete, as with all legal systems, but even this is contracting. The territory of the *lex lokasi* is expanding. In legal terms it is being received, albeit in a *sub rosa* fashion, from township to suburb. Above, I included universities in the wider definition of the suburb. From the relatively well-resourced and governed university where I have worked for some thirty years that is largely correct. However, it is not so for all South Africa's universities, something brutally exposed by Jonathan Jansen (2023) in his book *Corrupted*. The same applies, *mutatis mutandis*, to the other institutions I have included as components of the suburb where the rule of the *lex constitutional* is eroding. Nevertheless, despite this caveat, I retain the division between township and suburb and their respective legal systems for analytical clarity.

A key feature of the transition from apartheid to democracy was the move from a whites-only parliamentary system of government to a non-racial constitutional democracy. Under apartheid, parliament was the supreme legal authority, the courts' role was to apply parliament's laws. In South Africa's constitutional democracy, the Constitution is the supreme law of the land which the courts are responsible for interpreting. The higher courts, with the Constitutional Court at the apex of the legal system, determine what is constitutional. That which is not is invalid. There is "one system of law."[17] At least that is what is proclaimed.

In the suburb, widely defined, the Constitution still, for the most part, holds sway. The law of the land, the *lex constitutional,* is, by and large, obeyed. In the township it is different. There is a more complex system of law, or laws, the *lex lokasi*, in which the *lex constitutional* is present but is only one element. Three key features of the *lex lokasi* are illustrated in Chapter 4.

The first is that the *lex lokasi* results from the limited access to constitutionally defined justice in the township. The result is that township residents, drawing on past and new repertoires, operate with a different form of social control to that of the suburb. The second is that the *lex lokasi* consists of a plurality of power resources that are brought to bear as individuals seek, in the absence of one system of law, to defend or advance their position. The third is that the *de jure*, but not *de facto*, supremacy of the *lex constitutional* creates

17 Chaskalson (2000) Paragraph 44.

menyetla for those operating within the *lex lokasi*, but that this advantage remains illegitimate and cannot be taken too extensively or openly.

Menyetla case studies

Chapters 5 to 11 are cases studies of township *menyetla*. Each case study provides insight into the life of the township, the *lex lokasi*, and the country's entropic trajectory.

Chapter 5 tackles what must be the most ubiquitous township *monyetla,* electricity theft. There are few township homes where the electricity meter isn't, temporarily or permanently, *tshipered* (bridged), bypassed, or loaded with "ghost" (fraudulent) coupons. Elsewhere, particularly in informal settlements, electricity is supplied via improvised connections. This theft is so widespread as to be effectively decriminalised and a *de facto* practised norm, at least where the *lex lokasi* operates. For an act to be criminal it must be deviant, and everybody can't be deviant.

Chapter 6 looks at the newly introduced Social Relief of Distress (SRD) grant which provided a small social security payment for close to 10 million recipients without work or other social grants. *Menyetla* were created by the inefficiencies of implementing the new grant. What emerged in and around post offices, the initial payment point, were opportunities for petty or hustle corruption as claimants were informally assisted to access the grant. A standard "service charge" or "token of appreciation" (depending on how the assistance was framed) of R50 for the R350 grant payment was soon established. The chapter explores the range of actors that took advantage of this R50 a pop *monyetla*. Some were equally destitute as the grant recipients, such as the "*nyaopi* boys" who took control of the SRD queues outside township post offices. Others, such as post-office employees, were earning salaries twenty-five, fifty times, and sometimes more than the SRD grant. These *menyetla* have largely been closed following reforms of the grant's distribution systems, something that illustrates the precarious nature of *menyetla*, which must be taken while they can.

Mangobers are those who ride the commuter trains without a ticket, fare evasion as it is formally termed. Chapter 7 looks at this fare evasion and how it illustrates limits to the *lex constitutional* in the township. The chapter also illustrates the feedback mechanisms and cascading consequences when social actors respond to opportunities in increasing numbers and how this must be factored into understanding South Africa's entropic trajectory. What starts at the margins can, when unchecked, create dynamics with escalating consequences.

The illegal sale of alcohol in the townships during the COVID-19 lockdowns is the focus of Chapter 8. A large percentage of alcohol sales in the township takes place under conditions of what Andrew Charman *et al.* (2020) describe as enforced informality. This was magnified in four periods of prohibition decreed during the pandemic; legally, no alcohol could be sold, whether from licensed or unlicensed outlets. The chapter illustrates how *menyetla* are accompanied by risk, but how the writ of the *lex constitutional* operates only at particular nodes or pinch points in the township. Yet, limited as this writ is, it can, paradoxically, create *menyetla*.

Chapter 9 looks at medical aid fraud. One area where private medical aid coverage has expanded post 1994 is among civil servants and employees of state-owned enterprises, for whom it has been introduced as a benefit and condition of service. This allows employees and family members to use private healthcare and skip long queues and indifferent service that is the hallmark of South Africa's public healthcare. Often, however, despite a high level of subsidisation, it is a benefit that employees cannot afford and becomes a grudge purchase providing justification for fraud.

Medical aid fraud requires cooperation between scheme members and healthcare providers: doctors, dentists, pharmacists, psychologists, and so on. Earlier chapters identify how some *menyetla* require networks or syndicates of confederates to operate clandestine joint ventures. Medical aid fraud requires such networks, which include healthcare professionals. This underlines that taking *menyetla* is not only about surviving but also about taking advantage to get ahead.

The tension between individual, short-term gain and collective, long-term provision is explored in Chapters 10 and 11. Chapter 10 describes the looting of Metrorail stations and lines during the COVID-19 lockdowns of 2020. Chapter 11 deals with the looting of shopping malls and warehouses during the unrest of July 2021. These cases examine how, within the *lex lokasi*, short-term gain will prevail over long-term interests. Chapter 11 also describes how, paradoxically, attempts to defend long term interests, with the emergence of citizens defence groups, conflicted with the *lex constitutional*, illustrating the increasing gap between constitution and social realities.

These case studies demonstrate people doing things for themselves. Self-help is something to applaud, but what these chapters describe is how individuals, and temporary networks of confederates, pursue narrow, short-term gain at the expense of long-term, collective development. This agency, and its individual orientation, is a response to the failure of South Africa's post-1994 transformation in which there was to be a better life for all, yet it is also an accelerant of that failure.

However, if the building of a better South Africa has stalled it does not mean that social dynamics are frozen in place. It is now individual agency that is shaping micro and macro level developments. Change is happening, but unplanned. The drivers of change lie outside the formal structures crafted in the Constitution of 1996.[18] What we are witnessing is a widening gyre of social disintegration. Looking around us, we know this to be true but struggle to acknowledge that what has been vaunted as the best constitution in the world isn't working.

An outsider in the township

At this point it is customary to bludgeon the reader with statistics on the volume of research conducted and an account of how the different research methods employed constitute a rigorous and coherent investigation. Valuable accounts of research also describe the ups and downs encountered and lessons learned. However, since I am a white professor writing about the underbelly of South Africa, I should first explain something about my own position and describe my insider–outsider status in the township from which I have written this account from below.

Let me start at the beginning: the research on which this book is based did not begin as research. When I came to South Africa in January 1994 from the UK, for a one-year teaching post at Wits University, it was to see the country's transition to democracy. I saw no point in confining myself to the suburb. My initial "passport" to enter the township were students who invited me to visit. But it was when conducting my PhD research on shopfloor relations in South African factories in the late 1990s that I began visiting townships on a regular basis, facilitated by shop stewards in the factories I was researching. Going into townships was not only a matter of curiosity, but also of political and moral conviction. A non-racist society does not create itself. White people needed to do more than adopt a new vocabulary. Unfortunately, it became increasingly obvious that most chose to *laager* in the suburb. That has been deeply disappointing, but it has not discouraged me from continuing: my township life can be challenging, but it is also enriching.

I have benefited from my township life. Not only in terms of personal integrity, and learning, but also in terms of my academic career. This is my third book on life in African townships. All have been based on extensive, long-term involvement and research, and all have been written from below or about township life as it is lived. The books dig deep into HIV/AIDS beliefs, resistance to precarious employment, and now *menyetla* and social order. Each raise sensitive issues, at least for some readers: non-scientific beliefs about disease, strike violence, and now theft, fraud, and fiddling.

[18] Nor are they contained by *ubuntu*, an African version of solidarity, in which it is understood that a person's humanity rests in their relationships with others. In chapters 6 and 9, I explore the idea of bounded *ubuntu* and how this facilitates the taking of *menyetla*.

Some uncomfortable issues make appearances in all three books, such as the widespread belief in witchcraft.

As for making some people uncomfortable, I make no apology. Especially if they are residents of the suburb. We residents of the suburbs should understand what township residents, as much South African citizens as ourselves, believe and do. To condemn inequality but eulogise, or alternatively blame,[19] township residents from a distance may be comfortable, but it provides no foundation to tackle inequality, South Africa's key fault-line. This requires uncompromising analysis, neither condemnatory nor hagiographic. I attempt to provide that in what follows.

But why should I, a white, male professor with my primary residency in the suburb, undertake such research? I am not alone in researching and writing about the township, but it is remarkable just how little scholarship focuses on the township.[20] The research I draw on in Chapter 3 describing townships today is thinner, and often shallower, than that I have drawn on in Chapter 2 describing the apartheid township. Contemporary scholars, irrespective of age or race, are not keen on the township as a field of study. I teach a Masters'-level research methodology course for sociology and development studies students at my university. The course includes assisting students to develop a proposal for their research report. Although some students' choices are influenced by funding opportunities, the vast majority choose what interests them.[21] Most topics address policy formulation, institutional studies, and identity politics, all valuable, but it is noticeable just how few students choose a township-based topic that requires research from below. If the township was crowded with researchers with backgrounds closer to those of residents than my own, I would reconsider where best my time and energy could be spent. But it isn't.

More important than any sensitivities of suburban residents are those of the researched who deserve honest treatment and respect. That I hope is clear in the chapters that follow. As with previous books, I have anonymised those whose stories I tell should there be risk of embarrassment, legal jeopardy, or other sanction.

The division between suburb and township in South Africa is not only about race but also class. When I visit Katlehong or stay in Mashaeng, I must cross both social divides, which in the township are tightly interwoven. We need to constantly remind ourselves that the inequalities of South Africa are not normal, that we are the most unequal society on earth. The *menyetla* described in this book are, at least on the scale that they are being practised, a product of an unequal society. Yet, they are not simply the mechanical outcome of

19 See Dickinson (2015).

20 Even more so if surveys, rather than in depth studies, are excluded.

21 We then find a supervisor able to supervise the student's chosen topic.

poverty. It is conduct that is learned, adapted, and replicated. The taking of *menyetla* is agentic behaviour.

My visits to Katlehong became more frequent from 2004, but it was not till 2007 that I started to regularly write up fieldnotes. These recorded and reflected on what I had seen and heard. Writing fieldnotes generates questions. My visits to Katlehong are anchored with a Sesotho lesson which has become a conversation in Sesotho-heavy *kasi* idiom about ongoing local and national events, lunch – whether *kota* or *hlooho*[22] – and street socialisation with (largely male) friends. But they are also about deliberate inquiries into township life which take me far and wide. If you're taking fieldnotes, you're researching. And since I'm an academic who is expected to be researching, I am working. That is correct, but it does not exclude other reasons for being in the township. Driving into Katlehong, or to Mashaeng, does not feel like work. It is something I look forward to.

In 2007, to improve my Sesotho, I stayed for two months in Mashaeng, the Fouriesburg township close to the border with Lesotho in the Eastern Free State. I had already visited a few times; it was the *mahae* (rural origins) of a Katlehong friend. It was, I realised, an ideal place for language immersion. I enjoyed my stay and in 2009 began renting a two-room building where I have since lived on a part-time basis. Here too I take notes as well as conducting formal research. But these are, as with Katlehong, only one aspect of my township life. It is also an unconventional holiday home. There is the slower pace of life in a rural township compared to Gauteng (though not as slow or as placid as I first imagined), walking in the surrounding commonage and hiking in nearby mountains, playing board games with visiting children, running micro-level interventions, such as providing children with school stationary that families cannot afford, visiting friends (*ho tjhakela*), attending funerals and community meetings, befriending squatters during a land occupation, attending the township's St Elizabeth Catholic church as a warmly welcomed visitor despite my lack of religious faith, and so on. Some of these are what township residents do; others are linked to my outsider–insider status.

During research projects and road trips, I visit other townships, though with nowhere near the frequency of Katlehong and Mashaeng. However, in 2016 I lived for six months in the village of Sehlajaneng while on sabbatical leave at the Free State University's Qwaqwa[23] campus, also in the Eastern Free State. As with my journey from Katlehong to Mashaeng, it was facilitated

22 *Kota* (quarter) is standard township fast food; a quarter loaf of white bread stuffed with chips and other fried food depending on price. *Hlooho* or *inhloko* (head) refers to a stew made from the meat of a cow's head and is eaten with pap, the staple stiff maize porridge of the South African township. Traditionally, *hlooho* is considered as men's food.

23 Qwaqwa is the old Basotho "homeland" established under apartheid.

by friends, this time from Mashaeng who introduced me to my Sehlajaneng host family. Again, more involvement, more conversations, and more notes.

I've always been open about my status as an academic, whether conducting a formal research project or otherwise in the township. I also let people know that I'm keen to know more about life in the township. "How people really live" is the way I put it. This desire to understand has been, with very few exceptions, welcomed. Most people go out of their way to explain something if you show interest. Some take it upon themselves to point out things they think I should know about. This opens new avenues of inquiry. Some lines fizzle out (though not without something learned); some go far. Some I have taken up as formal research projects with interviews and other orthodox sociological methods of collecting information. Others remain as long-running, muti-factored themes within my fieldnotes.

Finally, since early 2022 I have worked with Lawyers for Human Rights (LHR),[24] the Casual Workers Advice Office,[25] and the Orange Farm Human Rights Advice Centre,[26] all of which provide township residents with legal advice and support. These experiences have provided a different perspective on conflicts within townships, as well as between township and suburb.[27]

Researching *menyetla*

The *menyetla* described in this book involve illicit, unlawful, and illegal activities. Surveys cannot provide reliable data and the standard sociological research tool of in-depth, open-ended interviews[28] has its limits. Much as a researcher might underline the confidentiality of the interview,[29] with

24 An NGO established in 1979 committed to social justice and human rights enforcement (https://www.lhr.org.za/).

25 A centre focused on advising and organising precarious workers based in Germiston on Gauteng's East Rand (https://www.cwao.org.za/).

26 A community advice centre based in Orange Farm south of Johannesburg (https://orangefarmadvicecentre.org.za/).

27 I spent a sabbatical year with Lawyers for Human Rights (while also serving as a candidate attorney and drafting this book) and have continued to assist with several cases before joining the organisation in 2025. I spent two months voluntarily working with the Casual Workers Advice Office in late 2023. I have been assisting the Orange Farm Human Rights Advice Centre since early 2024 on a part-time basis.

28 That is, the researcher has a series of prepared questions, but the respondent is encouraged to elaborate on their answers, which in turn generates new questions to further explore the issue in conversational form.

29 A process made, paradoxically, more difficult by ethics committees' insistence on participants giving formal consent, often to multiple components of the research. The Wits University's School of Social Science ethics committee's current example consent form for use by researchers provides the following clauses for consent: the interview

rare exceptions they are a stranger who, irrespective of race, is an outsider. Additionally, a one-off interview cannot hope to contextualise something that is an integral part of the individual's family, street, and township life. Much as this book highlights the individual agency of township residents, this is embedded within a wider context that needs to be understood.

Further, one-off interviews cannot accurately account for people's actions over time. It is not that the researcher must spend decades in the township to understand the lives of its residents. Well thought-through research projects that include the classic methods of surveys and interviews[30] can and do produce valuable accounts and data. But *mara* (still), long-term engagement and time-tested trust, along with constant curiosity, are critical assets if we want to know how people really live.

In the areas of Katlehong and Mashaeng where I am known, people are willing to be open, if not in front of others, then certainly when talking privately.[31] Not because I tell them that our talk is confidential but because they know that it is, having watched my behaviour over years and decades. The reach of this trust is multiplied, when those assisting me introduce me to others and, with full insider credentials, vouch for me.

As well as trust there is the question of the researcher's own beliefs. I am, with the occasional slip, a responsible and law-abiding citizen.[32] But to pronounce this perspective when seeking to understand *menyetla* would amount to moral condemnation. It would cut off honest communication. You might be able to joke about the *menyetla*, but to criticise or condemn them will end the conversation.

Menyetla are rooted in the lives of township residents, less behavioural choice based on abstract principles, more behavioural adaptation to actual circumstances. A Katlehong friend of long standing rhetorically asked during a street conversation late one Saturday afternoon why I was still with them

itself; that they understand the purpose of the research; recording the interview; the use of quotes in publications; that they will remain anonymous; and, that other researchers may access the transcript. Not all these listed aspects need be used, but the template form completely overlooks the limited education of many township residents and their suspicion of authority, in particular the legal trap of signing documents or otherwise providing consent to something they do not fully understand.

30 Even returning for a second or third interview can make a huge difference in what a respondent is willing to say since you are no longer a stranger. The value of repeat interviews is well documented – see, for example, Ellis (1998); Laslett and Rapoport (1975); and, Luttrell (2005) – but rarely practised. What typically counts is the number of people interviewed, not the quality or reliability of the content.

31 Typically, this is not a formal interview but simply conversations to which nobody else is party.

32 Though a professorial salary provides me with resources to facilitate this with relative ease.

after all these years. Because, he told me, I hadn't tried to change what I found and was, as a result, accepted. That is not entirely true; I have already confessed to involvement in micro-grassroots development initiatives, but the observation has enough truth to validate the point.

An advantage of long-term relationships with members of a community is that contemporary events are talked about informally. Indeed, this talk is central to community life. Call it catching up, call it gossiping, call it what you want, it happens. Sometimes from a distance as observers of others, sometimes from within events as protagonists or affected parties. Sitting on a sofa, eating a seven-colour Sunday lunch[33] as a friend of the family, or sitting in a dirt yard on beer crates as a joint is passed around, it doesn't matter; you talk about what is important. You can talk about politics and international affairs if you want, but what really seizes people is what is happening around them. This is a part of community life in which any member, full or part-time, must participate. For the curious it also provides an opportunity to directly enquire as to what was, in the view of those present, exactly happening when X said or did Y to Z.

Now for those promised statistics. Excluding interviews and field visits specifically linked to research projects that have been written up elsewhere,[34] this book draws on my township fieldnotes. As of early 2025, I have written notes for some 380 Katlehong visits. Each entry, supplemented with photographs, covers multiple issues. They usually come out at between 1,000 and 3,000 words, occasionally upwards. From my Mashaeng stays I have some 120 visit entries, which vary between 2,000 and 10,000 words, reflecting that stays are up to a week at a time, sometimes longer. My six-month stay in Sehlajaneng adds further notes. My civic life in the township and the communications that arise, whether emails, phone calls, or WhatsApp groups, along with membership of township Facebook pages, adds further information, which are sometimes written up as fieldnotes. Then there are my ongoing 'legal diaries' in which I record *inter alia* what insights I have gained since 2022 as a legal practitioner: as of early 2025 running collectively north of 450 pages. It is, however, my Katlehong fieldnotes on which I mostly draw, and which are referenced with the date in year-month-day format, for example: Fieldnotes: 230115 being the 15 January 2023.

Importantly, however, for this book it is not the number of words written or tally of visits that matters. Rather, it is the quality of observation, and the insights gained, that are important. I have striven over the years to focus on accurate recording, careful reflection, the testing of ideas within my circle of township friends and contacts, and ongoing analysis.

33 The name for the typical township Sunday lunch (or Sunday *kos*), based on the variety of colours on the plate.

34 See, especially, Dickinson (2014) and (2021b).

Analytical dichotomies

The argument developed in this book differs from the well-ventilated view that state capture is key to the country's current crisis. A focus on state capture is important, but it is not the sum of challenges that confronts South Africa. Corruption has penetrated throughout society, or, to use Andre de Ruyter's term, metastasised.[35] But even the widest concept of corruption does not embrace everyone. Many do not have power over others that can be turned into cash, or cash that can be turned into power. But that doesn't mean that they are unable to work out how to gain something outside of legitimate channels. It is this underbelly of South African society that is explored and explained in this book.

To do this, I use analytical dichotomies or binaries. The central pair has already been introduced, the binary of township and suburb and their corresponding social orders: the *lex constitutional* and the *lex lokasi*. One is set against the other in order to parse post-apartheid South Africa. Binaries cannot capture every detail of the social world since there is much that is between and betwixt. As already acknowledged, the boundary dividing township and suburb and their respective *leges* is not static. Yet, the difference between lives in the suburb and the township is stark and clear. It reflects the reality of different lives in the most unequal society on earth.

Other binaries are used in this book: injunctive (or articulated) and practised norms; collective action and individual agency; and long- and short-term time horizons. In practice, social variables are spread unevenly along spectra, and salience along this spectra changes with time and context. However, binaries assist in making sense of complex detail when multiple social variables are simultaneously present. This does not mean that an analysis based on binaries is simple. Even with the five binaries mentioned an accounting approach produces thirty-two analytical combinations.[36] Not surprisingly, I do not follow such an approach, but the analytical scaffolding that binaries provide assists in building the perspectives outlined in the book.

Changing social order

Stepping back from the immediacy of the case studies, what must be engaged with is the failure to transform South African society and the resulting crisis of social order. Under apartheid there was order based on racist ideologies. A white minority used parliamentary supremacy, and military might, to maintain control and exploit the country's majority. It was a diligently organised system

35 de Ruyter (2023:135).

36 Two to the power of five (2^5) or 2x2x2x2x2 = 32.

of bureaucratic repression and exploitation of black people: African, coloured, and Indian, but above all Africans.

The end of apartheid was achieved through negotiations, backed by a sober view of what would eventually happen without an agreement. The "final" Constitution of 1996 was a compromise based on political expediency as well as high ideals. The promise of 1994, a better life for all, has not materialised. Realistically, there is now little prospect that the social and political forces aligned to the Constitution of 1996 can prevail in bringing about the hoped-for change. As described in the following chapter, the aspirations of 1994 have evaporated. But that does not mean there is no social order. The question is, what form and what direction is that order taking?

1

South Africa's entropic trajectory

"Our horses are facing Zimbabwe:" Katlehong Township, mid-July 2021

KATLEHONG[1] IS a sprawling township southeast of Johannesburg. Typical of South Africa's urban townships, it is a mixture of formal housing, backyard rooms, hostels, and informal shack settlements. It merges, to the east and the west with two neighbouring townships, Thokoza and Vosloorus. Collectively the fused townships are known as Kathorus. Not that anyone would say that they hail from Kathorus. Rather, with local identities salient, they will tell you which townships they live in and, likely, which section. The census of 2011 records 737,000 people in Kathorus, of which 98.7 per cent were African.[2] This racial homogeneity, a defining characteristic of South Africa's townships, is an enduring historical legacy. Africans, coloureds, and Indians with rights to reside – permanently or temporarily – in urban areas could only do so in separate, racially designated townships.

It's a forty-five-minute drive from my home in the Johannesburg suburb of Westdene to Katlehong. As you enter the township passing Huntersfield Stadium there is a sign greeting visitors: "Welcome to Katlehong." It could be welcoming you to another country, another world.

Late on Saturday afternoon, I drive with friends down Sontonga Road to Tsietsi Section at the southern tip of the township, a good 12 kilometres

1 Colloquially also known as Spruit, a shortened version of Natalspruit, the name of the river that runs along the eastern edge of the township. A third name, of unclear origin, is Spyland.

2 Compared to 79.2 per cent of South Africa's population in the 2011 census. The 2022 census gives a population of 676,000 for Kathorus (also 98.7 per cent African). It is not clear why the Kathorus population would have dropped by eight per cent given inward migration and densification of housing observable in the area. The 2022 census had an undercount of 31 per cent (compared to the 2011 Census undercount of 14.6), the highest yet recorded by the UN Population Division and has been criticised on methodological grounds as to its statistical reliability (Kahn, 2024a). I use 2011 census data in this book.

from Huntersfield.[3] For the last week, Kwazulu-Natal and Gauteng provinces have been convulsed by looting.[4] A political struggle within the ruling ANC morphed into an insurrection triggered by the imprisonment of former president Jacob Zuma. The insurrection then turned into an orgy of looting by the poor, and the not so poor, who stormed shopping malls and warehouses. We pass Sontonga Mall, one of the new township malls built in the last twenty years. It stands wrecked and empty. The streets, however, are busy with hawkers. The wrecked mall excepted, it looks like business as usual, but that's deceptive; these micro businesses cannot substitute for supermarkets, stores, or ATMs.

Now that the paroxysm of looting has subsided, the cheap transport of the Metrorail to Germiston, "town," is sorely missed. In 2020, during the first COVID-19 lockdowns, the lines' overhead cables were cut and taken while stations in the township were stripped clean, down to window frames and roofing.[5] Now, to shop in Germiston for groceries you must take a minibus taxi. People grimly joke that it will cost R50 to buy a loaf of bread.[6]

In Tsietsi I walk with my friend Morena Thulo to a tavern a few streets away. We are in COVID-19 Level 4 lockdown and alcohol sales are outright prohibited. In the township, however, the ban amounts to less choice and higher prices. The tavern owner is outside chatting with friends. One I recognise as a policeman, we have socialised together. We greet and Morena asks what is available. The options are Gordon's gin or cans of Heineken, at more than double normal retail prices. The tavern owner says we're lucky, he had a delivery only yesterday, which given the ban and the brands he's offering means it's looted stock.[7]

Back at Morena's place we sit around a fire in his backyard. It is fuelled with chunks of warped chipboard and cracked plastic buckets. The women are in the house. We talk as the air chills. In more comfortable surroundings, the country's opinionistas are providing long-range analysis for the unrest and what it means for the country.[8] Around our fire, the mood is subdued. I hear the fear that has been long smouldering in the suburbs. Township and suburb are different worlds, but the unrest is a moment of shared clarity. We see the future and are afraid. Around the fire the fear is framed less by race than nationality. My friends are, metaphorically, looking across the borders. They point to the countries from which immigrants come to South Africa: Zimbabwe, Malawi, Mozambique, the DRC, Somalia, and elsewhere. Around the fire, it is seen in zero sum terms: what they take, South Africans lose.

3 This account is based on fieldnotes: 210717 and 211106.
4 See Chapter 11.
5 See Chapter 10.
6 i.e. because of the minibus taxi fares to find a shop selling bread.
7 See Chapter 8.
8 Myself included (Dickinson 2021a).

Now South Africa's economy is on a downward spiral. The hopes of a better life sinking fast. Jerry Kgodu sums the fears around the fire; "Our horses are facing Zimbabwe."

I put an uncomfortable question to Morena, though I am addressing everyone around the fire. Why didn't *Kopano ke Matla,* a local community security initiative,[9] defend Sontonga Mall? It is the closest place to shop for groceries, buy airtime, or draw cash. It was not impossible to face down looters: 8 kilometres north residents defended Hlahatsi Mall for over two weeks.[10] Morena can only offer lame excuses, and I pursue it no further.

There is black humour around the fire, we joke about circulating memes: "South African saying: I'm so hungry I could steal a TV!" But when months later I talk to Thabo, who was caught looting in one of the township's malls, I am struck with the banality of his crimes. He had arrived long after the mall had been breached by the vanguard looters focused on the ATMs. Wading through the wreckage, he had collected tins of fish and cartons of juice. It turned out to be an expensive trip. The police, unable to defend the malls, saved face by arresting *smallnyana* looters. Thabo ended up in a crowded prison cell in Boksburg Prison for two weeks and was dismissed from work for absconding.[11]

The drive back through the township is in darkness. It has been load reduced, Eskom's ongoing rotational power outages of low paying areas. Load reduction is additional to the periodic load shedding that affects the suburbs when national generating capacity drops. The high mast lights of the township are out and so too the robots (traffic lights). When I complain about having to negotiate each darkened junction, somebody, in a fit of alcohol-lubricated righteousness, says that people must start paying for their electricity. At this we laugh. We know that everyone is stealing electricity in one way or another.

The expression that our horses are facing Zimbabwe is a metaphor. The two countries are distinct in many ways, but the idea of South Africa following Zimbabwe's post-independence path to dysfunctionality: a corrupt elite, a collapsed economy, and crumbling physical and social infrastructure, is now widely held. Fear of the future is no longer the prerogative of white South Africans, but also township residents who were given hope only to see it dim.

Nostalgia, state capture, and looting from below

There is nostalgia in the township for the past. Or at least for what is remembered as better then than now. What is emphasised is that under white rule there was order in the township, the bylaws were enforced, there was

9 For which I had facilitated a workshop a few months earlier.

10 See Chapter 11.

11 See Chapter 11.

work. A man (for this is a narrative most often offered by men) could put bread on the table.

All this can be challenged. If there was order, it was one maintained by black policemen or *kitkonstables*[12] who policed the township by benching[13] offenders. As the joke about *kitkonstables* of the time suggests, the order of yesteryear wasn't as rosy as now imagined:

> If a man was walking alone and they stopped you: "Where are you going?"
>
> If you were two: "What have you got [that you shouldn't]?"
>
> If you were three: *Phafa!* [Sjambok!]
>
> If you were four: Off to jail![14]

Less ambiguously, there was full employment in the township, but only because of influx control with unemployment hidden in the so-called homelands.[15] Given this, township men were family breadwinners and so head of the house, with the dignity that came with this status, yet they remained second-class citizens in the country of their birth and their ancestors.

Those who narrate this version of the past are not unaware of these caveats. As one man qualified his narrative of a better past; "the whites ruled well, but wrongly."[16] Moreover, this narrative of order and work in the past exists in parallel to that of the past as oppression. When someone wants to emphasis just how bad their precarious employment as a casual worker is they will quickly compare it to the apartheid workplace.[17]

In the suburbs, as I define them in this book,[18] concern over South Africa's trajectory focuses on corruption. This narrative has been dominated by the concept of state capture, in which individuals located within state structures, including state-owned enterprises, syphon public resources into private pockets. How this took place is documented by the *Zondo Commission of Enquiry* reports and elsewhere.[19] This looting from above has leached resources

12 See Chapter 2.

13 Being beaten while being forced to lie on a bench.

14 Fieldnotes: 180303.

15 See Chapter 2.

16 Fieldnotes: 210417.

17 See Dickinson (2021b) for a detailed account of precarious employment conditions under labour broking in post-apartheid South Africa.

18 See the Introduction.

19 Myburg (2017); Chipkin and Swilling (2018); February (2019); Pauw (2022); Haffajee and Chipkin (2022); Jansen (2023); and De Ruyter (2023).

available for infrastructure development and maintenance as well as social spending. This narrative also posits the past as better than the present. Again, this needs to be caveated, the extensive corruption of apartheid's twilight is documented,[20] though nobody thinks this has not been far surpassed.

This chapter describes how the diversion of public funds into private pockets is increasingly apparent and destructive. Yet, this is not the dominant narrative in the township on corruption. The reaction to the money stolen from the public purse in the township is less indignation and more jealousy. In honest moments, there are admissions that if given the chance they would do the same. But with a difference: they would not, they claim, be greedy. A racially inscribed morality tale is sometimes used to illustrate this:

> When a white man [it could be a woman, but that's how the story is told] gets a contract, he skims 10 per cent for himself and builds the road [or whatever it is]. When a black man gets a contract, he puts 90 per cent into his pocket, and the road doesn't get built.

This is not a moral judgement over corruption *per se* since black and white are skimming their cut, but criticism that Africans are taking too much. They are being greedy or selfish. We can throw caveats at this morality tale also. Nevertheless, the tale points to a truth about corruption in contemporary South Africa; it is out of control from top to bottom.

Township residents, imbued with agency that is overlooked by political and educated elites, grasp, develop, and expand *menyetla*. This looting from below is justified by looting from above. State capture provides a blanket justification for theft, fraud, and non-payment for those in the lower rungs of society who are struggling to survive or scrambling to get ahead.

The focus of this book is not on state capture, looting from above, but looting from below. I have consciously resisted the gravitational intellectual pull to place state capture at the centre of the book's analysis. This choice is not to minimise the effects of state capture. State capture is a central facet of South Africa's entropic trajectory, but it is not the only factor. We need to understand each factor, as well as the ways in which they interact and reinforce each other.

While state capture by the big fish clocks up fraud in the billions of rand, the gain of individuals looting from below are, in comparison, chicken feed. Yet their actions are not without consequence. The pursuit of small *menyetla*, such as the theft of electricity by households or fare dodging by commuters on the Metrorail, when conducted at scale, has a significant impact.

Our understanding of the elements of this unfolding crisis is uneven. In contrast to state capture, how township residents seize *menyetla* is poorly

20 Hyslop (2005).

understood. It's not that people don't know that it's happening. It would be hard not to recognise that the theft of electricity is rife given widespread media coverage. Yet, to understand why and how this is happening is more difficult. This book attempts to do that.

Structural imbalances and subverted policy

In South Africa's first democratic elections of April 1994, the ANC campaigned with the slogan of "A better life for all!". It was an ambitious promise. Whether a development state driven by a selfless cadre of politicians and civil servants working with civil society could have fulfilled the promise is now an academic question.[21] While there were committed people in the ANC leadership, it is now clear that the noble intentions of 1994 have been hollowed out. Nevertheless, the failure to deliver a better life for all cannot be attributed only to state capture.

The country's history of colonialism and apartheid bequeathed a dysfunctional society and economy. Apartheid policies of separate development based on a racial hierarchy resulted in the under-development of the majority. The psychological damage this created remains in place, as have the economic effects which transformation policies, including affirmative action, have failed to overcome. This is nowhere more evident than with the structural imbalance of workplace skills.

Apartheid restrictions on education and training for Africans and, to a lesser extent, coloureds and Indians, created a skills profile out of kilter with evolving economy needs. The result is that those with access to quality education and training command a super-premium in the labour market. Conversely, those without these qualifications and skills greatly outnumber opportunities for low-skilled employment. In the last quarter of 2021, unemployment reached 35.3 per cent narrowly defined and 52.2 per cent broadly defined.[22] These figures are particularly high, coming after the impact of the July 2021 looting and the COVID-19 lockdowns, but even putting these effects aside the trend of increasing unemployment is relentless. What can be clearly seen within these statistics is the legacy of racial policies. Unemployment at the end of 2022, narrowly defined, was 39 per cent for African; 30 per cent for coloured; 28 per cent for Indians, and 9 per cent for whites.[23]

21 Though the question as from where and how such cadres may yet emerge is very real.

22 The narrow definition includes only unemployed people who are actively seeking employment. The broad definition includes 'discouraged work-seekers' who while wanting work have given up on seeking employment.

23 Stats South Africa (2022).

The failure to promote a job-creating economy is not only the result of state capture. Sociologists testify to the stubborn intergenerational transfer of social disadvantage in any society. Despite a raft of legislated policies intended to overcome the legacies of apartheid there has been – outside the creation of a black middle class – limited success.

The ANC ambitiously set the target of reconstructing South African society. With hindsight, much of the policy reform was over-ambitious and naïve. The attempt to address the country's skills imbalance is an example. The promotion of workplace training to increase the skills of workers and their economic productivity was well-intentioned but ended up entrenching inequality while doing little to increase economic output. The one-percentage skills development levy (with the intention of it being increased) on companies' payroll was to fund the training of workers. An elaborate system of sector-based training authorities meshed workplace training with a complex system of training accreditation. Yet, the result has not been to significantly upskill the workforce. Rather, much of the levy has ended up funding the sector training bureaucracies, consultants, and training providers. It is middle-class graduates who have primarily benefited from the skills levy.

Where legislation has tipped the balance towards low-skilled workers, as with the *Labour Relations Act* which governs workplace relationships, this has been extensively bypassed. Faced with legally empowered unions, employers – both private and public – introduced new and complex employment relationships. The most notorious being labour broking, the preferred method from approximately 2005 to 2016 of creating a precarious labour force unable to assert the legal rights that legislation decreed. Legislative reform to close the loophole of labour broking was a bumbling affair and when finally achieved proved to be a pyrrhic victory. Employers migrated to alternative employment configurations that maintained precarious labour.[24]

Developmental overreach

In the early 2000s, as the Zimbabwean economy collapsed, a mordant joke circulated in South Africa.

> Q: *What did Zimbabweans light their homes with before they used candles?*
>
> A: *Electricity!*

At the time, South Africa still had cheap electricity, and a massive programme of electrification had extended supply to a large percentage of the population.

24 Dickinson (2021b).

With load shedding and load reduction from the mid-2000s the joke has come home to roost. You could make similarly barbed jokes about South Africa's roads, water, education, criminal justice system, or pretty much anything else.

Over-ambitious and complex policies, aimed at transforming society post 1994, provided cover for self-enrichment practices. The complex system of government established by the country's Constitution illustrates this with its system of cooperative government. This requires three levels of government: national, provincial, and local or municipal, to coordinate their actions. Yet, as Louis Picard and Thomas Mogale outline, the Constitution resulted in "... a governance theory emphasising decentralisation and local control and a political (fiscal and administrative) process that is both highly centralized and often inefficient."[25]

Governance is more convoluted than cooperative, and this makes it difficult to know exactly who is failing to deliver basic services or maintain infrastructure. A public housing development involves myriad processes of approval, finance, and tenders spread across levels of government, state agencies, and contractors. The detail is often maddingly complex and opaque; ideal terrain for corrupt practices,[26] difficult ground for genuine public participation, and an obstacle to implementation. Every municipality is required to produce an Integrated Development Plan (IDP) every five years through a process of consultation.[27] There were high hopes for the IDPs. As Edgar Pieterse optimistically put it in 2002, "... the genius of the policy design for the IDP is that it reconciles the democratic aspirations of South Africans with the service-delivery imperative ...."[28]

For Dihlabeng Municipality, under which the township of Mashaeng falls, the IDP typically comes in at a hefty 200 pages. It is, we are told, "the key instrument to achieve developmental local governance for centralised, strategic, participatory, implementation-orientated, coordinated and integrated development."[29] The IDP delivers adjectives, but can it deliver development?

In Mashaeng consultations are held on Dihlabeng's draft IDPs in the township hall. Councillors and municipal officials arrive in smart cars. Residents arrive on foot and fill out the attendance register. Initially, we saw these events as a chance to influence service delivery. Water, land for houses, and of course anything that would provide jobs. People spoke with passion and the officials diligently wrote down what was said. But once you'd been to a couple you could see the picture. The politicians were making promises and officials were going through the motions. We might talk, complain, reason, or

25 Picard and Mogale (2015:245–6).

26 Njilo (2022).

27 In terms of Chapter 5 of the *Local Government: Municipal Systems Act* 32 of 2000.

28 Pieterse (2002), quoted in Dlamini and Reddy (2018:14).

29 Dihlabeng Local Municipality (2016:14).

plead from the floor, but the way to push things your way was to have your councillor on the mayoral executive committee. Then at least something would be delivered. Even if only in the run up to the next elections.

This cynicism took a while to take hold. In the decade and a half or so after 1994 there was a sustained attempt to re-prioritise resources from the previously privileged, in effect from white suburbs to black townships. White suburbs had enjoyed comprehensive municipal infrastructure and services. When I came to Johannesburg in 1994, suburban streets not only had street signs, but at each corner a kerbstone was painstakingly stencilled with the street's name, an arrow, and the number of the next house in that direction. Handy, in the days before GPS, should you reach your street but didn't know if you should turn left or right. It was an extravagance based on the availability of cheap black labour. In townships, where municipal workers tasked with stencilling suburban kerbstones lived, most streets did not have names, never mind street signs. Houses in a township are numbered. The house numbers reach, three, four, sometimes five, figures. My Mashaeng address is 396 Mashaeng Township. If I lived elsewhere in the township, it could be 1396 or 2396 Mashaeng.

Service delivery to the township residents began prior to the fall of apartheid. In part, an attempt to establish a black middle class as a buffer against revolution. However, the pace picked up dramatically post 1994. The roll out of services made a difference to people's lives, more so for women given the gendered division of domestic labour. It also supported public health, facilitated children's education (as with the simple boon of having electric light with which to do homework in the evening), and more. Such interventions would, it was anticipated, build society, economy, and social justice. Delivery of houses, electricity, street lighting, piped water, storm drains, and more, in short service delivery. It also gave dignity to township residents, perhaps no more so than with waterborne sanitation, or more straightforwardly put, flush toilets.

I started visiting Mashaeng in the mid-2000s. The bucket system was still in place. We sat on a wooden bench in a small outside privy and crapped through a hole into the bucket below. The shit was collected weekly. Flies patrolled and the smell sharpened as the week progressed. You avoided looking down. If the bucket filled before collection day, as would happen over the Christmas break,[30] you needed to go elsewhere. One option was to use a neighbour's toilet, but since they were in the same situation, this was a source of tension best avoided. You ended up squatting *thoteng*, in the open land around the township.

Then flush toilets came. It was a considerable investment with pipes installed and sewage treatment works constructed. It was a cause for celebration. The

30 With additional family members visiting over the holidays and disruptions to collection.

bucket system was no more. However, the flush toilets increased water usage, as did the growing population of the township with people coming off the farms and from Lesotho. Yet, the bulk water supply for the township was not increased. Water is life, a fact only really appreciated when it is scarce. At its most basic we need water for drinking, cooking, washing clothes and dishes, and to bath. It's also needed to flush the toilets that now resided on every Mashaeng stand. Periodically the township is without water. Sometimes for hours, sometimes days, sometimes longer. Sometimes, it's just some sections of the township that are dry. Sometimes it's the entire township.

A flush toilet without water is no cause for celebration. As an elderly neighbour described it, you become a slave to the white throne. It demands water after every use, bucket after bucket. If you are old and cannot carry the water, you must pay somebody to assist. If you fail to appease the white throne, the smell sharpens, and the flies arrive. Almost twenty years after flush toilets came to liberate us from the indignity of the bucket system, the problem of water has not been resolved, though the explanations and the promises have been legion. Households have adapted as best they can. We store water in 20 litre *dikupu* (buckets), but when the water is out for days or weeks this doesn't suffice. Women and children carry water in buckets on their heads[31] from township streets where the taps are still running. Occasionally, a municipal water tanker makes an appearance and there is a scramble as we rush out with buckets. When the whole township is dry, women trek to springs around the township as they did before piped water came, de-development before our eyes.

The turds that we flush away with the water we have collected in buckets now flows through sewage plants which no longer work.[32] Raw sewage flows through them and into the river systems of the Free State. At least with the old bucket system excrement was dumped in trenches away from streams and rivers to avoid contamination.

With hindsight, the statistical success of service delivery to township residents was a case of more haste, less speed. Supporting infrastructure was not installed, or insufficient. Nor were maintenance costs adequately budgeted. It was political show: high profile delivery for today without a plan for tomorrow. Services delivery has not completely halted, but its continuation is faltering, and often chaotic. The neglect of maintenance programmes erodes what has been achieved.

31 Reflecting the established division of labour. It is rare to see a man fetching water, unless they are using a vehicle.

32 Nationally, 39 per cent of South Africa's wastewater systems were regarded as being in a critical state based on the Green Drop standard in 2022. In the Free State this stands at 67 per cent, an increase from 51 per cent in 2013 (Carnie 2022).

In part, this was engendered by political pride that skews spending to the new and the flashy. The slog of maintenance does little to profile politicians or help them win elections. New projects also provide opportunities for the class of tenderpreneurs that has emerged within political–business nexuses. The tenderpreneur provides a kickback or bribe in return for receiving the contract, takes a percentage, and passes the contract onto a contractor, that contractor likely repeats the process passing the work along again. By the time it gets to the contractor who does the work, profit has been cut to levels that ensure shoddy work and corners cut.

Responding to South Africa's entropic trajectory

The failure of development, visible in townships years ago, has now reached the suburbs. In Johannesburg, the economic centre of the country, grumbles and frustration over chaotic municipal billing has turned to outrage and apprehension as water and electricity becomes increasingly unreliable. It's one thing to fight over meter readings, it's another to collect water from a tanker in the street. The entropic trajectory of post-apartheid South Africa is less the centre being unable to hold, than it is society's economic and social infrastructure collapsing from the periphery into the centre.

The response of suburban citizens has been to fork out for private provision.[33] This has long been the case for security and healthcare, with those able to pay subscribing to armed response companies and medical aid (insurance) plans. But now private provision extends to purchasing generators, installing water storage tanks, and, once the City of Johannesburg conceded it had no working fire engines at many of its fire stations, subscriptions to Fire Ops, a private, subscription based fire-fighting company.[34] At school in 1970s Britain, I was taught how municipal fire brigades were created in the nineteenth century because private fire-fighting arrangements proved inadequate as towns and cities grew. Like Mashaeng residents collecting water from springs, that Fire Ops exists is development in reverse.

The same applies to other services: collectively organised provision of water, sewage, electricity, roads, and more is far more efficient than each household attempting to be self-sufficient. The same applies to security. But, if collective provision fails, then citizens must provide for themselves. Suburban residents pay for private provision with resentment; questioning why they pay taxes but must pay again for services which the state fails to provide. Yet, they have little choice but to pay, if they are able, since the state neither serves nor protects them.

33 A response found across the globe where there is inequality and the provision of services inadequate (Kalina 2020).

34 Fire Ops SA (N.D.).

The response of township residents to South Africa's entropic trajectory is different to that of the suburb. One reason is depth of pockets; private provision is expensive. But it is also down to cynicism over what democratic South Africa has and will provide. In other words, disenchantment with the *lex constitutional* and its promises. David Kirk and Mauri Matsuda, looking at disadvantaged American neighbourhoods where upward mobility is limited, argue that "disadvantage breeds cynicism toward societal institutions."[35] Narrowly defined, legal cynicism refers to the criminal justice system and the control of crime, explored in Chapter 4. But the cynicism of township residents is wider. It is not only the justice system, criminal and civil,[36] that is failing, but the entire spectrum of state functions: service delivery by municipalities, the state housing programme, the issuing of identity documents by Home Affairs, services provided by the Department of Labour,[37] the Master's administration of deceased estates,[38] compensation for traffic accidents by the Road Accident Fund, and more.

It is not that these state and quasi state institutions no longer function (though some are close to the brink). Rather, their services are all too often slow, indifferent, confusing, inefficient, and frustrating. Frustration leads to the conclusion that the institutions and individuals within them are corrupt, even if they aren't. The cynicism of township residents should be understood widely. However, we should not conceive of a corrupt/inefficient set of institutions on the one side and a cynical but passive population on the other. The two are not separate entities since township residents work within, and are part of, those institutions.

But whether in or outside these institutions, township residents have, as this book underlines, agency. They will, if they believe the institutions are stacked against them, engage with these systems to best advantage. What Patricia Ewick and Susan Silbey refer to as being with the law. Here the legal system – or in our case the wider gamut of state institutions – is understood as "an arena of competitive tactical manoeuvring where the pursuit of self-interest is expected…."[39] This cynicism opens up additional options for pursing disputes.[40]

35 Kirk and Matsuda (2011:448).

36 Including the Commission for Conciliation and Arbitration (CCMA), which constitutes the lowest rung in the resolution of employment disputes. See Dickinson (2021b) for an account of precarious workers experiences with the CCMA and labour courts.

37 Including the administration of the Unemployment Insurance Fund and compensation for occupational accidents.

38 Morrison (2023).

39 Ewick and Silbey (1998:48).

40 Kirk and Matsuda (2011).

One township response to stalled transformation is the now endemic service delivery protests, riots, and localised insurrections. These seek to divert the state's shrinking resources to the protesters' community. Peter Alexander's (2010) suggestion that these protests constitute a rebellion of the poor has resounded in academic circles.[41] Yet, Alexander describes these protests as "plac[ing] demands on people who hold or benefit from political power."[42] If rebellion is resistance to state authority, then these protests are not part of a rebellion, but are rather petitioning the state, albeit through disruptive and sometimes violent repertoires of action (Von Holdt et al. 2011). While these protests *are* based on common causes of frustration, the demands of service delivery protests rarely transcend local concerns.[43] Such protests can be tactically effective but are strategically fruitless unless the state is able to increase the resources available overall.[44] In the context of South Africa's limited economic growth and growing population, such protests can only succeed in temporarily shifting resources, before protests elsewhere demand attention.

Another township response to the country's entropic trajectory is linked to the state's failure to provide security. This takes the form of community security initiatives, ranging from Community Policing Forums members patrolling townships streets in reflector jackets through to enraged locals lynching suspected criminals. This so-called mob justice is meted out by frustrated township residents who, caught between an ineffective criminal justice system and *tsotsis* (hoodlums), periodically take matters into their own hands, something outlined in Chapter 4.

However, the prevalent and ubiquitous township response to the development failure of post-apartheid South Africa and the country's entropic trajectory is grasping opportunities or *menyetla*. As the prescribed, lawful, means of advancement have shrivelled, townships residents do what they can for themselves, loot from below.

41 As of October 2024, Google Scholar records Alexander's 2010 article "Rebellion of the poor: South Africa's delivery protests" as having been cited well over 1,000 times.

42 Alexander (2010:26).

43 In contrast, township protests against foreign nationals, that is xenophobia, while played out in local formats, is unified by a widely shared perspective.

44 In contrast, Partha Chatterjee's argument as to the ability of political society (see the Introduction) to use the resource of electoral mobilisation to force concessions takes place within the context of a rapidly growing Indian economy (Chatterjee 2008).

2

The apartheid township

Introduction

THIS CHAPTER outlines the history of South Africa's African townships up to the transition to democracy in 1994. The focus is on the township under apartheid, but the history of racial segregation and control long predates the election of the National Party in 1948. However, once in power the National Party vigorously tightened and extended the separation of races, intensifying structural violence on the African majority, justified by legally coded racist beliefs.

I draw on an often-brilliant scholarship as well as some of the laws and regulations used to control Africans in urban areas. Two key points emerge which assist in understanding the townships under democracy, the subject of the following chapter, the law of the township, and looting from below.

The first is that the township was a key component in a system of exploitation under colonial and apartheid rule of Africans by whites that created and consolidated an unequal society. Those in the township were permanently pauperised. This pauperisation meant that it was impossible for township authorities to raise sufficient finance for infrastructure development and services provision. Further, and equally important though less well understood, this prevented the creation of large scale, sustainable employment within the township. This impossibility stemmed from the very purpose of the township: to provide cheap labour for whites. This legacy remains and given the failures of the 1994 transformation project is a key explanation as to why township residents grasp *menyetla* in concealed defiance of the *lex constitutional.*

The second point is the psychological impact of apartheid's bureaucratic regulation on the lives of township residents in which they had to manoeuvre within stifling systems of control. This psychological legacy is transmitted to succeeding generations through folkways that are far more efficient than didactically proclaimed values of the Constitution. This influences township residents' relationship to democracy's *de jure* laws and provides moral validation for the *de facto* rule of the *lex lokasi* in the township.

South Africa's long history of racial segregation

The townships have their origins in the pass laws restricting movement of people of different races within the country. Racial segregation laws have pervaded South African history. Segregation entailed the separation of races, but in practice meant the restriction of racial groups deemed not to be white[1] to limited areas, the rest of the country being for whites. The earliest pass law was enacted in 1780 to control the movement of slaves in the then Dutch Cape Colony.[2] The passing of the *Native Land Act* in 1913 restricted where Africans could reside, eventually stabilised at just 13 per cent of the land. As Sol Plaatje (2021) documented in 1916, it also ended sharecropping[3] on white owned land, reducing African farmers to labourers.

In 1922, the Stallard Commission[4] recommended that Africans should only be in urban areas to serve whites. This applied the principles of the 1913 Land Act to urban areas.[5] What became known as the Stallard doctrine was to form the heart of apartheid urban policy. This doctrine expressed what was at the time "taken for granted throughout white-settled Africa"[6], that:

> … [T]he commingling of black and white is undesirable. The native should only be allowed to enter urban areas which are essentially the white man's creation … to minister to the needs of the white man, and should depart therefrom when he ceases to so minister …[7]

In 1923, Jan Smut's South African Party passed the *Urban Areas Act* in what was then the self-governing British Dominion of the Union of South Africa. The Act, which was to be amended numerous times, provided a consolidated

1 The terminology is clumsy. The term 'non-white' is pejorative, implying that not being white is inferior. South Africa's employment equity legislation uses 'black' to refer to Africans, coloureds, and Indians collectively. However, the term black is also widely understood to mean African. The overlap is manifest in the various use of African, black, and native in pre-1994 legislation referring to Africans.

2 Savage (1986).

3 Sharecropping, also known as 'farming on the halves,' involves the sharecropper farming another person's land in return for receiving a percentage of the crop. The system is often used when the owner of the land does not have sufficient labour and/or capital to farm what they own. That a significant impact of the 1913 Act was to turn sharecroppers into paid labourers indicates that whites had already alienated the indigenous population from most of the land in a process of often violent expropriation. Sharecropping by Africans continued despite its prohibition under the Act for decades, something described in detail by Charles van Onselen (1996).

4 Transvaal Local Government (1922).

5 Davenport (1970).

6 Davenport (1969:95).

7 Stallard quoted by Pauline Morris (1981:18).

framework for the management of African townships,[8] then termed locations, and repealed a large number of national and local laws, regulations, proclamations, and ordinances that had previously enforced racial segregation.[9] The Act was presented as providing improved conditions for "natives in or near urban areas and the better administration of native affairs in such areas."[10] The Act also provided for the control of residence and movement of Africans, or influx control.[11] Permission to reside in a township was controlled and African men were required to carry a *dompas* (identity book), endorsed by their employer. Pass control was enforced until the mid-1980s. Before then, permission for Africans to reside in townships was determined by the needs of white employers for industrial and domestic labour.

White authorities controlled almost every aspect of township life, including the brewing, sale, and consumption of "kaffir beer" (beer brewed from sorghum, now commonly known as *umqombothi*) in the township. This began in 1908 with the Natal *Native Beer Act* that, along with subsequent legislation, provided for municipal monopolies on alcohol sales in the township. The resulting profits were an important source of revenue to offset the costs of providing facilities and administrating townships by white authorities.[12]

The *Urban Areas Act*, however, provided only a framework for local authorities to manage African townships, which they did with different levels of effectiveness. Doug Hindson outlines how the provision of housing for Africans failed to keep up with inward migration to the urban areas from the 1930s to the 1950s. The result was that: "Housing within locations was overcrowded as householders took in lodgers to supplement low incomes. Backyard shacks were erected and sublet. Squatter settlements were established on vacant land in and around the industrial centres on the Rand."[13]

The apartheid township

In 1946, the United Party government (a coalition of the South African Party, part of the National Party and the Unionist Party), also led by Smuts, appointed the Fagan Commission[14] to review "native laws." The report recommended a relaxation of influx control and the establishment of a permanent African urban population that would provide a pool of reliable workers and generate

8 Coloureds were explicitly excluded from the Act.

9 As Alan Mabin (1992:409) points out, prior to apartheid racial segregation was conducted through legislation that was not explicitly segregationist, such as the *Slums Act* of 1934 which allowed local authorities to clear slum areas and re-settle people in a racially segregated way.

10 *Urban Areas Act* (1923) Preamble.

11 Posel (1997).

12 Kane-Berman (1978).

13 Hindson (1987:56).

14 Government of South Africa (1948).

consumer spending. The faction of the National Party[15] then in opposition established its own commission chaired by a party member, Paul Sauer. The Sauer Commission[16] recommended, in opposition to Fagan, that a policy of complete racial segregation should be implemented. The National Party won the 1948 election, with a minority of the vote but majority of seats. As Alan Mabin outlines, it did so "on the basis of a manifesto which made clear the party's commitment to compulsory urban segregation."[17]

It was the recommendations of the Sauer Commission that the National Party government was to follow. South African urban policy now diverged from that in other colonised sub-Saharan countries which shifted to supporting the orderly urbanisation of Africans.[18] The National Party initially moved cautiously regarding its urban policy, mindful of its limited support base within the white electorate.[19]

Ivan Evans (1997) describes the three core policies of apartheid: the labour bureau system, the planned native location (township), and the Bantu Authorities system (or homelands). The labour bureau system controlled the flow of African labour between the ethnically demarcated homelands and African townships in the urban areas.

Simon Bekker and Richard Humphries (1985) identified the major flows of African migration within South Africa that these policies created: first, migration from the homelands and white rural areas to the white urban areas (i.e. African townships); second, from white rural and urban areas to the homelands; and third, oscillatory migration of Africans between homelands and employment in mines and urban areas.

The first flow, to white urban areas, resulted from the shifting requirements of the white economy for labour from agriculture to industry as agriculture mechanised and manufacturing expanded. The second flow of Africans from white areas to the homelands was a result of the implementation of apartheid policies aimed at "cleaning up" the so-called "black spots" where Africans resided in white areas. In large part, this was achieved through forced removals. The Surplus Peoples Project estimated that 3.5 million people were forcibly relocated during apartheid.[20] The third flow, in which Africans moved back and forth between homelands and employment in white areas, was the responsibility of the labour bureau system, charged with providing white employers with African labour.

Since Africans were confined to designated ethnic homelands when not employed and permitted to reside in urban township, the labour bureau system meant that there was full employment for African men (since residential

15 Then the *Herenigde Nasionale Party* (Reunited National Party).

16 Herenigde Nasionale Party (1948).

17 Mabin (1992:409).

18 Davenport (1969).

19 Evans (1997).

20 Platzky and Walker (1985).

permits were issued to men as household head) in urban townships. This situation continues to be looked back on with nostalgia by long-term township residents as a time when there were jobs for all. Though, in fact, Hindson estimates that the overall unemployment rate in South Africa was 18 per cent in 1960 and 20 per cent in 1970 (at a time when white unemployment was almost non-existent).[21] In other words, while under apartheid urban townships were sites of full employment, mass unemployment was hidden in the homelands. But while there might be full employment for African men in the townships, their position was precarious, since to leave employment risked losing the right to remain in the urban areas.[22] Thus, the system of influx control permitted the super-exploitation of African labour.

Planning and paternalism

Much of apartheid policy was driven by H. F. Verwoerd who forged systems of bureaucratic control over the African population through the Department of Native Affairs (DNA).[23] In the early years of apartheid, state officials drove the construction of new urban townships with zeal, determined to eradicate the housing backlogs for Africans in urban areas that had led to chaotic overcrowding, backyard rooms, and informal settlements. The 1957 PhD thesis of James Mathewson, *The Establishment of an urban Bantu Township,* illustrates this well. The township was Daveyton established in 1952 for the white town of Benoni on the East Rand. Daveyton, named after a former Mayor of Benoni, William Davey, was a greenfield development and model township.

Mathewson's enthusiastic account of Daveyton's planning and development illustrates many features of the apartheid township. His focus was on the engineering and finance of the project, and he lauds how the project team rose to the challenge with limited resources. Indeed, it was a massive undertaking. Forty-thousand Africans were provided with 8,000 serviced houses, divided into seven ethnically defined blocks, relocated from what were considered slum areas within two years.[24] In line with the policy of influx control, township houses were rented through a permit system, linked to employment of the male head of the household, and were not available for freehold ownership.[25]

21 Hindson (1987:72).

22 Davenport (1969:105).

23 Evans (1997).

24 Mathewson (1957:47).

25 In accelerating the building of township houses in the early 1950s, a thirty-year lease had been introduced. However, this was abolished in the late 1960s with the shift of emphasis to developing the homelands under the scheme of 'grand apartheid' (Kane-Berman 1978; Picard and Mogale 2015).

When it comes to technical detail, Mathewson's work is hard to fault. He provides specifications for every aspect of the township's construction. This went as far as making an adjustment over how much water was required for an effective sewage flow considering the diet of the Bantu, in comparison to Europeans, and the greater amount of faecal matter this produced.[26]

What comes out from the technical detail and accompanying financial prudence are the imperatives of cost and order: "The two prime factors in effective administration," Mathewson writes, "are to keep overhead costs as low as possible and to have uniform and coordinated control."[27] These two concerns, finances and control, are written large across the history of the apartheid township.

Nevertheless, control was clothed in paternalistic ideals, at least in the early apartheid years. Mathewson was concerned that in urban areas, "the Bantu are inclined to discard what is worthy in their own culture in return for what is inferior in others."[28] Consequently, he stressed the need for a cultural organiser to be appointed for the township. Put differently, what was required was that Africans, temporarily in urban areas, were to be kept as apartheid ideology perceived Africans should be: rural, traditional, simple, and loyal. Ultimately as inferior human beings.

Mathewson asserted that, "The chief value of wholesome living amenities [planned for the township] lies not only in creating better racial relations but also in producing a more responsive, satisfied and cooperative community."[29] It was, however, the white administrators who would be in charge. Mathewson again: "Administrators of native towns will find that constant consultations with all its imperfections can contribute considerably to efficient administration … [Through consultation] a feeling is thus created that they [Africans] form a part of the machinery responsible for the progress of their own town."[30]

This paternalism was not completely rejected. As Evans points out, resistance to the infamous 1955 Sophiatown removals in Johannesburg was, despite later embellishment, limited.[31] The ANC had called for resistance under the slogan "We shall not be moved!". However, it was speaking to the interests of an elite of Sophiatown homeowners who were also landlords renting out rooms and backyard space. "For the majority of tenants and sub-tenants, Verwoerd's clearance schemes were not without a silver lining, for it meant an end to the immediate squalor and high rents that prevailed in the slum areas."[32]

26 Mathewson (1957:109).
27 Mathewson (1957:182).
28 Mathewson (1957:189–90).
29 Mathewson (1957:225).
30 Mathewson (1957:196).
31 Evans (1997:156).
32 Evans (1997:156).

State control

What the apartheid urban planners brought was "soulless and regimented [townships] ... abundant testimony to the state's predominant interest in controlling the reproduction of Africans in easily monitored zones within the urban areas at minimum cost."[33]

Under apartheid, white municipalities initially administered neighbouring townships, with occasional consultation from a township advisory board. In 1961 the advisory boards had the option of becoming Urban Bantu Councils (UBCs), derogatively labelled "Useless Boys Clubs," which had limited administrative and executive powers while the white council, using a Black Revenue Account kept separate from that of the town, continued to control taxation and finance.[34]

In 1972, twenty-two Black Affairs Administrative Boards, covering the entire country, were established and took over much of the responsibility for running African townships from white municipalities. The introduction of the Administration Boards consolidated ministerial control over African townships. On most issues, the white township administrator reported directly to the relevant Administrative Board, that were effectively extensions of the national Department of Cooperation and Development,[35] as the DNA had been renamed.[36] With a larger geographical footprint than local municipalities, the Administrative Boards now oversaw influx and labour control.

Francis Kendall, writing in 1991, summed up how, "under apartheid, South Africa has developed one of the most highly centralised political systems in the western world. Both white and black (but especially black) local governments have had almost no powers of their own."[37]

The control of townships was however not just administrative but also physical. While townships had to be close enough to employment to allow daily commuting, they needed to be at a distance from the residential area of other races. Townships had to be surrounded by a buffer zone. In Mathewson's Daveyton, the then Minister of Native Affairs required a buffer zone of 500

33 Evans (1997:120).

34 Bekker and Humphries (1985:16).

35 Bekker and Humphries (1985:18).

36 The Department of Native Administration was reorganised into the Department of Bantu Administration and Development in 1958 when the Department of Education and Training, dealing with the education of Africans, coloureds, and Indians, was split off into a separate department. In 1978 it was reorganised as the Department of Plural Relations and Development, then the Department of Cooperation and Development (1979), and finally in 1985 as the Department of Development Aid, with many functions transferred to other departments (Picard and Mogale 2015; Platzky and Walker 1985).

37 Kendall (1991:29).

yards (475 metres).[38] Ideally, a township would be separated from the white town by an industrial area and there should be only one road between town and township, preferably running through the industrial area.[39] Even today, most townships have few entrances, making them easy to isolate in the event of unrest and, as we will see in later chapters, providing "pinch points" where the state retains some control.

Finances

If physical control of the apartheid township could be secured, it was far harder to manage financially. Indeed, finances were a perennial problem that plagued every configuration of township administration. The basic problem was how to pay for township facilities, upkeep, and services when its residents provided cheap labour for white employees and had limited incomes. Revenue collection was further constrained by restrictions on business activity in townships[40] – in order that township residents patronised business in white towns. John Kane-Berman outlines that in 1978 only one in ten purchases by Soweto residents took place in the township.[41] This restriction limited the business rates that could be levied and therefore the revenue to improve township facilities and infrastructure.

Revenue for the township came primarily from four sources: subsidies from the white town's account, until responsibility for the townships was transferred to the Administration Boards in 1972; rent for houses (a charge that included payment for municipal services as well as actual rent); a levy on the employment of African workers by white employers; and, the sale of alcohol.[42]

Not all municipalities established beer halls or otherwise permitted the sale of alcohol in townships. However, the municipal and later Administration Board's monopoly on the sale of sorghum beer, and from 1962 "European liquor,"[43] was an important source of income. When subsidisation from the white town's general account ended with the 1972 administrative reforms, the Administration Boards mounted advertising campaigns to promote beer sales in the townships.[44] The Johannesburg council had exercised its monopoly rights to brew sorghum beer in 1937 and opened beer halls in Soweto. In the 1975/6 financial year, sorghum beer and other liquor sales in Soweto raised R177 million, of which R30 million was profit out of a total township

38 Mathewson (1957:34).
39 Philip (2014:34).
40 Kendall (1991:29).
41 Kane-Berman (1978:62).
42 Bekker and Humphries (1985).
43 i.e. beer brewed from malted barley, wine, and spirits.
44 Kane-Berman (1978:60).

administration income of R321 million.[45] To maintain this monopoly, and the revenue it supplied, municipal police regularly conducted *klopjags* (raids) on those suspected of brewing sorghum beer for private sale.

Municipal beer halls, the only place in townships where alcohol could be sold, were bleak industrial caverns with metal benches and tables. The Daveyton beer hall could accommodate 1,000 drinkers.[46] As tastes shifted from sorghum beer to European liquor, revenue from alcohol sales in the township had to compete with white businesses circumventing the township administration's monopoly, something described in Chapter 8 that looks at alcohol sales in the township.

Bureaucracy, resistance, and reform

The apartheid township was a world of petty indignities for Africans at the hand of the apartheid bureaucratic system. John Kane-Berman, writing in the aftermath of the 1976 Soweto rising, outlined how, "urban Africans in South Africa are probably subject to more regulation and restriction than any other race or class on earth. To many of them, the business of daily living must seem like a Pilgrim's Progress through a world invented by Kafka."[47] At night, the 1930 amendment to the *Urban Areas Act* provided for municipalities to impose curfews between 10pm and 4am.[48]

African men were required to carry and produce their passbook on demand.[49] This had to be endorsed by employers. Until 1976, employers had to endorse passbooks monthly. Failure to carry a correctly endorsed passbook led to arrest and prosecution. In 1977 over 400,000 Africans, approximately 10 per cent of African males between the ages of 16 and 64 in South Africa, were arrested for pass offences, breaking curfews, or being in white areas without permission.[50] The enforcement of pass laws, and of other regulations, such as the prohibition on brewing, was carried out by African policemen, known as Blackjacks,[51] Green Beans,[52] and later, during the 1980s states of emergency, *Kitskonstables*,[53] under white command.

45 Kane-Berman (1978:66).

46 Mathewson (1957:148).

47 Kane-Berman (1978:ix–x).

48 Davenport (1970:81).

49 Legislative attempts by the apartheid government to require African women to carry passbooks were successful resisted, notably with the 1956 Women's March in Pretoria.

50 Burns (1978).

51 Kane-Berman (1978). For Soweto Township.

52 In Katlehong and Vaal township. Fieldnotes: 161206 and 241015. The nickname has reemerged for the Gauteng Crime Prevention Wardens established in 2022.

53 That is, "instant police" because of their poor training (Bonner and Segal 1998:126).

Township residents had to navigate myriad regulations, giving enormous power to officials, over for example allocation of housing.[54] Family houses were allocated to married men and a marriage certificate was required. This resulted in marriages of convenience to obtain housing.[55] Yet, officials also colluded with residents to arrange matters. In the case of housing allocations, Deborah Posel describes how African men and women were paired off for marriages of convenience by officials to allocate housing. This was done by women choosing one of the hats set out on a table. The hat owner, sitting in another room, was to be their husband.[56] When it came to employment, the labour bureau was often bypassed by employers issuing a work seeker's permit after the worker had arrived and a contract had been registered.[57]

Rule by regulation maintained a racist social order for decades. Evans describes how apartheid bureaucratic administration "underpinned racial domination and was surprisingly effective in conditioning the compliance of the African majority … coercion was systematically leached into issues of everyday administration."[58]

However, this compliance was not to last. On one side was the legislation, administration, courts, and police of the white minority. On the other, millions of Africans seeking employment and opportunities available in the urban areas and needing a residential foothold to realise them. Attempting to prevent the urbanisation of Africans was, Davenport described, "to do battle with a tempest."[59] And it became increasingly difficult as the growing manufacturing and service sectors of the economy required more skilled, educated, and therefore permanently urban-based workers.

It was at the level of local government that apartheid values were implemented most clearly: the separation of communities by race with white areas enjoying privileges denied to others.[60] As Colin Bundy puts it, "the issues around which township residents sought redress sprang directly from their experiences of coercion, tight-fisted administration and the bony grip of want."[61]

Townships became centres of revolt against the apartheid government. Nevertheless, the spark for this revolt was not over the issues identified by

54 Posel (2006:70).

55 Posel (2006:65).

56 Other systems to the same effect also operated. At a Wits University seminar on the family house (see Chapter 4) in 2017, an African attendee outlined how his own marriage had been organised by housing officials, with his to-be-wife in a separate room picking a number to pair him up for house allocation. He went on the say that this was the only thing that he thanked apartheid for as it had been a happy marriage!

57 Hindson (1987:65).

58 Evans (1997:x).

59 Davenport (1969:108).

60 Cloete (1995).

61 Bundy (2000:32).

Bundy, but over the implementation of Afrikaans as a language of instruction in the Bantu Education system.[62] This triggered the 1976 Soweto uprising directed against apartheid control of the townships. State institution, beer halls included, were targeted in months of unrest across the country during which hundreds of young people died. By revolting, the youth also challenged the complicity of their parents who had, since the crushing of internal opposition to apartheid in the early 1960s, largely submitted to their oppression.

In the wake of 1976, reform efforts attempted to improve conditions in the townships. These had deteriorated since the early years of apartheid, in part due to the 1968 shift in spending from urban townships to the homelands.[63] This was in line with the strategy of grand apartheid that intended the ethnic homelands to become independent states, albeit vassals of white South Africa.

Government policy now shifted towards stabilising the urban townships. The *Black Local Authorities Act* of 1982 attempted to establish local township authorities. This shifted the all-but-impossible task of improving township living conditions onto locally elected residents. Without any significant businesses operating within the townships, these township authorities could only raise funds through the unpopular measure of increasing rents and service charges on residents.[64] The Black Local Authorities (BLAs) had little real power and lacked popular support. While those supporting them might have seen them as a move away from white domination, opponents saw them as attempts to defuse pressure for genuine non-racial local government.[65] Harry Mashabela outlined in a survey of townships in the PWV (now Gauteng) that, "Many residents see [the BLAs] as powerless bodies and see councillors as self-serving individual who are often corrupt and usually unresponsive to residents … [township] councils are in effect still run by white officials …."[66]

Widespread unrest in the 1980s saw many townships, particularly in larger urban areas such as the Vaal townships southwest of Johannesburg,[67] rendered ungovernable as a result of protests, strikes by increasingly militant independent trade unions organising African workers, direct attacks on township police and councillors, and rent boycotts that hit back at apartheid repression and eased the bony grip of want.

Attempted political reforms failed to address the economic inequalities generated by centuries of racial segregation and decades of apartheid. The 1983 constitution, approved in a whites only referendum, created a racially segregated tricameral parliament for whites, coloureds, and Indians. This

62 The education system for African school students.

63 Bekker and Humphries (1985:38).

64 Kendall (1991).

65 Moolman (1990).

66 Mashabela (1988:7).

67 Noonan (2011); Rueedi (2021).

attempt to buttress white rule by giving other racial minorities voting rights, but continuing to exclude the majority African population, failed to end mounting internal and external opposition to apartheid. In 1990 the then State President, F. W. de Klerk, unbanned the ANC, PAC, and SACP, the main anti-apartheid parties. In 1992, another whites only referendum approved the introduction of non-racial democracy and democratic elections were held in April 1994.

Conclusion: Freedom and expectations

This chapter has drawn almost exclusively on the work of others that demonstrate how the apartheid township, an intensification of earlier colonial policies, was a key component of racial exploitation. The apartheid township entrenched and increased racial inequality. The impossibility of townships to balance their financial accounts is equally clear. So also, how the exploitations of Africans in the townships led to revolt and the defeat of apartheid.

What is more difficult to grasp is the psychological impact of the apartheid townships on those who lived in them. It is always difficult to say what the collective impact of oppression or trauma has on a population. People's experiences differ, as do their reactions and responses. Even harder to establish is what psychological impact is passed on to successive generations who remain in the townships thirty years into democracy.

Nevertheless, I make two suggestions as to the psychological legacy that are relevant to the looting from below that his book engages with. The first extrapolates from what Bundy describes as the "surveillance, harassment and constant control" of the township.[68] When the talons of apartheid finally loosened, the desire to be free was overwhelming. Small wonder if township residents reject, in practice if not by public pronouncement, any yoke that limits freedom.

The second is that having learned informal ways of managing the system to best advantage, given their oppressed position within it, such methods are germane when the 1994 promise of upliftment fell short of expectations.

68 Bundy (2000:31).

3

The post-apartheid township

Introduction

To the visitor, one African township looks much like another. Under apartheid, townships were dormitories for the African workforce. Despite many being the size of cities,[1] there is no central business district or centre, no central square, and few parks or open spaces beyond dusty football fields and empty wasteland. Only the occasional building rises more than one story. One street looking much like another, it is easy for the visitor to become disorientated.

Yet beyond this monotony of form, townships are varied and complex places. This chapter describes the contemporary township. The following section looks at evidence on how many people live in South Africa's townships before the differences and divisions within townships' racially homogeneous population are explored.

This is followed by a description of the formal governance of townships under democracy and the state's approach to their economic development. There are, however, other dimensions to the township beyond its governance and economy.

Culture is made and remade as social norms are enacted and, over time, changed. To attempt to describe the culture of the township risks over-generalisation and simplification. What is attempted is a description of three dimensions of the township that contribute to understanding the *lex lokasi* – the *de facto* law of the township described in the following chapter. First, the extent to which African systems of law and belief, with their origins in pre-colonial society, continue to operate in urban townships, contributing to the plurality of residents' beliefs. Second, the configurations of private and public space and how secrets can be maintained. Third, the importance of consumption for social status; social success measured by money.

The chapter concludes with the argument that the state has only limited control in the township. Rather, social order in the township is for the most

1 There is no standard definition of what constitutes a city, however Dijkstra *et al.* (2020) define a city as a population of at least 50,000 inhabitants with a density greater than 1,500 inhabitants per km^2.

part in the hands of its residents, though not in the way hoped for by the draughters of the Constitution.

The population of the township

Establishing how many people live in South Africa's townships is not straightforward. Stats South Africa's (SSA) census records whether people live in formal housing (made of brick or concrete), traditional housing (mud walled and thatched), or informal dwellings (shacks, usually constructed with wooden frames and galvanised metal sheeting), and not by settlement type. This means that while a house in the township is formal housing, shacks in its backyard are recorded as informal housing.

A 2014 World Bank Study[2] used three different national surveys conducted by SSA[3] to estimate, for 2000 and 2011, the population of different settlement types. For urban areas the study differentiated between townships and informal settlements.[4] The combined population of townships and informal settlements in 2011 was some 18 million people, more than half the total urban population. The 3 million people living in informal settlements represented a doubling over the period, the 15 million in the township an increase of almost 40 per cent. Both percentages represent far higher increases than in other urban areas (at around 20 per cent), while the rural population declined. These trends have continued since the study. Vast informal settlements now ring metropolitan centres while townships continue to densify with unregulated building of backyard rooms and shacks, and the widespread construction of *maline* – lines of rented rooms with each room rented separately.

A 2009 study,[5] used a different methodology to calculate the township population, again from SSA data. These findings, similar to those of the World Bank, calculated how township populations varied as a percentage of the total urban population across South Africa's major urban areas. This ranged from a low of 38 and 42 per cent for eThekwini (Durban) and Tshwane (Pretoria) respectively to a high of 70 per cent in Ekurhuleni (Gauteng's East Rand) where much of the fieldwork for this book took place.

The post-1994 RDP[6] housing projects have replicated apartheid's monotonous townships layout described by Evans (1997). Nor have they

2 Which focused on the economics of South African townships (World Bank Group 2014).

3 The *Income and Expenditure of Households Survey*, *General Household Survey*, and *Labour Force Survey*.

4 Though exactly how is not clearly outlined.

5 Department of Co-operative Governance and Traditional Affairs and European Commission (2009).

6 Reconstruction and Development Program; the short-lived economic policy on which the ANC based its 1994 election manifesto. The acronym has stuck to state provided houses.

closed the physical separation between town and township. As Kate Philip outlines, under pressure to deliver housing, the cheapest land available, typically the worst, has been used, resulting in a "persistent spatial divide" between townships and economic opportunities.[7]

Unconstrained by such budgetary pressures, squatters establish informal settlements in urban areas wherever vacant land is left unguarded. Given low wages and high transport costs, the closer these informal settlements are to town centres and industrial areas the better. Some extend up to the boundaries of suburbs and office parks. Others are nested within formal township housing or form township extensions.

Division and diversity

The World Bank's study found that while almost 80 per cent of the South African population was African, Africans made up 96 per cent of the population of urban townships and 97 per cent of informal settlements. The balance of these areas was made up largely of coloureds who constitute four per cent of urban townships and 2.2 per cent of informal settlements.[8]

While there is close to total racial homogeneity in urban townships and informal settlements,[9] African townships are not socially homogenous. One difference is ethnicity. South Africa's eleven official spoken languages,[10] nine of them African, illustrates, albeit far from comprehensively, the ethnic diversity of the country. To formulate disputes or grievances around ethnic lines is publicly taboo.[11] Nevertheless, in as much as such ethnic

7 Philip (2014:41).

8 The World Bank category of other urban areas, that is all urban areas excepting township and informal settlements, was far more racially mixed: 43 per cent African, 27 per cent white, 22 per cent coloured and 8 per cent Indian. The almost total absence of Indians in township and informal settlements in the study figures must involve some decisions over categorisation. For example, Phoenix, within the eThekwini municipality, was established in 1976 as a township for Indians during apartheid. In 2011 it had a population of 179,000 and was 85 per cent Indian. It is described as a "working class township" by Laganparsad and Xolo (2021) but has presumably been categorised in the World Bank study, along with other similar Indian and coloured townships, as forming part of their category of other urban areas. Nevertheless, adjustments to statistics along these lines will, given South Africa's demographic statistics, make only limited changes to the overall picture of townships being African.

9 Under apartheid all townships, African, Indian, or coloured, were, by definition, racially homogeneous. To a large extent these geographical racial divisions remain.

10 Since 2023 South African Sign Language has been an official language.

11 See for example the immediate backtracking of President Ramaphosa over his assertion, early in the July 2021 unrest, that it was the result of Zulu mobilisation

reference is censored in public discourse,[12] awareness of ethnicity is salient in social interactions.[13]

Ethnic identity is buttressed in long-established townships by the apartheid policy of ethnically demarking township sections. The names of these sections often indicate the originally designated ethnicity. Over time there has been some dilution of this ethnic homogeneity, though much less so in hostels which, in Katlehong Township, are predominantly Zulu.

Only in more recent township developments, formal and informal, are ethnically mixed neighbourhoods the norm. Education and entry into the middle class, generally among those in more established sections, mutes the salience of ethnic difference, though rarely completely. The ethnic "other" remains a potential dividing line in social disputes while, conversely, ethnic consanguinity assists in establishing informal networks of trust.

Neighbourhoods within townships, known variously as sections, zones, units, extensions, and blocks, are themselves markers of identity. There can be fierce loyalty invested in sections, that becomes salient over the distribution of resources, such as employment opportunities on infrastructure projects, for which project managers must maintain a careful balance over who, from where, is employed.[14] Sections differ in terms of the socio-economic status of residents, most markedly between long-established sections and new informal settlements. Nevertheless, the historical legacy of the township and the tendency of those who significantly improve their economic position to migrate to the suburb means that these differences are compressed in comparison to the country as a whole.

A person's employment position provides the most pertinent marker of class. Since there are few township residents with substantial wealth independent of employment, it is those with secure, permanent, jobs, who form the apex

(which clearly was a factor in the early stages of the unrest after the Zulu former President, Jacob Zuma, was imprisoned for contempt of court).

12 Not least by the ANC which has, since its inception, strived to suppress "tribalism" as divisive of the African majority.

13 Ethnic stereotypes should be treated with caution: everyone has their own individual behavioural characteristics. Nevertheless, there are tangible differences between, say, Basotho and amaZulu. I am generally immersed in Sesotho township environments and interact in what could be called "Sesotho-kasi" culture and behave differently than in my predominantly white suburb or at university. However, if in an urban township I am interacting with one or more Zulu residents, my 'Sesotho-kasi' cultural practice must shift to "Zulu-kasi" culture, particularly with Zulu men. In this environment, I must be far more assertive and directly counter challenges thrown at me. This should be done without resorting to personal criticism, with confidence, and preferably with humour. Once a parity of challenge is established, things go smoothly.

14 Typically, failure to carefully negotiate this results in such work, whether organised by a private company (such as fibre installation) or state contracted work (such as road upgrading), being obstructed.

class of the township. State employment provides generous wages and benefits relative to equivalent employment in the private sector. Next come those in precarious employment, the working poor, who are employed on short-term contracts without security, at or below the national minimum wage and with few benefits. By and large permanent and precarious employment is in surrounding industrial areas, towns, and cities and not the township itself. "Stipend employment," in the form of government and NGO employment schemes, usually in the form of short-term contracts, often rolled over indefinitely, form a sub-class of township-based precarious employment, often below the national minimum wage.[15]

Given the limited formal businesses in the township and that much of the small business sector, notably *spaza* shops, are run by immigrants, the class of South African petty bourgeoise business owners is small. There is however an extensive class operating micro enterprises selling township fast food, running drinking establishments of varied degrees of formalisation, operating hair salons, collecting bottle, paper, and cans for recycling, or hawking from street stalls or door to door. These informal enterprises are often adjunct to families managing on the threadbare social security system of pensions, disability, and child grants. Last in the employment hierarchy there are unemployed adults relying on relatives and the recently introduced SRD grant described in Chapter 6.

Nationality forms another line of division. Immigrants, Asian and those from other African countries, are a source of complaint for outcompeting locals in township businesses and undercutting them in the labour market. Such criticism, ubiquitous in conversation and periodically escalating into xenophobic violence, is increasingly appearing in national discourse as scapegoats are sought for the country's entropic trajectory.

Other social stratifications further diversify township populations. Within African society age and gender differences are keenly understood and maintained. Those attending a township *mosebetsi* (plural: *mesebetsi*), part ritual and part social gathering, quickly gravitate to appropriate age and gender-based groups that occupy different physical spaces. Effortless as this may seem, these social norms are enforced. If, for example, a woman lingers when greeting men at a *mosebetsi* she will likely be rebuked should she not take the hint that she's overstepping what's proper. It's not that the men don't want female company, but there are ways that things should be done in public. Gender and age differences are maintained through physical location, not only at *mesebetsi* but also in township churches and, indeed, the township as a whole; streets are the social domain of men, homes those of women.[16]

15 The state's expanded public works programme hourly wage in 2024 was R15.16, exempted from the national minimum wage rate of R27.58 per hour.

16 Children and adolescents are free from this norm and can utilise both street and home.

Democratic local government

The history of townships is interwoven with the question of governance. Under apartheid, the township administration became an extension of national policies. With democracy, responsibility has been shifted to local or municipal government. As the third tier of government, along with national and provincial structures, municipalities' legislative sphere is demarcated by the Constitution. The objective of this reform was outlined by Pravin Gordhan in a forward to the 1998 *White Paper on Local Government*: "The process of transforming the institutions of the South African state is premised on the fact that the new democratic state has a specific mission; that of meeting the new developmental objectives which will help to create a better life for all."

The *Local Government Transition Act* of 1993 began a process of municipal reform. Transitional Councils were established that temporarily united towns and townships with the first non-racial local elections held during 1995 and 1996. The 2000 local government elections followed a comprehensive reorganisation of local government into the current metropolitan, district, and local structures in "wall to wall" municipal structures across the country. The size of these new municipal structures was increased in the belief that this would generate greater administrative professionalism and economies of scale. An important implication of this reorganisation is that previously linked towns and townships are now subsumed into larger political entities. This has contributed to a pervasive lack of accountability as local government has become increasingly remote, bureaucratic, and corrupt.

Local government is now recognised as an unmitigated disaster. Three major, interlinked fault lines can be identified: organisational complexity, funding, and corruption. The complexity of South Africa's three levels of governance, along with the superficiality of public engagement, has been sketched in Chapter 1. Tracy Ledger and Mahlatse Rampedi (2020) outline how the 1998 *White Paper on Local Government* incorrectly predicted the revenue raising ability of local government. In addition to being underfunded, municipalities also carry "unacceptable levels of unfunded mandates,"[17] that is responsibilities for which they are not allocated resources.

Only forty-one of the country's 257 municipalities achieved unqualified audits in the 2020/2021 local government audit report. The uncontroversial summary by *Business Day* journalist Luyolo Mkentane is that "most of the country's 257 municipalities, which are at the coalface of service delivery, have been run into the ground due to maladministration, looting and corruption …."[18]

[17] Picard and Mogale (2015:166).

[18] Mkentane (2022).

Malls and stalls: the township economy

In terms of annual consumption per capita, the World Bank 2014 study on South African townships found that "the distribution of consumption across settlement types is extremely skewed relative to population distribution."[19] In rand terms this was calculated for 2010–11 at R18,000 in townships and R12,000 in informal settlements compared to R66,000 in other urban areas.

Townships have remained essentially dormitory or commuter settlements. The frantic early morning weekday exit, and tired afternoon return to the township, bears witness to this. Despite the lifting of apartheid restrictions on township businesses, and the almost total absence of bylaw enforcement, there has been only limited economic development in townships.[20]

The most visible local economic change in the township since 1994 can be summed up as "malls and stalls." Over the past twenty years shopping malls have been established in most large townships, giving easier access to, largely white-owned, supermarkets and stores. At the same time, the informal economy has expanded with informal stalls at street markets around every shopping mall. Small scale businesses, often based in people's houses, garages, and yards, abound but are for the most part limited to *spaza* shops, food outlets, drinking venues, and hair salons. Generally, they are under-capitalised and prone to failure due to poor financial control and social tensions within families. Given this, an easy and common option is to rent out these sites to entrepreneurial immigrants who are typically able to buy stock cheaply in bulk using ethnic-based collective purchasing and are willing to work long hours.

Much of the stock for these informal businesses is purchased outside the township. So, despite the opening of myriad business in the townships the economic impact on the local economy has been limited. The World Bank study of Diepsloot Township calculated a low economic multiplier. Multiplier analysis measures the overall rise in the income of the township compared to an initial financial injection. As the study reports, "this finding reflects weak economic linkages within Diepsloot that result in large leaks to the wider economy outside. Diepsloot residents and firms use much of [their] income to make purchases outside Diepsloot; even the goods and higher-end services purchased within Diepsloot are ultimately sourced from outside."[21]

One business that benefits from the township's dormitory status is the black taxi (i.e. minibus) industry. Drivers are required to pay a set amount per day to the taxi owners. What they take in fares above this amount is what they keep. The incentive system promotes reckless driving as they chase fares. Routes are controlled by a multitude of taxi associations and there are periodic shootouts

19 World Bank (2014:75).

20 For a comprehensive review of the township economy see Charman *et al.* (2020).

21 World Bank Group (2014:14).

over turf. The black taxi industry illustrates the hard scrabble nature of most township businesses: a high level of informality and the need to assert oneself against rivals by making rather than following the law.

Despite the dramatic political rupture of 1994, the enduring spatial divide between suburb and township and limited economic development in the township has meant that inequality is now "set in concrete."[22]

A plurality of belief

Racial segregation emphasised the different cultures of whites, Africans, and other races, framed with the assumption of white or European cultural superiority. The extent to which urbanisation resulted in Africans abandoning traditional ways of life, its norms and its rules, in favour of those of the coloniser, has long been the subject of investigation.[23] The move from rural to urban environments influences social norms as people adapt to their new environment. Prior to the abandoning of influx control in the mid-1980s, urbanisation was strictly regulated. The ending of these restrictions has seen an acceleration of urbanisation while links to rural origins, or *mahae*, are maintained with the continuation of oscillatory migration patterns, established by apartheid policies.

The resulting urban "*kasi* culture" synchronises African tradition with modern institutions, such as school education; contractual employment; and access, albeit financially restricted, to mass produced consumer goods. This *kasi* culture is far from monolithic, but a starting point is to recognise that the township has its own culture that is different to the suburb.

One distinctive aspect of the township is the presence of African customary law. Its significance is less in its formal recognition under the Constitution of 1996 and more in its use in legitimating social norms at odds with other systems of law. In practice, though with some exceptions,[24] South Africa's Dutch-Roman common law and parliamentary legislation dominate legal procedure. Yet traditional African law provides a moral-counter point. The significance of this in the township, where the writ of constitutional law is limited, should not be underestimated.

Under traditional African law, land used for agriculture is allocated by chiefs and not inherited, but re-allocated based on need. This principle does not apply to occupied residential stands to which there is a general right of

22 Philip (2014:41).

23 See for example Philip and Iona Mayer (1961) and Pauw (1963). Both books had several impressions and editions published.

24 Such as the recognition of traditional marriages and the legality of polygamy under apartheid and democratic legal dispensations.

inheritance within the family.[25] The idea of a right to the land of one's birth remains deeply rooted in an African collective cosmology and is a powerful adjunct to the narrative of how Africans were dispossessed under colonialism. When working with LHR, I have been struck at how difficult it is to explain that being born on a property does not give right of occupation, let alone ownership, in court.[26] South Africa's current eviction laws were enacted in reaction to summary evictions under apartheid.[27] These new laws frustrate landlords and landowners who must engage in protracted and costly legal action to remove unlawful occupiers.[28] Yet they provide no right to property based on birth. LHR clients, for the most part Africans, threatened with eviction are interviewed to establish their rights of occupation. If, during these interviews, I explain that there is little basis to oppose a lawful eviction, clients will not infrequently produce what they think is a trump card which I have neglected: "I was born here!" When I explain that, in the eyes of the law, this gives them no rights, the response is incredulity, sometimes disbelief, and sometimes despair.

LHR clients are poor by any definition. To lose their lifetime home is a blow, little cushioned by the prospect of temporary emergency accommodation that will only plunge them deeper into poverty.[29] Suddenly, their life narrative of disadvantage resonates with a national narrative of dispossession. The laws of democracy may provide rights on paper, but from their perspective we are back to the Land Act of 1913 and the forced removals of apartheid. Do those who lack legal rights then comply with the notice to quit and court orders? No, they resist, even if only by sullen refusal to comply, until the Red Ants[30] arrive with a court order and crowbars. Their resistance draws on a powerful counter narrative of an alternative legal system that would, if followed, produce a different result.

Customary African law is a far more flexible system than the common law with its system of *stare decisis* (the rulings of higher courts binding lower courts) and the clarity (for the most part) of legislation. As Ian Hamnett (1975) outlines, since customary law is based on maxims or principles rather than

25 There is a grey area between what is clearly land used for agricultural production, and gardens attached to homesteads which are used to grow vegetables, see Hamnett (1975).

26 At least outside of the so-called "tribal areas," largely the old homelands, where chiefs continue to operate.

27 Primarily the *Prevention of Illegal Eviction from and Unlawful Occupation of Land Act* 19 of 1998 and the *Extension of Security of Tenure Act* 62 of 1997.

28 Or bypass these laws as in the case of constructive eviction where pressure is applied in a range of ways to force people to leave without having to approach a court.

29 Dickinson and du Plessis (2023).

30 The best-known South African company providing eviction and removal services.

detailed codification, it is possible to reach different conclusions in a dispute depending on how the principles are applied.[31] This flexibility underlines how appeals to customary or African law may provide advantage, rhetorically if not with the force of constitutional law, in disputes. But even as rhetoric, an appeal to customary law has real effect as in the example of conflict over a family house in the following chapter.

This plurality of social resources also exists in the metaphysical world. Understanding township culture requires a recognition of ancestors existing in a parallel world that has bearing on the world of the living. The degree to which it is believed these worlds intersect, that is how influential ancestors are in the affairs of the living, varies between individuals.[32] Some Pentecostal churches take a militant stand against ancestral belief. Yet, while belief in ancestors may be mocked by pastors, to break completely with respect for ancestors is another matter. Funeral rituals are a litmus test; to openly take a stand against traditional rites at funerals, such as slaughtering an animal, is to risk family strife. Christian belief further complicates the metaphysical world of township residents. Not only is the Christian God added to the spiritual world but also a visceral role for satanic forces and possession by evil spirits.

In practice, most township churches operate with some degree of syncretisation of traditional African and Christian beliefs. This may be explicit and celebrated as with apostolic or Zionist churches; accepted but regulated with acculturation practices[33] in mainline churches that Africanise their liturgy; or covert as when church members continue with traditional practices and beliefs discreetly or in secret.

Traditional rituals around death and marriage are also syncretised with Christian practices as well as state requirements. Thus, a marriage may involve a civil registration at the magistrate's court, traditional wedding ceremonies at the home of the groom and bride, and a white wedding in church – if family finances stretch that far. Similarly, funerals combine a range of traditional and modern practices: a night vigil before the burial, funeral policies to fund the most lavish burial that can be afforded, a church service, wreaths

[31] This flexibility allows for pragmatic rulings that provide justice in situations where less flexible legal systems may produce unfair outcomes. But it also permits outcomes reflecting unequal power of the litigants (or interests of the chief/presiding officer of the traditional court). This contrast between legal systems is relative, not absolute. Within South African courts operating with common and statute law, paying for more skilled and experienced lawyers provides a distinct advantage against less well funded opponents.

[32] It is, however, far greater than the European/white respect for, grief over, and remembrance of departed loved ones.

[33] In which Christian theology and practice is supplemented with indigenous African beliefs and customs.

and messages of condolences, orders of service with a list of speakers, and an animal slaughtered at the home of the deceased with its hide, or *lekoko*, sometimes draped over the coffin at the moment of burial. Orders of service are scrupulously collected at the graveside and buried with the deceased, or alternately burned, lest they be put to malicious use.[34]

If there is one key point to draw out of this long section it is that township residents live in a diverse and plural world of meaning, and equally of reference points for action.[35] This is not unique to the township, but it is particularly intense and necessitates juggling multiple, not always compatible, beliefs and obligations. This has bearing on why and how *menyetla* are justified on a widespread scale, even when illegal or illicit.

Secrets in public

The township is crowded and there is limited privacy. Suburban residents can, if they wish, keep themselves to themselves. Low density housing, high walls, gardens, and car ownership means they can choose who, where, and when they interact with others. A township resident may not have the privacy of their own bedroom. And even if they do, once they step out of house, room, or shack they enter a bustling *de facto* public space shared with others and with whom they must interact whether they wish to or not. Yet, much remains hidden.

At the centre of the previously mentioned *mesebetsi* are family members, but the attendance of neighbours is importance. This is not through invitation, but simply notification. Indeed, you don't even need notice. The unwritten rule of a *mosebetsi* is that all are welcome. If resources permit there will be food and home-brewed *umqombothi* provided for allcomers. If a neighbour is holding a *mosebetsi* it's expected that you attend, even if only briefly to show goodwill. Not to do so could suggest you do not wish the family well.

A *mosebetsi* is therefore to a large degree public. Yet, those attending may never know why it is taking place, and it is not polite or politic to ask. Unless the host volunteers that it is to thank the ancestors for good fortune, then it may be to appease them following misfortune. To poke your nose into others' troubles risks bringing suspicion on yourself.

Belief in witchcraft is widespread, yet open accusations are rare. More common is to accuse out of earshot or at most to *ho koba*; to speak indirectly or to insinuate. Such shielded or disguised accusations of malevolence provide explanation for failure or disappointment as well as censuring behaviour deemed selfish.

34 The usual explanation being that they could be used to turn the deceased into a zombie slave.

35 I make much the same argument, though in the context of health beliefs around HIV/AIDS, in *A Different Kind of AIDS*.

This supernatural world is largely veiled with public silence. *Sangomas* and prophets may claim to understand the ways of witchcraft or evil spirits, but only because their mission is to counter them. Beyond these practitioners, the only claim that can be publicly made with safety is that of victimhood. Early on in my township visits I showed a group of young men a picture on my digital camera (in the days before smart phones) of something I had come across:[36] a red candle pierced with needles. Obviously, it was ritualistic, but could any of them, I enquired, give me specifics? Nobody could. Until I was kindly told aside that everybody knew it was retaliation against witchcraft, the aim was to return the witch's curse back to sender. Nobody, however, was going to volunteer this knowledge in public, since it would reveal an intimacy with dark arts.

If witchcraft is a secret kept in public, then so too is money. At least when not being flaunted to provide status. Men in particular spend money freely as a *moreki* (the one who buys) at the end of the month or when they have a windfall. But outside of these status-buying splurges, it is wise to be *tjonne* (broke), even if you aren't really.

A wage earner may well not tell their partner how much they earn or will utilise opportunities to conceal bonuses, overtime payment, or money obtained from workplace theft. For men this provides a *mosefo* or discretionary fund used for drinking and girlfriends or "spares" on the side. Women likewise keep finances to themselves, though less for drinking, and almost never for boyfriends,[37] but more likely to ensure that there is money for children's *skaftins* (lunch boxes) and transport when money is tight at the end of the month. A mordant Sesotho ditty goes, *Ha mosadi o tsamaya, mona a kututsa*. (When the woman leaves [the house] the man searches high and low [being careful not to disturb anything]). He is looking for the money she has put aside.

Some home secrets are darker. Domestic violence is widespread across South African society.[38] Women in low-income brackets report the highest levels of partner violence.[39] Much domestic violence goes unreported, in part because the criminal justice system is not trusted. Violence against women

36 On Melville Koppies West, Johannesburg: a rugged area notionally under municipal control, but in effect common land used extensively by apostolic churches and *sangomas* as well as recreational users.

37 Not because they might not have them, but because of the gendered roles typical of these relationships in which the man provides resources to the woman as part of their relationship. The exception to this is the less common "cougar" and "Ben Ten," younger boyfriend, relationship.

38 Commission for Gender Equality (2022).

39 Stats South Africa (2020a).

is a social norm based on assumptions of male superiority[40] that conflict with the publicly proclaimed constitutional right to gender equality.

Secrecy may also be a reaction to legal vulnerability. As explored in the next chapter, while the *kasi* may have its own rules, too open defiance of national law brings risks. If not in the form of legal sanction, then the need to buy off state officials with bribes. The sale of *zol* or cannabis remains illegal even after the decriminalisation of its private use in 2018. It is, however, not hard to find a dealer in the township. These sales are often *maizisitse* (disguised) by a legitimate business that covers for the arrival and departure of customers.

That there are secrets within the public sphere is not unique to the township. As Georg Simmel explained, secrecy is a "universal sociological form in every society."[41] But what should be noted is how secrets are maintained in the township despite it being an intensely public space. A *sub rosa* world is maintained behind the thinnest of veils.

Achieving status

Individual and family status is determined in many ways. In African society, respect for elders and lineage is important. However, in South Africa displayed wealth announces status most clearly. This is true of the township, though these displays must often be achieved with limited resources and competing demands. The latter includes "black tax" levied by family members on wage earners. This results from the cocktail of high unemployment, extensive family ties, and limited social security. Black tax drains the pockets and patience of wage earners.

Achieving status through conspicuous consumption can take many forms; the car you drive, or having a car at all, the clothes you wear, the places you visit, the drinks you buy for others, and what you drink yourself. Status chasing through consumption conflicts with maintaining secrecy over disposable income on which claims can be made. This tension adds another stress to township life; one day you are splashing out to be someone, the next day you claim to be broke to stave off requests for assistance. If you are rich enough, the solution to the dilemma of displaying wealth but limiting demands is to move out of the township. You can return, in your expensive car and branded clothes, at weekends then retreat to the relative inaccessibility of the suburb till your next visit.

Within resource-tight environments, displays of conspicuous consumption can be achieved with minor gradations of signalled wealth. You could, for example, turn up your nose at Lion Larger, the cheapest brown bottle beer, in favour of slightly more expensive Black Label or Castle, or show that you

40 Saferspaces (2022).

41 Simmel (1906:463).

can afford green bottle beers such as Amstel or Windhoek. The differences in rand terms need not be large to be noticed. That gradations of status can be achieved in rand increments means that status differences can be displayed within as well as between socio-economic levels, something that fuels intense competition, jealousy, and resentment.

In the *kasi*, conspicuous consumption, however transitory, is *the* mark of success. More than anything else, it determines what a person thinks of themselves and what others think of them. The assumption from the suburb is that the poorer a person the more careful they should be with their money.[42] Yet, since self-worth is measured in large part by the standards of the community and if status is achieved through demonstrated material success, then few will rationally utilise what resources they have in line with Maslow's hierarchy of needs or some recommended purchasing formula for the poor.[43]

In 2007, during my first long-term residential township stay, I lived with two unemployed men. I bought groceries for the three of us *in lieu* of rent and we ate from the same pot, making communal life easy. But their poverty, demonstrated by their clothing and bedding compared to those I had brought for my stay, was obvious. One week I bought them blankets, another I gave money for them to buy clothes. Driving to the shops in town, I asked what they intended to buy with the money. One planned a jacket. That struck me as a good choice. The other socks. A very sensible choice I thought. I buy socks in packs from Woolworths. I thought it might not be a bad option for my housemate. He'd be able to stock socks aplenty with what I'd given. But he could buy cheaper in PEP, though they wouldn't match in quality and wouldn't last as long. Then I thought he might not buy in either Woolworths or PEP, but rather one of the "Indian shops" in the cheaper, African, end of town. He'd be sorted on the sock front for years. I parked the car, we parted, I got on with the grocery shopping.

Driving back home, I asked how the sock shopping had gone. It had gone well. My housemate had found what he wanted. I was still thinking quantity, but we weren't on the same wavelength. He was thinking brand. He hadn't purchased scores of socks as I imagined. It wasn't even double figures. It was three pairs. Pringle. Pringle of Scotland was then in the pantheon of South African fashion brands. I swallowed hard. I had imagined something thrifty, and it took me a while to think past my reaction of bewildered disappointment.

My housemate was taking the opportunity when it arose. My stay presented him with a minor windfall. He would flash his Pringle socks and feel proud. He would have his moment to *swanka* and be someone. We dismiss, to our analytical handicap, just how important status is, not only to those in the fast

42 Alongside exasperation at the reported or observed bad financial decisions of the poor, often coupled with amnesia concerning the financial mistakes we all make.

43 See Dickinson (2015) for a more detailed outline of this argument.

lane, but equally so for those at the bottom of society; a drawer full of socks is sensible; wearing Pringle socks is a dream fulfilled.

Contested control

Under apartheid, the African township was administered by white officials, with African representative structures little more than token. Residents had to comply with the demands of officials and the myriad rules which they imposed or find ways around them. Administrative control was backed by the police who maintained the pass laws that criminalised much of the African urban population. As Phil Bonner and Lauren Segal outline in their history of Soweto, the police's priority was preventing crime in white areas.[44] Townships were subject to sporadic mass raids, such as the *klopjags* on illegal brewing, but there was little crime prevention or detection. As a result, residents resorted to self-policing to deal with *tsotsis* (criminals or hoodlums), using corporal punishment, such as benching, to impose discipline.

With the end of apartheid, a new social order was intended. With respect to policing this was symbolically signalled by renaming the South African Police (SAP) to the South African Police Service (SAPS) and the military ranks of the SAP changed to civilian equivalents.[45] However, little has changed. Given the SAPS's inability to control crime, the benching of criminals has escalated to far more savage beatings and killings, addressed in the following chapter. The police have little authority and are largely restricted to operating "pinch points" at the entrances to townships where they can mount roadblocks. Only when *de facto* released from constitutional requirements and able to use brute force are the police able to claim any control over the township: the eventual suppression of the May 2008 xenophobic riots, the imposition of the first COVID-19 lockdown in March 2020, and the tardy response to the July 2021 looting, described in Chapter 11. But such manifestations of police power, resting on tear gas and rubber bullets, are fleeting spasms.

Beyond a new approach to policing, the intention was that South African society would be governed by consent. The liberation slogan, "The People Shall Govern!" was to take effect. The Constitution provided the framework for this new order with a complex system of cooperative governance and extensive consultation. However, much of this vision has turned out to be superficial. Social order in the township *is* to a large degree in the hands of its residents, but not in the way intended by the drafters of the Constitution.

Take the township's informal economy. Hawkers set up stalls wherever there is foot traffic to generate sales. Many of these enterprises are survivalist in nature, a response to the astronomical levels of unemployment. A

44 Bonner and Segal (1998:68).

45 The latter reform was reversed in 2010.

key anchor for informal markets in the township are shopping malls. These informal markets are in effect extensions of the mall, albeit established without permission on the pavements of the surrounding streets.

The largest such market in Katlehong is Sepetlele which surrounds the Letsoho shopping mall. Customers come from those shopping at the mall, adjoining taxi ranks, and, previously, the Natalspruit Hospital.[46] When the municipalities' Local Economic Development (LED) department commissioned a survey in 2006,[47] there were some 800 stalls operating in what initially looked a chaotic, edgy bedlam. The stalls, often no more than tables with awning rigged from plastic sheeting, encroach onto the roads. Cars had to drive slowly through crowds using the streets as throughfares. Smoke drifted from fires, rubbish littered open spaces, there was a cacophony of sound as hawkers shouted to potential customers and taxi horns blared. But under this surface chaos there was order: traders had, over time, established "their" place, if somebody didn't sell on a particular day their space would be utilised, but only until they came to set up stall the next day. The traders would cover for neighbouring stalls if one had to leave for a break, and it wasn't the place to *tshwara phoho* (rob somebody); a thief would not get far once the alarm was raised. In other words, this informality had rules. None were written, but the traders knew what they were and for the most part kept them.

These norms of traders' mutual assistance did not however translate into any real market-wide governance. There was a trader association which claimed to regulate the market but was little more than a liaison body for outsiders, including researchers, with business there. It claimed that only legal trading was permitted in the market. However, never mind bylaw infringements, there are stalls where phones can be unlocked without questions or pirated music sold. Regulation of the market in any significant way was beyond the association's power. Indeed, an attempt at enforcement of rules had resulted in a rival association being established.

None of the traders had permits to trade and were breaking bylaws by obstructing the pavement with their stalls. Other stalls, such as those selling food, were often in breach of health and safety standards. A few traders had been forced to pay bribes to municipal police, but the sheer size of the market provided a *de facto* right to trade. The research was commissioned with the objective of formalising the market. It was clear, from briefings, that the LED officials envisaged an ordered and clean set up in which entrepreneurial traders would formalise their businesses and graduate to better things. What

46 *Sepetlele* is Sesotho for hospital, hence the name of the market. The hospital has since been relocated, with little impact on the market.

47 The project, commissioned by Ekurhuleni Metropolitan Municipality, was conducted with colleagues and students from the Wits Business School (Dickinson *et al.* 2008).

we found was that although stall holders would like more customers, few were interested in changing how they operated. It was also apparent that while the municipality would like to see the market formalised, that wasn't going to happen. For better or worse, the traders governed themselves and the municipality's influence was marginal.

In the next chapter, I conceptualise, using socio-legal theory, the way in which the township is regulated, not by the state nor by constitutional law, but by the *lex lokasi* created by ongoing, everyday social struggles.

4

A crisis of social order: The *lex constitutional* and the *lex lokasi*

South Africa's crisis through a legal lens

IDEALLY, A country's laws, what citizens are required to do, are in harmony with its social norms, what people actually do, or at least what they say they should do. Such harmony is never complete. There is always some gap between law and social norms; whether because of criminals and deviants or otherwise upright citizens cutting corners. However, the *extent* of the disparity is important. When the difference is limited society is functional, but if social practice differs significantly from law there is a crisis of social order.

There are different ways in which the disjunction between law and norms exists. It could be that the law does not consider the plurality of a society and the disjunction between law and norms is uneven within the country. It could be that law lags social norms which have moved on. If so, the law is a conservative force that assists in preserving a past *status quo*, and with it the entrenched power relationship of a society. It could that the law is being used to engineer social change. If so, law is ahead of hoped for social norms which it has been introduced to bring about.[1] Likely, all three possibilities co-exist, but to what degree and in what ratio will determine the significance of these disjunctures.

Whether codified law is ahead or behind social norms is contestable since it concerns evaluating existing and desired social values and the social order that promotes, controls, or outlaws these. In South Africa, a project of progressive social engineering has been attempted following the fall of apartheid. Its failure has created a yawning gap between practised norms and law. This chapter explores the disjuncture between the formal law of South Africa, which I term the *lex constitutional,* and the informal law of the township, the *lex lokasi*.

The looting from below that this book explores occurs at the disjuncture between publicly professed social norms, which largely align with the law

1 Falk Moore (1973), what has come to be framed as the countermajoritarian problem (Cummings 2018).

of the land, and practised (rather than professed) norms. Looting from below does not define the *lex lokasi* in its entirety, but it does provide an analytical lens through which it can be viewed. The following sections outline the plural legal system in South Africa and how, in theory, all law and social practice is subject to the Constitution. This constitutional supremacy represented a triumph for those seeking progressive social transformation based on the Constitution's Bill of Rights.

There is increasing tension between rights and wealth; rights and accountability; and between rights and popular opinion, which are important elements of South Africa's entropic trajectory. However, the key focus of this book is how social practice in the township, governed by the *lex lokasi*, is diverging from the rule of constitutional law, the *lex constitutional*. A bifurcation of law in practice.

South Africa's plural legal system and constitutional supremacy

Prior to the introduction of the Interim Constitution of 1993,[2] South Africa was a racially restricted parliamentary democracy, in which a white parliament passed laws, otherwise known as statutes or acts of parliament, that could not be legally challenged. Thus, the apartheid project was enabled by the long-lived National Party parliamentary majority conducting a social engineering project based on racist beliefs.

In addition to statutory law and the subsidiary regulations that these statutes provide at national, provincial, and local levels of government, there is the common law and traditional or customary African law.

Common law, or the law of the courts, is developed by judges' rulings in cases brought before them. Rulings of higher courts take precedent over those of lower courts. While the common law was and is overridden by statutory law, it operates when there is no relevant statutory law. In contrast to statutory law that can be swiftly enacted in a parliamentary sitting, the common law, based on court judgements, moves slowly and unevenly with social norms. More precisely, the social norms that judges take into account.

Traditional African law operated before colonisation among the indigenous populations. Without a written record, customary law relied on oral transmission. As noted in the previous chapter, Hamnett outlines how "the 'rules' of customary law reside in concrete but general norms, whose ambivalence, or ambiguity, permits a variety of possible outcomes [for a particular dispute], which can be formally proposed and argued for as 'legitimate.'"[3]

The law of European settlers, common and statutory, was imposed on indigenous African populations.[4] Nevertheless, traditional African law, subject

2 That came into effect on 27 April 1994.

3 Hamnett (1975:114).

4 For imposed law see Burman and Harrell-Bond (1979).

to the so-called repugnancy clause,[5] was applied in areas of the country allocated for Africans. Some African customary law was codified for use in court proceedings, notably Zulu traditional law, forming the so-called official customary law.[6] Elsewhere African traditional law remained unwritten and Native Commissioners' courts relied on white experts and African elders to provide guidance on "living customary law."[7] Outside of the four short-lived, nominally independent ethnic states created during apartheid with their own parliaments and courts,[8] traditional courts were subordinate to the white court system to which serious cases had to be referred.

In a political system in which parliament is supreme, as was the case during apartheid, judges are entrusted with applying laws. Their role is to declare what parliament intended the law to achieve regarding any case before the bench and not to evaluate statute against any other benchmark. Until 1994, South Africa's white parliament made the law which judges had to apply. Indeed, in the early years of apartheid parliament passed legislation to prevent judges following common law principles and deviating from what it wanted to achieve.

In 1951, shortly after the National Party came to power, the government enacted the *Prevention of Illegal Squatting Act*. This criminalised squatting and assisted in enforcing racial segregation through forced removals.[9] It was also used to eradicate informal settlements established by Africans in urban areas. Africans, resisting these relocations, used common law interdicts in courts presided over by more liberal judges to counter the removal of informal settlements. In response, parliament passed the *Natives (Prohibition of Interdicts) Act* in 1956. The Act's long title stated that its objective was to "Prohibit the granting of interdicts or other dilatory [delaying] orders of court having the effect of staying or suspending the removal or ejectment of natives ...." The Act forced the courts to uphold the apartheid project as legislated by parliament.[10]

5 That African customary law could be over-ruled where it offended white sensibilities. The practice of bride wealth (*lobolo* or *bohadi*) was excluded from the repugnancy clause.

6 And therefore "frozen" since no mechanism was provided to repeal and amend this colonially captured version of indigenous law.

7 Until 1986 when their function was taken over by magistrates' courts. In 1988 the *Law of Evidence Amendment Act* allowed African customary law to be used in any court (Himonga and Bosch 2000:307).

8 The "TBVC" states of Transkei, Bophuthatswana, Venda, and Ciskei, none of which were internationally recognised. Any assessment of the independence of their political and judicial systems should consider that, overall, they were vassal entities of South Africa.

9 Platzky and Walker (1985).

10 In fact, carried out largely by ministerial-enacted regulations that parliament's laws provided for (Evans 1997).

The end of apartheid resulted in a transition from a white parliamentary democracy to an inclusive[11] constitutional democracy. The Interim Constitution came into effect on the 27 April 1994 and was replaced by what was termed the final Constitution of 1996,[12] which I refer to simply as the Constitution. Under the Constitution, it is the Constitution, not parliament, which is the ultimate arbitrator of law. Section 2 of the Constitution asserts that "this Constitution is the supreme law of the Republic; law or conduct inconsistent with it is invalid ...." Courts, above the magistrate level, are empowered to declare any law unconstitutional, though such declarations must be confirmed by the Constitutional Court. Any law – statutory, common, or customary – that the Constitutional Court declares unconstitutional is invalid.[13]

Thus, democratic South Africa has a plural legal system with different legal codes operating simultaneously, yet all subject to the supremacy of the Constitution creating, in principle, a single system of law being ever harmonised to the Constitution.

The Constitution

The Constitution was central to the optimism of South Africa's transition to democracy. Cheaply printed copies were widely distributed. Its objectives were laid out in its preamble: "South Africa belongs to all who live in it, united in our diversity." The Constitution, the Constitution says, was adopted by the freely elected representatives of the people and is to "improve the quality of life of all citizens and free the potential of each person ...." To achieve this, old laws were to be repealed, and new legislation enacted enabling this constitutional promise.

Chapter 2 of the Constitution, the Bill of Rights, outlines enshrined fundamental rights, as well as how those rights can be limited, enforced, and interpreted. The rights listed in Chapter 2 extend to socio-economic rights, noticeably on health, food, water, social security, housing, and education. It is these rights that have placed South Africa at the forefront of constitutions. There is however small print, these socio-economic rights are to be progressively realised within the state's available resources.

After the lofty pronouncements of the Bill of Rights, the remaining twelve chapters of the Constitution are dry material. They outline the political, executive,

11 In 1994, the right to vote was extended to every South African over eighteen years of age, including prisoners, but not those detained in psychiatric institutions.

12 On 4 February 1997.

13 Where the unconstitutionality of a law can be corrected by minor editing the Constitutional Court is empowered to amend the law. Where this is not possible, the Constitutional Court will instruct parliament to amend the offending law or practice to conform with the Constitution.

judicial, and administrative structures of the republic. Dry but important, since it is these chapters that determine the convoluted system of governance, and its unintended consequences, described in Chapter 1 (of this book).

The Constitution came into effect in 1997 and has been little changed. To date it has been amended eighteen times, but that number suggests more change than is the case. Many of the amendments are administrative in nature (the first, second, fourth, fifth, and eleventh). The eighth, ninth, and tenth allowed 'floor crossing.'[14] This was, however, reversed by the fourteenth and fifteenth amendments. The third amendment provided for municipalities to be demarcated across provincial boundaries, but this was reversed by the twelfth amendment. Both the twelfth and thirteenth amendments detailed new provincial boundaries. One of these changes was further altered by the sixteenth amendment. There were minor administrative changes to the judicial structure in the sixth amendment, and more substantial ones in the seventeenth amendment of 2013 which reorganised, but didn't change, the court hierarchy. Attempts to amend Section 25 of the Constitution to allow expropriation of land without compensation between 2018 and 2021 collapsed.[15] By contrast, the eighteenth amendment was passed with the required super majority in the National Assembly ten years after the seventeenth. It added South African Sign Language to the official languages of the republic. A progressive move, but which is hardly central to the country's challenges. Over more than twenty-five years, the Constitution has, other than cosmetic amendments, remained unchanged.

Constitutional transformation

The intention was that the Constitution would change society. To do this it was necessary to harmonise existing law to the Constitution. This was ambitious given the plurality of South Africa's legal landscape and even more so when law is viewed from a "law in society" perspective, in which law is understood as what is implemented, rather than what is written.[16] As Leopold Pospisil outlines, law is a mechanism of social ordering linked to social structure and is therefore a way of resolving *intra* group disputes.[17] If there is not, in fact, a single social order then irrespective of what is said, and as much as there

14 In which elected representatives could change parties without losing their seats (and salaries).

15 Though the entire endeavour was little more than political pantomime given that the Constitution already allowed for expropriation without compensation (Dugard and Seme 2018). In 2024, a new expropriation act was passed. If anything, this limited the situations in which property could be expropriated without compensations (Dickinson 2025b).

16 Harding (2021).

17 Pospisil (1978).

is a *de jure* single system of law, in practice this resolution of disputes will not happen. This book outlines a plural legal landscape, though not in the way that it is described in legal textbooks: common, statute, and traditional African law under the Constitution.

The Constitution was understood to be the primary mechanism by which society was to be reordered. The Interim Constitution's post-amble described itself as a "historic bridge" between past and future and the current Constitution's preamble outlines much the same, stating that its purpose is to "establish a society based on democratic values, social justice and fundamental human rights." The metaphorical bridge is a project of transformative constitutionalism, the process by which society will be recast from a racist order into an idealised society in which human rights are upheld. The courts are central to this process, their role being to harmonise law and conduct with constitutional values. Karl Klare describes transformative constitutionalism as "a long-term project of constitutional enactment, interpretation, and enforcement committed … to transforming a country's political and social institutions and power relationships in a democratic, participatory, and egalitarian direction."[18] This project of social transformation, progressive social engineering, is driven by constitutional interpretation, and Constitutional Court rulings are the acme of this project.

The vision of transformative constitutionalism is laudable, but there are obvious challenges. These include whether the Constitution will enable social transformation commensurate to the country's social and economic inequality; whether rights provided in the Constitution are being used to avoid accountability by the politically connected and the wealthy; and whether popular disagreement with some constitutional rights, such as the abolishment of the death penalty or outlawing of corporal punishment, can be contained.

However, what this book addresses is whether, if practised law is a product of social structure and if South Africa's township and suburb are not only apart but different, there exists, in anything more than proclamation, a single system of law.

Law and norms

Norms are shared standards of behaviour, what is done or should be done in situations ranging from greeting someone in the street through to the use of violence. Social norms and written law may converge or diverge. However, just as laws can be kept and broken, so too can norms. In psychology, a distinction is made between descriptive and injunctive norms. Injunctive norms are behaviours that are established as the right thing to do: social morality. The

18 Klare (1998:150).

term descriptive norm, what people report that others actually do, is clumsy. When people are asked to describe a social norm, they usually first describe the injunctive norm; what should be done. If the psychologists' descriptive norm is the actually practised norm deviating from injunctive norms, why not use the terms injunctive and practised norms? So, I use the term "practised norm" when it deviates from an injunctive norm.

In Chapter 5, we look at electricity theft in townships. Theft is a crime; it is against the law. But it's not that simple. Most people acknowledged that theft of electricity breaches the widely held injunctive norm that stealing is wrong. However, when people steal, the breach of this injunctive norm can be managed in several ways. It can be hidden from others, essentially the same strategy as is practised to avoid legal sanction. Alternatively, the breached injunctive norm can be justified in a range of ways, such as being unable to afford electricity, or that everybody else is doing the same. Such justifications provide a defence that parries the injunctive norm, even if not effective against legal prosecution. Another response to the breach of injunctive norms is euphemism, such as referring to buying "cheap electricity" when, in fact, fraudulent meter coupons are being purchased. Here the infraction is fogged by verbal camouflage.

This book explores how practised norms in the township diverge from injunctive norms aligned with the law of the land. When *menyetla* correspond to the legal categories of corruption, fraud, and theft, these are contrary to injunctive norms and contrary to law. Yet, they are increasingly conducted in practice, albeit concealed, justified, or euphemised.

The *lex lokasi*

Ewick and Silbey distinguish between law and legality. Seeing social structure as an emergent property of social action, they argue that legal consciousness (our understanding of the law as it applies to ourselves) arises from participation in social life and that what emerges from this is "legality," a term they distinguish from "law." Legality is, in their own words, "the meanings, sources of authority, and cultural practices that are commonly recognised as legal, regardless of who employs them or for what ends. In this rendering, people may invoke and enact legality in ways neither approved nor acknowledged by the law."[19]

The social historian E. P. Thompson (1993) used the concept *lex loci*, which translates as local law. Thompson asks his readers to step back not only in time but also into the *lex loci* of communities, which may be at odds with the proclaimed law of the land. The *lex loci* of the township, location, or *kasi*, I

[19] Ewick and Silbey (1998:22).

term the *lex lokasi*.[20] In the case studies that follow I draw out five key features of the *lex lokasi*. These are:

One: In the township it is the *lex lokasi* and not the *lex constitutional* that operates on a day-to-day basis.

Two: In an open challenge *the lex lokasi* will be defeated by the *lex constitutional*, if only temporarily. As a result, *menyetla* conducted within the *lex lokasi* remain largely *sub rosa*.

Three: The *lex lokasi* is not a unified system of law, but a multidimensional spectrum of power resources that are employed opportunistically. It is not only flexible but uncodified.

Four: The *lex constitutional* provides a resource not only for corrupt practices (as classically defined[21]) but also for *menyetla* (the grasping of opportunities) within the *lex lokasi*.

Five: Attempting to prevent these practices with greater regulation based on the *lex constitutional*, in the context of contemporary South Africa, proliferates such opportunities within the *lex lokasi*.

These five features do not reflect a complete separation between the *lex lokasi* in the township and the *lex constitutional* in the suburb. Feature Two indicates that they can come into conflict and Feature Four illustrates how one, the *lex constitutional*, can be used as a resource within the other. To a degree, there is flexibility; depending on context, township residents may move between the *leges*, either because it is to their temporary advantage or because the *lex constitutional* has been brought to bear. The case studies that follow in this chapter, and the *menyetla* described in the following chapters, illustrate how there can be oscillation between the *leges*. Nevertheless, the five features illustrate key analytical binaries between the *lex lokasi* and *lex constitutional*.

"We have no police station:" taking the law into their own hands

A Katlehong township yard with beer crates for seats. It is less than five minutes' walk to Katlehong South Police Station, yet Bheki Nonyane sums up the situation with the pithy observation that "we have no police station." This pronouncement is prompted by the police's failure to arrive at the scene

20 An alternative would be, following Ewick and Silbey (1998), "location legality."

21 See Chapter 1.

of a car accident on the street. The accident is not our business other than it happened in front of us an hour earlier. A drunk driver strayed into the oncoming lane. The incensed driver of a Golf IV, now parked up on the pavement with its front smashed-in, has rejected the offer to fix the car at a street corner panel beater. He has called the police, but they have yet to appear. Likely, they never will, Bheki asserted. Nobody disputes Bheki. We know the police are useless.

"What about the previous week?" Bheki continues. Anger in the area had boiled over and a drug dealer had been dragged from her house by locals tired of constant theft by the nyaopi *smokers she supplied. After some slapping and insults, the woman was handed over to the police. But what, Bheki asked, was the good of that? The woman was out the next day on bail; obviously a* diza *(bribe) had been paid. Bheki continued his derision of the police; if you went to the police station, any police station, the detective would ask you what your problem was and how much money you had to fix it. So much for a docket, so much for a judge, and so on. Not a Bill of Rights, but a bill of corruption.*

But call them when there is a serious problem! Bheki laughs. Maja takes over the narrative. He mocks the police. When cops get a call at night that somebody's in your yard they stay put till the criminals have gone. Then they'll arrive with blue lights flashing and jump out guns drawn. Maja mimics a cop, swinging a gun in front of him, like in the movies, shouting out "Where are they? Where are they?" as though he's going to take them on Rambo style. All show and bravado.

Whether Bheki and Maja are right about specifics can be challenged. But I don't bother; they are right about the bigger picture. The township is failed by the police night and day. They'll certify ID copies for you, but when it comes to crime – theft, mugging, robbery, and murder – they are useless. We are at one in this legal cynicism. Without resources to hire private security, township residents must protect themselves.

Yet, when they do, they are accused of taking the law into their own hands. It is called mob justice. The term is prejudicial and fails to account for the dilemma township residents face caught between endemic crime and inadequate policing. Rather, I term such self-help as community punishment. Community punishment draws on widespread support for the use of corporal punishment in the township to correct behaviour; whether for disobedient children or adult transgressors.[22] The term community punishment is not to glorify it; such punishment is not only extra-judicial but rough and ready. There is little consistency; anger is a fickle thing. One alleged *tsotsi* may be

22 For an account of corporal punished in South African workers' strikes see; Dickinson (2021b), Chapter 14: "The Mabarete strike II: Invisible violence."

beaten, hacked, and burned to death, but another escapes and returns to live in the area after things have cooled down.

Community punishment is generally spontaneous, albeit a spontaneity that draws on understood repertoires of action. There may be loosely constituted committees operating at the street and block level which set the ball rolling by calling people to a meeting, but without public anger little will happen.

There is a complex relationship between community punishment and the police, with Community Policing Forums (CPFs), statutory-established organisations, occupying a position somewhere in between. On the one hand, community punishment is doing the police's job for them, but it also presents a threat to their authority and, potentially, danger.[23] When police arrive at the scene of community punishment,[24] they may well standoff while the beating proceeds. The community is doing what they are unable to and to intervene would be risky when the crowd's blood is hot. Once the paroxysm of punishment abates, they take the victim(s) to the police station, hospital, or morgue as necessary.

Reports of so-called mob justice are now routine in the country's media, though what gets into print is the tip of the iceberg. To merit coverage there must be a minimum of one gruesome death, though even that is no guarantee.

On the night of 18/19 May 2021, nine young men were subject to community punishment in Zandspruit, an informal settlement north-west of Johannesburg. They were beaten and set alight, eight died. The police were prompted into action and arrested fourteen suspects, although some 200 people were reported to have taken part. The Roodepoort magistrate presiding over the case differentiated between the local CPF which she said wanted to hand over suspected criminals to the police and the "vigilante group [which] preferred taking the law into their own hands."[25]

The Magistrate went on to outline that; "A civilized society must respond to crime when and where it surfaces with fairness and justice, and vigilantism can only cause chaos in our communities."[26] Overlooking the chaos of endemic crime in the township (and elsewhere) she criticised the police for failing to control "vigilantism by necklacing" prevalent in Zandspruit.

Magistrates represent the *lex constitutional*. In that context, what the magistrate said was on point. But she mistakes symptom for cause. The real problem is not what she describes as vigilantism, but the conditions that give

23 Buur (2008).

24 That they *are* called to the scene illustrates that not every township resident agrees with such punishment, or at least the severity with which it might be being enforced. Another reason for calling the police in these situations is that the captured suspect is a friend or relative.

25 Seleka (2021a).

26 Seleka (2021b).

rise to such action. If there was efficient policing, then the *lex constitutional* and the *lex lokasi* regarding theft, robbery, and murder would align.[27] But in the absence of effective policing there is no alternative for residents but to take the law into their own hands. Lectures, however righteous, cannot rectify the gap. The *lex lokasi* operates when the *lex constitutional* fails. The weaker the *lex constitutional's* writ, the more it is replaced by the l*ex lokasi*. Yet, when the lex constitutional is brought to bear as with the Zandspruit arrests and "vigilantes" are brought before the courts it is the *lex constitutional* that prevails.

A plurality of power: The family house

Following colonial conquest, legal rights to land were differentiated by race. This was a long and varied process. In shorthand, what emerged was that whites could own property with title deeds registered in their name. By contrast, in the 13 per cent of the country allocated for Africans under the *Native Land Act* of 1913 and subsequent amendments,[28] land was held by designated tribal chiefs on behalf of their subjects. However, Africans were essential as workers for white businesses, homes, and municipal authorities. The African worker had to be available to their white employers in white areas yet return "home" at the end of their service. Single sex hostels provided the ideal way in which this could be achieved. However, townships of increasingly urbanised Africans emerged with the industrialisation of South Africa. Apartheid governments doggedly but unsuccessfully attempted to maintain residence in African townships as temporary. African ownership of township houses was not allowed. Rather, permits were issued to African men giving them the right to reside with permitted family members.[29]

It became increasingly difficult to maintain townships as places of temporary residence for the expanding African working class. In response, National Party policy shifted to creating an African property-owning class, permitting long-leases and then allocating the rights of home ownership to permit holders.[30] The policy was pragmatic; to give urban Africans a stake in the system. The

27 Excepting what punishment criminals should face, in particular popular support for the death penalty.

28 Which became the nine ethnic demarcated African homelands or Bantustans under apartheid.

29 The permits were referred to as Section 6 permits when it was for a stand on which they build a house, meeting municipal specifications, and Section 7 permits when renting a house from the municipality. The sections refer to *Government Regulation* 1036 of 1968 drawn up in terms of the *Bantu (Urban Areas) Consolidation Act* 25 of 1945.

30 Bolt and Masha (2019).

Conversion of Certain Rights into Leasehold or Ownership Act 81 of 1988[31] provided a framework for converting permits to ownership in the township.

A common ownership format for these erstwhile permit houses is the "family house."[32] As Maxim Bolt and Tshenolo Masha (2019) argue, the family house has no legal reality yet a very real existence. The title deed of a family house lists a family member who is custodian and holds the house in trust. How this operates in practice is left up to each family.

The family *home* holds deep significance in African culture as it is shared with the ancestors. This is irrespective of the legal form with which the *house* is officially registered. African culture has adapted to changing circumstances, including urbanisation. A legacy of colonial and apartheid rule is that Africans' urbanisation has taken place alongside long-established and enduring migration between rural[33] and urban environments. The family home is linked to historical origins but also settled by birth. As generation follows generation in the township and if links to the *mahae* (historical, rural, place of origin) weaken, a township house becomes the *home* where ancestors reside in spirit.

Thus, a family house is the appropriate place for *mesebetsi* (traditional rituals/gatherings) to be held. That the family house should be available for such rituals is a powerful injunctive norm.[34] The family house also serves as a family security net. This is a second injunctive norm; that it is available as a place where family members in difficulty or need are entitled to stay. But a family house is also an economic asset. It is often the family's most valuable property used to generate income from the rent of backyard rooms or *mekhukhu* and front yards and garages for businesses.

It is over the use of the family houses, particularly who can reside in them and who controls financial flows from rents, that disputes frequently arise.

31 Along with the *Upgrading of Tenure Rights Act (ULTRA)* 112 of 1991.

32 Other forms available in Gauteng are: individual title; co-ownership, with two or more family members as co-owners; and a family trust in terms of the *Trust Property Control Act* (Gauteng Province N.D.).

33 The concept of rural areas for Africans in South Africa is tricky. Given the crowded conditions of the homelands, agriculture (or wilderness) was limited. What many homeland residents lived in was "peri-urban" rather than rural. The African population that was geographically rural was those living in white rural, i.e. farmland, areas. Most of these lived in what amounted to worker villages under the control of farmers, but now increasingly in rural townships as farm workers leave or are evicted from farm properties. Any sharp distinction between rural and urban African culture isn't accurate or helpful – there are differences, but these fall on a complex gradient of beliefs that is constantly enriched by movement between rural and urban townships (see Dickinson 2014, Chapter 5).

34 Indeed, such rituals should be actively supported by other members of the family and at bare minimum attendance is expected.

While some families manage these family homes successfully, many become protracted battle grounds.[35]

Se ya voma!

When Violet Mashinini died her children inherited the four-room family house in Katlehong, though the house remained in the name of their late father, Abraham. Abraham had been given title to the property under the Conversion Act.[36] *A family meeting held after Violet's funeral agreed that Mpho, the last-born son, would remain in the house. Mpho was still without work five years after leaving school a grade short of matric. He was in most need. Keabetswe, the oldest child, had married and lived with her husband in Daveyton; Thabo, second born, was working in Durban. Dimakatso had a position with the Ekurhuleni Metro Police Department (EMPD) and had married another metro cop. It was understood that the house would be available when any of the siblings needed to hold* a mosebetsi.

Mpho was joined by his girlfriend, Thandi, and her two children. They rented out space in the backyard on which tenants erected mekhukhu *of zinc sheeting. Tenants paid rent to Mpho. This was tolerated by Mpho's siblings who understood that he had no income, though it made holding* mesebetsi *awkward at times.*

The problems started when Dimakatso asserted her right to build brick rooms in the back yard. She explained that she wanted to invest in the family house and the rooms could be used by Thabo's two sons who, having left school, had yet to find anything more than casual work. The fly in this ointment was that the rooms would take up the space Mpho rented out. The dispute between Mpho and Dimakatso escalated. The other siblings called in their malome[37] *and there was a family meeting. A compromise was reached. Dimakatso would build three rooms, one each for Thabo's sons and one would be rented out. Mpho would collect the rent and keep half. That worked for a while, but when one of Thabo's sons got work as a security guard in Rustenburg and vacated the room there was disagreement over who was now entitled to the rent.*

Mpho's case was that the room had displaced his previous rental income. He and Thandi were otherwise having to manage on social grants. He pointed

35 Disputes over rights to the house are compounded as subsequent generations increase the number of people with a claim. Further complications arise when custodians' names are not updated, and the houses end up in the name of departed parents or grandparents (Dickinson 2025a).

36 A composite account in that it is drawn from several family house disputes to which I have been party in different capacities.

37 A maternal uncle who holds a position of authority within a family and, among other responsibilities, may be called to assist in resolving family disputes.

out that Dimakatso had a regular salary and her own house. Dimakatso's argument was that she had built the rooms and she escalated maters by asserting that Mpho was not looking after the family house properly. Thandi had brought her younger sister to live with them. The siblings had not been consulted, it was Thandi who was calling the shots! Thandi, Dimakatso asserted, wanted to take over the house!

In fact, Dimakatso needed the rent to keep up bond payments on her house in the upmarket township section of Spruitview. After repeated rows, her husband had moved out and was no longer contributing to the bond payments. She was getting letters from the bank threatening repossession. However, she didn't share this with her siblings, it would be admitting that her life was not going well.

The tenants in the rooms were caught in the middle of the dispute; both Mpho and Dimakatso came to collect rent at the end of the month. Whoever got there first got the rent, whoever got their late shouted at the tenants that the rent should be paid to them.

It was Dimakatso who turned the squabble into a family war. Four men arrived at the house late on a Friday. They knocked on the tenants' doors and told them they were to pay rent to Dimakatso. They wore civilian clothes, but one was recognized as a colleague of Dimakatso. Mpho went to the CPF's office at the police station. They called a meeting promising to adjudicate the matter. Mpho was confident that as a local resident the CPF would rule in his favour, but Dimakatso ignored the letter instructing her to attend the meeting.

At the end of the month there was a shouting match between Dimakatso and Mpho. The matter escalated, insults were exchanged, and childhood grievances reemerged. Dimakatso threatened to deal with Mpho. At the advice of a neighbour, Mpho went to the Palm Ridge magistrates court for a protection order. The order was interim,[38] *the return date for confirmation three months away. Dimakatso was prohibited from visiting the house which knocked her out of the end of the month rent collection race.*

Dimakatso then hired a lawyer who commenced eviction proceedings against Mpho. He was, the lawyer's letter said, unlawfully occupying the house owned by his client. The letter ordered Mpho to vacate the property by the end of the month. Failure to do so would lead to legal action for his eviction and Mpho would be liable for the lawyer's costs. When Mpho went to the municipal offices, the house was listed under Dimakatso's name. Dimakatso, Mpho concluded, had bribed somebody at the office. Back at the CPF he was told that nobody could be evicted without a court order, so he stayed put. The

[38] Interim orders are issued routinely with a return date on which the facts of the situation can be tested if the person against who the interim order has been issued contests the order. Alternatively, the matter falls away as neither party turns up with the interim order having served its purpose within a family or neighbour dispute.

sheriff, a man with arms the size of tree-trunks, arrived one morning, handed over papers and demanded a signature. Mpho understood little of the papers, but he knew the eviction was proceeding and there was a court date.

Unable to afford a lawyer, Mpho planned to explain to the magistrate that Dimakatso had bribed somebody to transfer the family home into her name and was threatening him. He was confident that the truth would come out. However, the case was postponed. As was the date for the confirmation of the protection order against which Dimakatso's lawyer had filed an affidavit.

Mpho's neighbour, Simphiwe, warned him that he should be careful. Dimakatso would be frustrated, perhaps she would put a contract out on him to get him out of the way permanently? These things happen nowadays. "Look at it this way," Simphiwe said; "the house is worth what? Perhaps R300,000? Probably more. Especially with the backyard rooms. Maybe R350,000. You can hire an inkabi *for a few thousand rand."*[39] *Simphiwe made it clear he wasn't saying that's what Dimakatso would do, but it was best for Mpho to be careful.*

Mpho visited a sangoma. *In the dim interior of her low-roofed* indumba, *she burned a handful* imphepho *and threw an assortment of bones, coins, and shells onto a reed mat. She told Mpho there was a disagreement in the family. To this suggestion Mpho responded "*Se ya voma*!" (We agree!)*[40] *and clapped his hands. When she said it was a male relative that was angry Mpho was silent. It was, the* sangoma *pronounced, a woman. "*Se ya voma*!"*

The sangoma *stated that Mpho was in danger. She made two different mixtures, pouring powders and dried herbs from the glass jars that cluttered the room. One mixture was to be sprinkled around the perimeter of the yard at midnight. The other Mpho was to boil with two litres of water and drink a small cup of the brew every morning. Whatever his enemy threw at him would be returned to sender.*

Simphiwe, Mpho concluded, had given him good advice. After his visit to the sangoma, *things went his way. When the eviction hearing got to court, he had a stroke of luck. An aunt was there for a different matter. When she heard that Dimakatso was evicting Mpho she stormed over to where she sat in the court corridor. She was, the aunt berated her, disrespecting their culture. This was not how disputes were settled! What she was doing was shameful! She should know better. The disagreement should be resolved within the family, not at court. It was a public humiliation that Mpho wasted no time in disseminating.*

Keabetswe, the oldest sibling, now embarrassed by the public airing of the feud, called a family meeting. It was agreed that the house belonged to the family, whatever the municipality had on record. Dimakatso was to

[39] *Inkabi*: Zulu for ox, but in context a hired killer, typically from rural areas and who disappear back there after the hit. See Thomas (2018) for an account of hired killers in South Africa.

[40] The "we" refers to the ancestors.

withdraw her case and Mpho his protection order. They returned to the previous arrangement brokered by their malome. *Family peace was restored. Though likely temporarily. Mpho fully expected Dimakatso to return to the offensive with another angle of attack. To boost the* sangoma's muthi *he took out legal insurance at a monthly premium he could not afford.*

What this case illustrates is the plurality of power resources, generated from what Sally Falk Moore (1973) describes as semi-autonomous social fields, operating within the township.[41] The *lex lokasi* is not one system of law, but a multidimensional corpus of power resources. The value of each resource depends on context and the degree to which it can be mobilised by an individual or group.

The case also illustrates that the *lex constitutional* is one resource within the *lex lokasi*. In this dispute it was present in several forms: the municipal records, the protection order, and eviction law. But on each occasion the *lex constitutional* was being *used*, not *followed*. Protagonists in conflict can and do move between the *lex constitutional* and the *lex lokasi*. However, within the *lex lokasi* the *lex constitutional* is used as a power resource or weapon. It is not, as the Constitution proclaims, supreme. In the case of the Mashinini family house, it was trumped, at least for a while, by injunctive cultural norms, though in a different situation it could have been trumped by intimidation, a community structure such as the CPF, violence, sorcery,[42] or other source of power. The *lex lokasi* does not constitute one system as does the *lex constitutional*, rather it is a flexible, multipart structure of social regulation that operates without any overarching, apex, law or norm.

The border business

Lesotho and South Africa share a 900-kilometre border. The border came into being as the result of long conflict between the Basotho nation, drawn together by Morena Moshoeshoe, Afrikaner/white settlers, and British colonial authorities in the nineteenth century.[43] It is a border with little legitimacy.

41 See de Sardan (1999:37) for an example of how different legal systems can be mobilised over wedding negotiations, illustrating how pre-colonial, colonial, and post-independent legal systems are superimposed on each other and, "all [of them] can be called into service according to need."

42 Since sorcery or witchcraft is widely believed and practised and since what is believed has real effects, even if not in the way intended, it is a power resource within the *lex lokasi*.

43 For a concise summary of how the border was demarcated over time see Germond (1967:569–71). For an account of how borders were seen differently by the Basotho, Afrikaner settlers, and British authorities see Sanders (1975).

As David Coplan has described it, "the [Lesotho] border is not an international, political or economic boundary … but rather a business."[44] Since 1963 when identification documents were first required to cross, the business of the border has been up and running. Much of this is bribes paid to border officials to overlook document irregularities. Many Lesotho citizens, men and women, work in South Africa. The difficulty of obtaining and renewing travel documents, particularly for Lesotho citizens who may have their passports cancelled if they overrun their permitted stay in South Africa, keeps the border business humming. These requirements can be onerous. The *Prevention and Combatting of Trafficking in Persons Act* requires that a parent wishing to cross the border with their child provide:

- The child's passport;
- an unabridged birth certificate;
- an affidavit from the other parent/legal guardian giving consent;
- an ID copy of the other parent/legal guardian; or,
- a death certificate if the other parent is deceased.

If both parents are accompanying the child, it's "just" the passport of the minor and the unabridged birth certificate that is required. Certified copies of the latter are accepted, but the date stamp must not be more than three months old.[45]

Regulation provides opportunities for officials to accept bribes in return for overlooking citizens' failures to meet the requirements of one or both states that they wish to travel between.[46] This is corruption as defined by Nye (1967) and is part and parcel of the border business. The *lex constitutional*, or at least selected elements, are used to extract economic rents, bribes in plain language. In township idiom: *tjhotjho*, *diza*, cool drink, *nyoba*,[47] under the carpet business, or to use common euphemisms: "helping each other," "doing favours," or, a Sesotho saying, *matsoho a hlatsana* (hands wash each other). These opportunities for bribes are possible because the *lex constitutional* does not exist in its entirety at the border but can be mobilised selectively by agents of the state for their own benefit.

Paying bribes is one way to get across the border with document shortcomings, but there is another. The Caledon River, or in Sesotho the *Mohokare*, forms Lesotho's northern border with South Africa's Free State province. Other than in spate, the river can be waded with little difficulty. In sleepy

44 Coplan (2001:81).

45 Department of Home Affairs (2019).

46 The requirement during the COVID-19 epidemic to produce a negative test result to cross the border further increased the regulatory and financial burden for those wishing to cross between the two countries.

47 A Nguni influenced township term which also, potentially confusing, means sex.

dorps along the border there are dusty taxi ranks for destinations near and far. Those travelling back to Lesotho from work in Gauteng or elsewhere take long-distance taxis which go directly to the border. However, those without the necessary papers can alight at these local ranks and transfer to transport headed *nokeng* (the river). Since there is no formal signage indicating taxis' destinations, it is a matter of asking which taxi is going where. Hidden in plain sight, albeit veiled by the Sesotho vernacular, are two queues for Lesotho-bound travellers. One to the border, or *borokgong* (place of the bridge), for those with papers (or those intending to bribe their way over), the other *nokeng*.

On a busy day, before a long weekend or the Christmas holidays, the *nokeng* transport service is busy. There are well-used routes down dirt roads to the *Mohokare*. These areas have a wild feel. The farms are run down and stock theft a constant hazard. Farm prices are rock bottom and most farmers here are Africans struggling with inadequate capital.[48] Rough justice abounds.[49] Some South African farms next to the river have been abandoned, effectively annexed by farmers from Lesotho who bring their cattle across the river to graze. On Fridays at the end of the month, *bakkies* and taxis loaded with passengers drive to the river and return empty. The river can be forded at the drifts with no one to check documents.[50]

However, this alternative crossing can be expensive. The fare from town to *nokeng* may be ten times that to *borokgong,* even though it might be only twice the distance. Unless the *dorp* is right on the border those crossing *nokeng* have little choice but to stump up the steep fare. Some of this goes to local police or army units who make it their business to be elsewhere when the *nokeng* runs are operating.

Once at the river, payment is not necessarily over. Crossing the river in spate is dangerous[51] and provides further opportunities or *menyetla*. Locals, usually young men, offer assistance. This may be a rope tied between trees on either bank, inflated inner tubes, or other improvised flotation aids. These services are provided for a fee.[52] With heavy bags or a baby on your back it's best to pay.

The two branches of the border business, *borokgong* corruption[53] and *nokeng menyetla*, both extract economic rents from the legally vulnerable.

48 By contrast the vast majority of farms away from the border, and all high-value farms in the area, are owned by white farmers.

49 Chabalala (2020).

50 Indeed, local farm workers without transport regularly ford the river to buy groceries if shops on the other side of the river are closer (Fieldnotes: 141018).

51 Radebe (2021).

52 The joke being that it is doubled when halfway across.

53 Officials can also directly predate those intending crossing *nokeng*. Long distance taxis from Gauteng and elsewhere approaching border towns are targeted by police

They are in competition, offering alternative ways around the problem of documentation. When it is difficult to comply with the *lex constitutional*, openings for corruption and *menyetla* are created. In other words, the *lex constitutional* itself becomes a resource that enables corruption and *menyetla*. As developed in later chapters, the more the problems of corruption and *menyetla* are identified as the result of ineffective or insufficient regulation and responded to on that basis, the more openings for corruption and *menyetla* are created by attempts to supress these activities.

The different ways in which legal border requirements can be circumvented constitute the *lex loci* of the border, which given who travels without the required documentation and who takes the bribes or grasps the *menyetla*, can be seen as a part of the *lex lokasi*, even if it not physically in the township. The relative strength of the *lex lokasi* and the *lex constitutional* are asymmetric. The *lex loci* operates *sub rosa*. It may well be more relevant in the day-to-day lives of township residents than the *lex constitutional*, but the *lex constitutional* is the only legitimate authority. Should a spotlight be trained on *lex lokasi* practices, the *lex constitutional* prevails, even though its triumph may be fleeting and largely symbolic.[54]

There are rarely open and sustained stand-offs with one party standing by the *lex lokasi* and the other the *lex constitutional*. At least not yet, though later chapters on fare evasion, the looting of the Metrorail, and the July 2021 unrest explore where this is beginning to happen.

Now and again, those taking bribes at the border are caught in sting operations and face disciplinary action, dismissal, and occasionally criminal prosecution.[55] The periodic sting operations aimed at corrupt officials is an illustration of the power of the *lex constitutional* when push comes to shove. However, that these operations must be periodically repeated illustrates that after a show of strength by the *lex constitutional*, the *lex loci* quietly returns.

An example of the *lex constitutional's* public power *vis-à-vis* the *nokeng* dimension of the border business is the uncovering of a private border post in May 2021. This operated a few kilometres away from the Calendonspoort border post between the Free State and Lesotho. The drift over which this

---

and passengers are asked to show their documents. Lesotho citizens without valid permits for their stay in South Africa, or not having a passport at all, must cough up if they are to continue their journey. Advice to those who intend to cross the border *nokeng* is to alight at the town *before* the border town, take a local taxi to the border town which is less likely to be stopped by police than the long-distance Quantum taxis, and then take transport to the river.

54 This relationship follows De Certeau's (1988) idea of strategy and tactics and which I have previously used in other contexts (Dickinson 2014 and 2021b).

55 See Molosankwe (2021) for the eventual sentencing of several officials from the Calendonspoort border post convicted of taking bribes in 2013.

informal border post operated was accessed through land owned by a recently deceased African farmer. His widow, it was alleged, set up a "tollgate" and was "charging car thieves and illegal immigrants to use her property to cross [the river/border]."[56]

Setting up a private border post is pushing the *menyetla* of the border business too far. Tipped off by the local farmers' union, an operation was conducted by a Hawks (priority crime) team assisted by the police Crime Intelligence unit, the Tactical Response Team, and the military. Talk about cracking a nut with a sledgehammer! Illegal crossing of the border is ongoing, but it is best to keep a low profile.

The Constitution as a vehicle of transformation?

This chapter began by arguing that there is a gap between the law of the land in South Africa, the *lex constitutional*, and the law of the township, the *lex lokasi*. Much of the chapter has looked at the form and practice of the *lex lokasi*, contrasting it to the *lex constitutional* and exploring the relationship between the two.

However, since there is always a gap between the law and practice in any society, it could be argued that the process of transformative constitutionalism will bring social practice into alignment with the law. The raft of enabling laws, across the spectrum of social activity, promulgated after 1994, were a bold start to this project.

Along with a raft of new legislation aimed at dealing with land and housing in South Africa, the previously cited *Prevention of Illegal Squatting Act* was repealed and replaced with the *Prevention of Illegal Eviction from and Unlawful Occupation of Land Act* 19 of 1998 and, on farms and agricultural plots, the *Extension of Security of Tenure Act* 62 of 1997 or ESTA. These laws decriminalised squatting (occupation without legal right) and required landowners to follow lengthy civil legal processes before lawfully evicting occupiers. ESTA protects those who have worked and resided on farms, preventing them from being summarily removed from their homes when no longer wanted by the landowner. This shifts power from landowners to occupiers and in the context of inequality assists transformation.

Since 2022, I have assisted communities facing eviction in Muldersdrift west of Johannesburg.[57] The area is a volatile amalgam of private housing developments for the new middle class, weekend getaways retreats, agricultural plots, and informal settlements. Township and suburb intermingled in close proximity without the usual buffer zones between. But its socio-geographic

56 Times Live (2021).

57 Working with LHR, see the Introduction.

exceptionalism aside, it is a microcosm of South Africa's inequality and a cauldron of conflict.

Developers want the land clear of occupiers, often former farm workers and their families. One way to do this is to hire lawyers. The law is a resource of the rich, but it is not the only weapon available. Evictions are rarely by the book, rather there is a mixture of legal action intermingled with threats, legal bluffs,[58] bribes, and on occasion brute force[59] that bypass occupiers' legal rights. Much of this is to *avoid* using the courts. Though even if the matter ends up in court, there is no guarantee of justice. At a gathering of public interest law organisations in June 2024 the keynote speaker, Dunstan Mlambo, Judge President of the Gauteng High Court, spoke frankly. Summarising, his message: "There is decreasing confidence in the justice system. The system has become an instrument to increase vulnerability. Delays in getting to court are measured in years. It is commercially orientated judges appointed to the bench. Court orders are bought …."[60]

The use of precarious labour, aimed at avoiding the raft of progressive post-1994 labour laws, presents a similar strategy: avoiding and therefore undermining progressive labour legislation aimed at creating a more equal society.[61] These mêlées, visible on social fault lines, in which rich and poor struggle in close-quarter social combat see, for the most part, inequality maintained.

Yet, alongside these running battles there is an ongoing process of progressive legal development which, to paraphrase, is creating an ever more perfect constitutional framework. From complex and often confusing social struggle at ground level, human rights lawyers distil a legal point[62] on which strategic or impact litigation is waged. The aim of this litigation is to advance the rights of the poor and disadvantaged. To give power through law.

Despite limitations, the Bill of Rights lays a foundation for transforming an unequal society. Geoff Budlender, commenting on the Treatment Action Campaign's (TAC) court victory, based on the constitutional right to health, requiring the government to roll out antiretroviral drug treatment to

[58] For example, where a notice of motion is presented as an eviction order even though the case has not been heard and may not even be in the correct court.

[59] See Dube (2024) in the case of evictions at Tilly's Farm, Muldersdrift, that I was involved with after the unlawful demolition of fifteen families' homes by a developer in June 2022.

[60] Dickinson (2024).

[61] I document these "long tactics" of labour brokers in Chapter 12 of *In Precarious Battle* (Dickinson 2021b).

[62] See Abel (1995) for accounts and discussion of the disjunctions between events on the ground and what constitutes evidence presented in court over disputed points of law and fact.

HIV-positive pregnant women, explains that; "Social and economic rights are largely poor people's rights: the wealthy have [already] achieved most of the benefits which they promise."[63]

A list of legal victories asserting the social-economic rights of poor people can be compiled. Often these are hard fought successes, championed by NGOs with public interest law clinics. Legal cases make their way up the court hierarchy until the conduct or law in question reaches the Constitutional Court. However, to claim that we remain on the road of transformative constitutionalism jars with experience on the ground. This is not to deny that real gains have been achieved through strategic litigation, the TAC's treatment court victories, albeit supported by campaigns of social mobilisation, being an example. Nor is it to assert that the development of law to align with the Constitution has come to a halt. The Constitution Court continues to determine whether law, administrative procedures, and social practice comply with the Constitution. Yet, this project of constitutional transformation is increasingly detached from the reality of South Africa.

It could be argued that the problem is not the Constitution but rather a failure of the institutions of implementation,[64] the executive arm of government, the justice system, the civil service, municipalities, parastatal companies, and so on. This shift of blame for South Africa's entropic trajectory from the Constitution itself to the institutions responsible for transformation has merit, even if these institutions are themselves framed by the Constitution. As noted in Chapter 1, the dysfunctionality of many, if not most, of these organisations is not in doubt. However, this distinction makes little difference to the central argument of this book, that the *lex constitutional* has limited purchase in the township. Rather, there is a range of competing sources and forms of order that together make up the *lex lokasi*.

Law, if it is to be more than a charade, cannot operate separately from the society it is intended to regulate. Yet the law of the township, the *lex lokasi*, is conspicuously detached from the law of the land, the *lex constitutional*. Yet as conspicuous as it may be within the township, the social and psychological distance between township and suburb obscures this reality.

The following chapters describe township *menyetla*, ways in which advantage is sought and gained, even if fleetingly, outside of the law of the land. The study of these *menyetla* is a way in which to see the *lex lokasi*. *Menyetla* are not the *lex lokasi*, but rather behaviours arising from, and consistent with, the *lex lokasi*. It is within this *lex* that looting from below, the grasping of *menyetla* in the scrabble to survive or the scramble to get ahead, takes place.

63 Budlender (2001:131).

64 I am grateful to an anonymous reader for suggesting this line of argument.

5

Izinyoka: stealing electricity

Introduction: the transformer on Phiri Street

When thick black smoke billowed out from the electricity sub-station in Phiri Street every house was plunged into darkness. It was early evening in a July cold snap with temperatures set to dip below zero. Victor called a meeting. Standing in the street, the residents didn't need to discuss what had happened; too many houses and backyard tenants cooking and heating had overloaded the transformer. They quickly concluded that somebody needed to phone Eskom, the national generator and supplier of electricity. The next step was more difficult. Who was going to make the call? Those at the meeting melted away. Whoever rang would be asked their meter number. Their purchase of pre-paid electricity would be checked. This complication capsized the meeting. People went home to cold rooms and mute televisions.

Victor couldn't ring, being in the same situation as those who had melted away. But not a man to give up he found a neighbour who had a legit receipt. He gave the call centre operator his neighbour's meter number the following morning. The operator came back with the observation that he was a "low payer." The neighbour, it seemed, only bought the occasional coupon. Eskom would not dispatch anyone.

Fortunately, somebody knew somebody who worked for Eskom. Victor organised a collection and an Eskom team came out to replace the transformer. The electricians told those who stood around watching what everybody knew; the transformer was being overloaded.

When the transformer blew a second time, the contact in Eskom said he couldn't swing it again. But he knew somebody who could sell them a new one. There was another meeting and an agreement that each house would contribute R2,000. Only those who paid would be permitted to reconnected. The transformer arrived on the back of a battered TATA crane truck. The team of three worked fast. Lebohang, the supervisor, said he used to work for Eskom and assured Victor that the new transformer was up to the job.

Lebohang was lying. The new transformer went the way of the others only a few weeks later. When Victor rang to complain he was told that they must have exceeded the transformer's capacity and there was no guarantee. The conclusion in Phiri Street was that they had been ripped off and sold a dud. The whispers were that Victor had taken money for himself.

The story of Phiri Street is not unusual. Stealing electricity in South African townships is widespread. It may be theft, fraud, fiddling, or non-payment (with the intention of never paying), overlapping actions which amount to much the same thing, and I use the term stealing to cover all these illegal or illicit methods to obtain electricity without payment.

The story illustrates how stealing electricity creates further opportunities, or *menyetla* proliferation. A bribe paid to bypass Eskom's policies or the use of a parallel black market for electrical infrastructure that ranges from spider webs of cables to a transformer supplying an entire street or settlement.

With each step away from an enforceable contractual relationship, the riskier these *menyetla* become and the less possible redress, as the residents of Phiri Street found out. You can't complain about what you should not be doing. At least not publicly. And because of limited accountability, internal divisions are more likely, as Victor found out. He was honestly doing his best to assist his neighbours to steal electricity but was suspected of pulling off his own *monyetla*.

Much of this can be summed up as the pursuit of short-term gain by individuals resulting in escalating problems for the collective. In what follows, I develop this theme. However, some South Africans may be reading this by candlelight, or more likely courtesy of a generator, inverter, or other off grid "solution" to Eskom's failure to supply sufficient electricity. These readers may be thinking; "Yes, very interesting, but you can't blame Phiri Street for the failure of Eskom."

It's a fair point. The electricity crisis cannot be pinned on electricity theft in the township. The entire domestic sector, township and suburb, only consumes around 20 per cent of Eskom's output. Of course, what is going down in the township contributes to lower revenue by Eskom and higher infrastructure maintenance costs, but it's only one of several factors that brought the country to chronic loadshedding schedules. These include non-payment by large users or resellers, poor planning and management, underinvestment, over optimism, politically influenced decision making, infrastructure theft, and corruption. But I will conclude this chapter with a wider point, that the widespread stealing of electricity, along with other *menyetla* described in this book, are undermining our ability to act collectively or to hold leaders to account.

Electricity in South Africa

The majority of South Africans use electricity at home. Statistics South Africa's *General Household Survey* of 2019 estimates that 85 per cent of households are connected to mains electricity.[1] Additionally to household use, electricity is used in mining, industry, commerce, the public service, agriculture, and transport.[2] Most electricity in South Africa is produced by the state-owned enterprise Eskom, a vertically integrated (near) monopoly, overwhelmingly from coal-fired power stations, which transmits electricity along the high-voltage power lines of the national grid.

The task of distributing lower-voltage supply to consumers is shared with municipal distributors who buy electricity from Eskom[3] and sell it, at a markup, to domestic and commercial customers. Eskom has a range of different prices for its electricity depending on the customer, their location, the time of day, and season of the year.[4] Municipalities resell electricity with different mark ups adding further to the range of prices at which electricity is sold. While the domestic sector constitutes only 20 per cent of the total electricity consumption, it constitutes the largest number of users, some 14.6 million households in 2019, of which approximately 6.4 million are directly supplied by Eskom and some 8.2 million by municipalities.[5]

Electricity sales by municipalities is a source of income. It was billed in the 1998 *White Paper on Local Government* as being able to provide a third of municipal income. The white paper projected that 90 per cent of local government's operating budget could be raised by itself (rather than allocated from central government) and that 37 per cent of this could come from reselling electricity. As Tracey Ledger (2021) outlines, the country's local government funding model has been based on this hopelessly inaccurate assumption and is an important factor in the widespread financial collapse of municipal government. Many municipalities have consequently failed to pay for the electricity that they are supplying to residents. As of February 2023, Eskom was owed over R68 billion (of which R11bn was interest) by municipalities.[6]

Electricity in the home brings multiple benefits including lighting, cooking, heating, refrigeration, entertainment, and security. Using electricity to heat and cook eliminates harmful fumes generated from other energy sources such

1 The survey records 2.3 per cent of those having electricity obtain it from a source that they don't pay for. The reliability of surveys in recording illegal, grey, or sensitive information should be questioned. See Dickinson (2015) for an account of what was told to a Census 2011 enumerator compared to the actual household situation.

2 Some electricity is also exported.

3 A few municipalities produce their own electricity in addition to that purchased from Eskom.

4 Eskom (2017).

5 Using data from Eskom (2021), Department of Public Enterprises (2019), and Stats South Africa (2020b).

6 Ensor (2023).

as paraffin, wood, and coal, which contribute to respiratory diseases.[7] The use of TVs, radios, and smart phones keep people informed and connected. Electricity opens business opportunities. Finally, electricity, when correctly installed, is a safe form of energy in contrast to paraffin stoves and candles that are responsible for often devastating fires in informal settlements.[8] While these benefits accrue to all household members, it is women who benefit most, with the unequal burden of domestic work eased.

In 1987, Eskom embarked on its Electricity for All electrification programme focusing on black townships and rural areas.[9] Prior to this, most domestic connections had been provided by municipalities, primarily in white residential areas. There is now a complex mosaic of electricity supply across the country. Some parts of a municipality may be provided with electricity directly by Eskom, but in others the municipality resells Eskom electricity. A rural town may be on a municipal supply while "its" township is supplied by Eskom. In 1991, 38 per cent of households were connected to electricity, by 2002 68 per cent, rising to 85 per cent in 2019.[10] In the late 1980s and 1990s, Eskom's electrification programme took advantage of its then overcapacity, but was also aimed at raising the living standards of the black majority and promoting social stability in the wake of the Soweto Uprising of 1976 and the mid-1980s states of emergency.[11] Most of these new connections were installed with pre-paid meters,[12] meaning that the consumer must pay up front, rather than being billed monthly in arrears for what has been used.

To benefit, a household must not only be connected to the electricity grid but be able to afford the electricity used. Despite the cheap price of electricity in the 1980s and 1990s, payment for many of the newly connected proved impossible and poor households' electricity consumption was low.[13] If electricity was unaffordable to many households in the early 2000s, then even more so after tariffs rose sharply a few years later. Between 2007 and 2016 the average electricity tariff increased by not far off 150 per cent in real terms.[14]

Dramatic changes in the real price of electricity stems from the funding of what is a highly capital-intensive industry. Investment in new electrical

7 The health dangers of cooking with these fuels can be mitigated with well-designed stoves and heaters in good condition and with adequate ventilation. However, this presupposes that the household has funds to buy and correctly install such appliances and can afford the additional heating costs in maintaining adequate ventilation in winter.

8 Kimemia and van Niekerk (2017).

9 Van Heusden (2009).

10 Ruiters (2009); Stats South Africa (2020).

11 Eskom (1997); Van Heusden (2009).

12 Ruiters (2009).

13 Bond and McInnes (2007).

14 Per cent, calculated from Deloitte (2017) data.

generating capacity and transmission infrastructure requires massive expenditure. An electricity generating company either finances this from its own cash reserves generated from prior sales of electricity, or through borrowing which must then be paid back from sales revenue, or some combination of the two. In the early 1970s Eskom embarked on a large-scale capacity expansion programme, building coal-fired power stations. This was funded by a sharp increase in electricity tariffs (a 58 per cent real increase between 1973 and 1978).[15] It also resulted in the building of excess generating capacity. Public resistance to the increased cost of electricity led to the De Villiers Commission which, critical of the excess capacity Eskom had created, argued for lower tariffs. In real terms, average tariffs fell until the mid-2000s at which point new generating capacity needed to be built. Eskom, having failed to build up financial reserves as electricity became cheaper in real terms over the proceeding twenty-five years, had to borrow to replace its ageing fleet of power stations. It then proceeded to request tariff increases from the regulator to service the loans.

Two new coal-fired power stations, Medupi and Kusile, commissioned in 2007, would have allowed Eskom to meet electricity demand, though at a tariff high enough to pay back loans of some R300bn taken for their construction. However, rigging of construction tenders led to delays in completion, completed units running at below design capacity, and catastrophic failures of major components.[16] The result has been increasing power outages with electricity effectively rationed though load shedding schedules.

The Free Basic Electricity allowance

The post-apartheid government's response to the problem of electricity affordability was the Free Basic Electricity (FBE) policy.[17] This policy allows for registered indigent households to receive a limited amount of free electricity. However, the FBE has proved to be a policy that, impeccable in terms of legal pedigree, fails to address the problem it was introduced to address.

The national enabling regulation,[18] sets the amount to be provided at 50kWh per household, though some municipalities provide larger amounts. Ekurhuleni Metropolitan Municipality, under which Katlehong Township falls,

15 Data from Deloitte (2017).

16 Brederode (2023).

17 There is also the stepped tariff applied by municipal suppliers of electricity (in which the charge for electricity increases with greater use, effectively creating cross-subsidisation). Stepped tariffs do not apply to pre-paid Eskom meters, though Eskom operates a range of different tariff systems with cheaper rates for users agreeing to a low amperage connection (Ruiters 2009:249).

18 Department of Minerals and Energy (2003).

provides double the statutory minimum; 100kWh. Ekurhuleni Municipality (2021) outlines the objectives of its policy with a cascading set of statutory requirements, beginning with the Constitution:

- To comply with the provisions of the Constitution of the Republic of South Africa;
- to comply with the provisions of the Electricity Regulation Act 4 of 2006;
- to ensure compliance with the Municipal Systems Act No 32, 2000;
- to comply with the provisions of the Municipal Finance Management Act 56, 2003;
- to comply with the Electricity Pricing Policy Government Notice 1398 of 2008;
- to comply with the Electricity Basic Services Support Tariff (Free Basic Electricity) Policy Government Notice 1693 of 2003; and
- to ensure affordability of basic services to the community.

Ekurhuleni's FBE is twice as generous as the statutory minimum of 50kWh. Having listed the Constitution, three statutes, one government notice, and one policy, the critical question is whether the FBE does ensure affordability of basic services? Unfortunately, the answer is "no." The national guideline of 50kWh was based on research on how much electricity poor households used. As Greg Ruiters pithily puts it, this was a "conflation of use and need."[19]

Nor does Ekurhuleni's more generous 100kWh FBE allowance meet basic needs. An energy audit of low-income households in Gauteng townships by Earthlife Africa in 2010 found that the average use of electricity was some 750kWh a month. Desktop projections of the minimum amount of electricity required for essential household use range from 260 to 420kWh a month depending on the season and what is counted as essential.[20]

There are further limitations to the FBE. The allowance is given per erven or stand rather than per household,[21] meaning that the allowance is not available to backyard tenants, even though there are an estimated 1.4 million such dwellings in the country.[22] Another limitation is the means tests of municipalities, responsible for approving household FBE applications, whether supplied directly by Eskom or by the municipality.[23] Tracy Ledger calculates that only 2 million households are receiving FBE out of almost 10 million that

19 Ruiters (2009:251).

20 Earthlife Africa/Ferrial Adam (2010).

21 Jackie Dugard (2009).

22 Stats South Africa (2019).

23 Where a subsidy is then provided, via the municipality, for directly purchased Eskom electricity, the municipality is re-imbursed by Eskom.

are eligible and for whom funding is transferred to local municipalities.[24] One way in which applications for FBE are choked off is through extensive qualifying criteria[25] and onerous application requirements.[26] As Ruiters puts it, "The economic logic here is that the state can keep control over the welfare budget by making welfare as demeaning and difficult to access as possible."[27]

High profile resistance: the Soweto Electricity Crisis Committee

The electrification of Soweto, South Africa's iconic township, began in 1979[28] and preceded that of most other townships. As a result, Soweto homes had credit meters (i.e. payment is retrospective and based on electricity use in the proceeding period) installed and are billed monthly, rather than pre-paid meters which featured in Eskom's later electrification drive.

Post-1994 efforts at cost recovery, part of the shift to a more market-orientated approach to services, were met in Soweto with widespread non-payment, illegal reconnections when disconnected, and opposition to the introduction of pre-paid meters. The role of the Soweto Electricity Crisis Committee (SECC) and Operation Khanyisa, in which disconnected households were reconnected by volunteer electricians, was hailed by a number of academics as heroic collective resistance to neo-liberalism.[29] The disconnections were a reflection of unaffordability and not as argued by Eskom and the South African government because of a culture of non-payment hanging over from the rent[30] boycotts aimed at the apartheid state.[31]

In October 2001 Eskom announced a moratorium on disconnections. Jeff Radebe, then Minister of Public Enterprise, acknowledging that there were genuine problems, offered an amnesty on illegal connections and a 50 per cent write-off for residents' arrears.[32] This was rejected by the SECC as insufficient. It was also rejected by Soweto residents, many of whom have continued to ignore their electricity bills. In 2017, only 17 per cent of the electricity used

24 Ledger (2021:31).

25 Ruiters (2009:253).

26 Ledger (2021:29).

27 Ruiters (2009:253).

28 Spink (1991:14). Initially, the supply was a municipal responsibility but was taken over by Eskom in the early 1990s (Eskom 1997).

29 Naidoo and Veriava (2009); Bond and McInnes (2007).

30 "Rent" in the township under apartheid was payment to the municipality for the house (i.e. rent) and included payment for municipal services. The term continues to be used, even with the transfer of house ownership, for what most readers would understand as rates and municipal service charges.

31 Fiil-Flynn/SECC (2001).

32 Egan and Wafer (2004).

by Soweto small power users was paid for, a shortfall of R289 million.[33] The township's debt to Eskom amounted to almost R19 billion in June 2019.[34]

The prominence of Soweto in resisting cost recovery for services is due to the SECC and the academics who aligned themselves with the anti-commodification/privatisation struggles of the early 2000s. However, what made this form of resistance so visible was that Soweto was electrified largely with credit meters. With a credit meter you can refuse to pay your bill, on a "can't pay" and/or "won't pay" basis. Once bills are not paid, the dispute moves into the terrain of disconnections. These can be prevented by residents calling for assistance from neighbours, using whistles, when Eskom technicians arrive.[35] The installation of pre-paid meters short-circuits this process; no credit in the meter, no electricity. Hence the struggle of the SECC focused on resisting pre-paid meter installation.

Soweto was not the only township that had credit meters installed when they were originally electrified, but it was the largest that successfully resisted their replacement with pre-paid meters.[36] However, as we shall see, there are ways to avoid paying for electricity even when pre-paid meters are installed.

Persuasion and deception

Outside of providing electricity for free and financing it through taxation, there are three ways of preventing people from stealing electricity. The first is to persuade them they should pay. The second is to make it impossible not to pay. The third, should the first two fail, is to deny them electricity.

Attempts to persuade people to pay for the services they receive have stretched across the span of South Africa's democracy. The first major attempt was the Masakhane (Let us Build Together) campaign launched in 1995 by then President Nelson Mandela, who outlined how:

> Government is putting massive investment into programmes for housing and services. We all have the responsibility to pay for what we use, or else the investment will dry up and the projects come to an end. We must ensure that we can, as a nation, provide for the millions still without the basic needs.[37]

33 Yelland and Groenewad (2017).

34 Department of Public Enterprises (2019:11).

35 Fiil-Flynn (2001).

36 There was extensive resistance to the installation of pre-paid meters in Tembisa on the East Rand (van Heusden 2009).

37 Mandela (1995).

Eskom runs its own Operation Khanyisa, in sharp contrast to the Operation Khanyisa of the SECC. Launched in October 2010, Eskom's Operation Khanyisa implores people to pay for the electricity they used.

> Why is there no public outcry about electricity theft? … The perpetrators are found everywhere – whether it's those who offer their services to "fix" the electricity, or the power consumers who choose to accept these "services" to tamper with or bypass their meters or power-supply points, make illegal connections or not pay for the power they consume … Operation Khanyisa is a national partnership, a movement that works to mobilize, inspire, empower and encourage all South Africans to join the fight against electricity theft, and to use electricity legally, safely and efficiently.[38]

President Ramaphosa's State of the Nation Speech in 2019 followed much the same lines; "It is imperative that all those who use electricity – over and above the free basic electricity provided – should pay for it."[39] These appeals have been to no effect. Attempts to construct a post-apartheid South African collective morality, often using the concept of *ubuntu*,[40] have been unsuccessful. Instead of acting as members of a collective, South Africans – and electricity theft occurs in township and suburb – have pursued their individual interests, ignoring the impact of their summated acts.

The SECC was an exception; it openly and collectively defied the economics of electricity distribution. In 2001 when Eskom agreed to a moratorium on electricity disconnections in Soweto, Jeff Radebe accused the SECC of being part of a criminal culture and unrepresentative of Soweto residents. More than twenty years later, it would be worth asking if it is not better to deal with an organised opposition such as the SECC than millions of households doing the same thing but in secret.

Izinyoka

Despite steeply rising electricity tariffs, the use of electricity by households has not decreased. Official statistics show that the number of households using electricity for cooking, a heavy user of electricity in the home, has risen. In 2002, 57.5 per cent of households reported that electricity was the main source of energy used for cooking. By 2019 that figure had risen to 75.1 per cent. Meanwhile, the use of the main alternative cooking fuels, wood,

38 Operation Khanyisa (N.D.).

39 Ramaphosa (2019).

40 The philosophy that a person is a person because of other people.

paraffin, and coal, had collectively dropped from 39.1 per cent to 12.1 per cent over the same period.[41]

In 2007, Eskom released a short video aimed at countering the theft of cables and illegal connections. It stressed the outcomes of such activities; an Intensive Care Unit (ICU) patient's ventilator stopping as the lights went off, a young child electrocuted by illegally laid cables. Those who stole and endangered the community were, the video said, *izinyoka*, isiZulu for snakes, a reviled creature. These snakes were hurting the community. The video ended with Eskom's crime line number, and the message that the snakes needed to be put where they belonged, "in a hole."[42] It seems unlikely the video had any impact on electricity theft, but the term *izinyoka* caught on, though without the stigma intended. An insult that can be levelled at almost everyone is an insult that can be laughed off. In the township, few people aren't *izinyoka* when it comes to electricity.[43]

Stealing electricity allows households to keep their head above water financially or increase disposable income. Additionally, it brings social harmony within families and between landlords and tenants over who is to pay for the electricity consumed. The question, and the fights, simply disappear.

There is nothing unique about electricity theft in South Africa. Electricity is stolen wherever it is produced and sold. Electricity theft can be estimated but is hard to measure precisely because between electricity generation and use by consumers there is loss of electricity along the transmission and distribution (T&D) network. Thus, simply subtracting the electricity that has been paid for from the electricity leaving the power stations, gives a figure that includes T&D losses as well as what has been used but not paid for. Thomas Smith's (2004) study of T&D losses in 102 countries found rates between 4 and 53 per cent of initially generated electricity. Smith used a cut-off of 16 per cent (which could possibly be accounted for by T&D losses rather than theft) beyond which, he concluded, countries have a "serious problem."[44] On this basis, 40 per cent of countries included in the study have such a problem. Higher

[41] Stats South Africa (2020b). Use of electricity for cooking peaked in 2014 at 79.9 per cent, but the subsequent decrease has been taken up largely by the category of "other", which in 2019 had risen to 8.7 per cent from 2.1 per cent in 2014. It's not clear what "other" fuel includes or why its use has increased so significantly. One possible explanation is that "other" is given to the research administrators to avoid follow up questions about an illegal electricity connection.

[42] Eskom (2007).

[43] Singular: *izinyoka*. The term *izinyokayoka* can be used to refer to the spider webs of illegal electricity connections.

[44] Smith (2004:2070).

rates of theft were associated with poverty along with political, economic, and social turmoil.[45]

Nevertheless, it is not only those struggling to make ends meet who steal electricity. Smith outlines how in Pakistan when the government authorised the army to conduct house to house checks to detect meter tampering, of over 100,000 cases of power theft, "many … were discovered in the houses, farms and mills of the ruling party legislators, 13 of whom were WAPDA [the water and energy authority] officials, while one cabinet minister had to resign after caught stealing electricity."[46]

In 2018, Eskom estimated losses due to electricity and infrastructure theft at R20bn a year,[47] though this can only be a thumb suck given the difficulty of such calculations. In August 2021, the Johannesburg City Power company said that non-technical losses, that is electricity theft, was costing it R2bn a year.[48] Whatever the margin for error, these are large figures which contribute to a crisis of electricity supply in South Africa.

Illicit reconnections

Once a customer is disconnected, cables, circuit breakers, and meters are removed. Reconnection charges are set at punitive rates. Johannesburg City Power clients who have been disconnected, which it points out are not only residents of informal settlements but businesses in the suburbs, had to pay a reconnection fee penalty of between R10,000 and R50,000 in 2021.[49] The problem with punishing the original offence with a punitive reconnection fee is that it is often easier to reconnect illegally.

Thuso's connection

When Thuso was disconnected for non-payment in the mid-1990s, he quickly organised reconnection with a "township electrician." [50] *Unemployed, his only income came from three backyard tenants who paid rent, electricity inclusive, each month. He had little cash for the reconnection and hadn't been able to afford an 80 Amp circuit breaker for the supply box, or* lejwe *in local lingo, in the street. Instead, he was reconnected directly to the street supply. The*

45 Smith (2004:2071).

46 Smith (2004:2068).

47 Van der Merwe (2018).

48 City Power (2021).

49 City Power (2021). For comparison, the monthly national minimum wage in 2021 was approximately R3,500.

50 This section is based on Fieldnotes: 170513; 170527; 170617; 170701; 170930; 171007; and 171011.

cable to the house ran a few centimetres under the earth of the yard. A hole had been drilled through the wall into the kitchen and the cable threaded through to join the distribution box inside the lounge. This entry was shielded from view by a casually placed paving slab.

The backyard shacks were supplied by overhead wires connected to a single plug in the kitchen. This would regularly trip and was a problem if Thuso was out. Although there was no protection in the event of a surge from the street supply, the distribution box was fitted with an earth leakage breaker that would come into action in the event of a short circuit. That, however, created another problem. The cable running under the front yard was not in great shape and would trip the earth leakage when it rained, cutting the power to all households until the frayed section of the cable was repaired. Thuso would dig up the wire to find the damaged section and, as there was no breaker at the lejwe, *tape the damaged sections on the live wire.*

The tenants complained about being left in the dark, pap *half cooked on the stove, and blank TV screens. Luckily, a neighbour was able to sell him ten metres of 4mm cable at half what it would have cost at Cashbuild. As for* matsoho *(hands or labour), Vuyo a self-taught electrician agreed to do the job for R200.*

There are a range of township electricians with different qualifications and skills. Vuyo is towards the bottom of this range. He has no formal training and has picked up what he knows from working with others. Most of the electrical work was done with a pair of pliers and an Allen key. For working on the live wire at the lejwe, *he had a pair of gardening gloves. But first, Vuyo rolled a joint to relax for the job ahead.*

A neighbour's car provided a screen as Vuyo worked on the lejwe. *A couple of neighbours stood around chatting while he worked. There was only one scare when an Eskom van drove down the street. Everybody froze except for Vuyo who left his tools and started walking briskly down the road. But it was an Eskom work bakkie, not an inspection van, and it drove past. The group reassembled and there were relieved jokes about avoiding a R500* tjhotjho. *Once Vuyo had disconnected the live wire at the* lejwe, *the old cable was ripped out and a deeper trench dug across the front yard for the new cable. Vuyo said that it would be best to run the cable into the empty meter box, rather than through the hole in the kitchen wall. It would, he suggested, make it easier for Thuso to legally reconnect when he could afford to do so. Thuso agreed.*

Once Vuyo had connected the cable to the distribution board and reorganised the wiring of the house and backyard rooms, it was back to the lejwe *to reconnect the live wire. He gripped the Allen key with the insulated electrician's pliers which he turned in his gloved hands. Then he carefully picked up offcuts of wire and brushed over the filled-in trench so that it blended into the rest of the yard.*

What struck me most about Thuso's re-reconnection was the banality. True, there was the scare over the passing Eskom van, but that soon passed. Neighbours and passers-by saw what was happening and carried on with whatever they were doing. One or two, with nothing more pressing, stopped and watched for a while, just as they might watch a bricklayer build a wall.

Out of Thuso's earshot there were however reservations. It was not that Thuso should not have electricity, they understood his difficulty. Nor was it that Eskom wasn't going to be paid. The criticism was rather about the amount of electricity consumed by the four households on the stand. Was it any wonder that the electricity tripped for the entire block on winter afternoons as people returned from work and the evening meal was cooked?

It was also noticeable that Thuso had no problem with having this reconnection less concealed than the previous one. It reflected how the situation had changed since his first illegal reconnection. By the time Vuyo was re-installing his illegal connection in 2017 most of his neighbours were, in one way or another, also *izinyoka*.

After Vuyo's departure, Thuso congratulated himself on having upgraded the connection. That the supply was now safe was especially important given that there were children staying in the yard. Vuyo's suggestion to connect through the empty meter box had also brought him closer to legality. He mused that at some point he would ask Eskom to reconnect him. The chances of that happening were, in my opinion, close to zero, but I said nothing. What I realised was that Thuso was not thinking, as I did, of legal or illegal connections. Rather, for him there was a spectrum. By improving safety and holding out the possibility of formal reconnection in the future, he had moved along that spectrum in the direction that would be approved by anyone who understood his situation.

Spiders' webs

Rapid urbanisation around South Africa's urban centres has resulted in widespread informal settlements. Stats South Africa's *General Household Survey 2019* estimates that there are close to 1.5 million households living in "Informal dwelling/shack not in backyard"[51] which approximates to informal settlements. Over a third of these are in Gauteng province. Of the 1.5 million households living in informal settlements, the survey records that some 650,000 use mains electricity for lighting and 256,000 use another source of electricity for lighting.[52]

51 Stats South Africa (2020b).

52 This may include illegal connections, but it could also be a car battery, charged for a fee at local businesses, to run a 12-volt system, or lights run from solar panels.

Many informal settlements which are not legally connected to the grid are supplied by tapping electricity from a nearby source. This can be street lighting, hostels, connected houses, transformers, or even overhead lines. Here, township electricians act as informal suppliers of electricity, stolen from Eskom or the municipality. Electricity is distributed through cables often strung above the *mekhukhu* roofs, forming a spider's web of wires.

Thanduxolo Doro (2016) records how in Ramaphosa Informal Settlement on the East Rand, some *mekhukhu* were electrified from either high mast "Apollo" lighting or nearby formal houses. They were charged an installation fee of between R300 and R500 and a monthly flat rate of R200 for which they had electricity to use a two-plate stove, refrigerator, lights, and television. The cables running from the lights would be periodically disconnected, but then swiftly reconnected.[53]

Too many illegal connections overloads transformers. Repairing or replacing transformers is a problem for power suppliers and in 2019 Eskom declared that it would not be restoring power when a transformer or other infrastructure failure was the result of illegal connections.[54] Attempting to avoid the problem, Johannesburg City Power has been removing networks of illegal connections in informal settlements at the rate of one a week.[55] Such operations require joint operations between City Power, private security, and police, though once removed cables are soon replaced.[56]

Bridging the meter

Bridging a meter involves taking the electric current past the meter reader. It is done by opening the meter box and inserting two short lengths of wire, allowing the current to flow past the measuring unit. In township lingo, to bridge a meter is to *tshipa,* a Sesotho word meaning to pinch or to nip. The words bridge and *tshipa* can be used broadly to describe any arrangement where some electricity is diverted past the meter, as with the T-junctions I describe in the following section. However, I use the term for when an electricity meter remains in place with current flowing through but not measured.[57]

53 Doro (2016).

54 Eskom Media Desk (2019).

55 City Power (2021).

56 See for example, SABC News (2021).

57 It is possible to tamper with some meters so that it records less units than are flowing through (Smith 2004:2068). Fiil-Flynn (2001:22) refers to rumours of such a device being offered to Soweto residents, but that it was unclear if the device worked. I have not come across or heard about such devices.

Lucky: winning on the swings and the roundabouts

Lucky is good with his hands and makes a living as a handyman in a small Free State township. He has no formal training but can install electrical wiring and fix appliances. He can also tshipa *your meter. In fact, this is his speciality. His charge ranges from R150 to R250 depending on how much money you've got. It's a good business. People, he says, are afraid of electricity and don't want to touch the meter box themselves.*

Meter boxes used to be sealed with a simple loop of wire closed with a crimp. You can buy crimps at any hardware store. Then Eskom made things difficult by using their own seals with a plastic tag. Fortunately, Lucky has a friend who works for Eskom who sells him seals. To complete the authenticity, Lucky puts an orange Eskom sticker on the side of the meter box with the fraud line number for reporting meter tampering.

Many of his clients call him when they are struggling and need some way of making ends meet. With the meter bridged it's a load off their mind. Things in the house return to normal; the fridge is back on, they can cook, they can boil a kettle, they can keep warm, they can charge their cell phones, they do not have to buy paraffin or candles. This is all good, but when Lucky helps them he also gives advice; buy the occasional coupon.

Buying small amounts of electricity is expensive per unit. An additional surcharge of up to 20 per cent is added by spaza *shops.*[58] *But, Lucky explains, Eskom can see if you've been buying electricity or not. It'll be hard to explain why you've suddenly stopped using any electricity. He councils them further, they can "bank" these purchases for when they want to* tshipolla *(un-bridge) the meter. Eskom knows you've bought a coupon, it doesn't know when, or if, you've entered it into the meter.*

"Why would somebody pay to have their meter un-bridged?" I ask Lucky. His answer is that people are afraid of Eskom as well as electricity. He thinks the fear is unfounded, but he's not complaining; it's the same charge to un-bridge a meter as it is to bridge. He wins on the swings and the roundabouts. It's not as though you can't get around an inspection, but some people are nervous, they are thinking about somebody looking at the meter and wanting to know why the display says 0.0 yet the lights are on. So, when things improve financially, they will call him, cushioning their return to legality with the coupons bought and banked while getting mahala *electricity.*

Recognising the nervousness of some of his clients, Lucky provides a discreet service and tells people that he came around to fix your kettle or give a quote on re-wiring the place. There's always the danger that a neighbour might loma

[58] Fieldnotes: 110723. Purchasing a R20 coupon of electricity in the township cost R24. The additional R4 was over and above whatever commission the *spaza* shops officially received from Eskom.

(inform). It's a good way to get even if you've fallen out. Lucky counsels on this also: just because you are getting electricity mahala *don't flaunt it. He gives the example of boiling sugar beans. Do as you would normally and boil a large pot of beans to last a few days, don't boil fresh each day.*

The pre-paid meter was intended to control households' use of electricity remotely, without the need for letters of demand, physical disconnection, and possible confrontation. But instead, the struggle over electricity supply moved onto new terrain. This has provided opportunities for those who know something about electricity and new *menyetla* for those able to supply township electricians with official Eskom seals and stickers.

By helping people to help themselves (to electricity), Lucky was giving people dignity. Not just the dignity of a clean power source at home, but also the social dignity of not having to scrimp, and bicker and fight over not enough. Yet, the dignity gained is also dignity lost. In learning how to avoid detection, Lucky's clients erode further their ability to call out the wrongs of others. If they accuse anyone, they must think carefully, in case a finger is pointed back at them.

Nkosinathi's T-junctions: value for money

Nkosinathi has a red seal certification as a qualified electrician.[59] *He is rarely short of work and prides himself on the quality of what he does. He always insists on using the right materials so that there aren't problems later. Much of what he does is above board, but he combines this with helping clients to manage their electricity bills.*

As he explains, assisting clients came naturally to him. He likes to help people. He gives an example: he is asked by a pensioner to fix a burned-out socket. Even the materials needed for this small job are hard for the pensioner to afford. They are using R600 of electricity a month, it's close to half of what they get from their [2017] social grant. They are not managing. Things are expensive. They can't afford to eat. So, he helps them out.

He sits down and discusses how much they are currently paying and what they can afford. He councils against making a dramatic reduction. It is best that they keep paying something. Maybe the pensioner should keep paying around R200 a month or so. They can explain the lower usage saying they installed a solar geyser, or perhaps they are saving on the bill by cooking with a paraffin stove.

Once it's agreed how much they would like to save, Nkosinathi works out which electrical appliances should be run past the meter. If possible, he

59 Fieldnotes: 170214.

does the job in a single day to minimise questions being asked. Ideally, he'd disconnect the house at the supply box in the street, but that could attract attention. Instead, he digs in the front yard and uncovers the cable between the street and the house distribution box. Cutting this wire is the risky part, but he wears industrial gloves and uses electrician's plyers. Once it's cut, he tapes the live wire and can now work without worry.

His speciality is the T-junction that he joins into the supply cable. One wire now leads, via the meter, to the distribution box. The lights and perhaps the bedroom plugs run from this cable. The second wire bypasses the meter and is connected to the kitchen and rooms that are regularly heated in winter. Once that's done, he re-joins the cut cable and fills in the hole.

The client need not worry if Eskom sends somebody around, they are still paying for electricity and the lights will not shine if the meter has no credit. He gives an informal 15-year guarantee on his T-junctions. People want reassurance that they've done the right thing and that they needn't worry about something going wrong. It's a point of pride that he won't be called back. There isn't a fixed price for his matsoho *(labour), it depends on how much the client is going to save.*

Nkosinathi places his T-junctions within a wider context. The township electrician might be making a few thousand rand with illegal connections, but he will get away with it. "Because he is a small fish?" I ask. "No," Nkosinathi laughs in response, "it's because the bosses are making tens or hundreds of thousands of rand. Corruption is everywhere. So, everybody must help themselves."

For Nkosinathi, it was obvious that Eskom knew what was happening. It might complain, but it didn't really want to do anything. It was a way of delivering to the people. Eskom and the ANC know what is happening. They know and they are winking. And in return the electorate votes them back at the next election. That, he says, is the way it is and that's why he doesn't have a problem assisting people to cut their bills.

T-junctions, splitting electricity between paid and stolen components, is hybrid electricity theft. It falls between bridging the meter, as with Lucky's clients, and an illegal connection without any meter, as with Thuso's set up. Once a T-junction is installed it is hard to spot and easy to forget. Indeed, some of the muted criticism of Thuso's connection came from neighbours whose own electricity supply was split with a T-junction. They had re-calibrated their own moral position. Since they regularly bought electricity, even if only for part of what they used, they were "known to Eskom." They were, in their own minds, doing the right thing.

Cheap electricity

There are ways of cutting energy costs without electricians. "Cheap electricity" or "ghost coupons" sold through clandestine chains cost only a fraction of legitimately purchased pre-paid electricity units. It is usually women, at the bottom of the chain, who take orders for individual households. She knows the person above her, but how long the chain is and who is the "kingpin" with access to a pre-paid vending machine, she doesn't know. She puts in orders, using the client's meter number to the person above her and receives ghost coupons, or simply the twenty-digit number that the client must input into their meter.

The common assumption is that Eskom employees are the kingpins at the top of the chain. However, in the few court cases where kingpins have been tried, they were using stolen Eskom vending machines. Such operations churn out ghost coupons on an industrial scale. In a 2010 prosecution, five stolen vending machines had generated 78,280 pre-paid vouchers between February 2007 and May 2008.[60] Although the number of units issued on ghost coupons varies, the purchaser typically receives upwards of 800kWhs. If 800kWhs was the average amount disbursed in this case, Eskom was defrauded of revenue for some 62.6 million kWh of electricity, worth approximately R12.5 million at 2008 electricity tariffs, or R115 million using 2021 electricity tariffs and rands.

"We are all hungry!" Nomvula's business

By 2021, Nomvula had been selling ghost coupons for over eleven years after her cousin introduced her to the business.[61] *Nomvula is entrepreneurial and retailing ghost coupons is one of several businesses she pursues. She bakes scones and sells them by the 20-litre tub when there is a funeral or other event. Cheap electricity, as she describes her product, is her most risky business and the one she takes care to conceal.*

When she first started selling cheap electricity, she went door to door in Batloung, a township some 40 kilometres away from where she lives. She picked up a client base and developed a weekly routine. She would collect meter numbers on a Monday, give the list to her cousin, one step up in the sales chain, and collect a list of coupon numbers on Friday which she would deliver the following Monday. When she first started, she was charged R10 for a coupon of 900 units. By 2021 that had risen to R35 which she sells on for R150. At 2021 tariffs this is worth in the region of R1,500.

Nomvula charges just 10 per cent of the value received in electricity because of competition with other vendors in Batloung. Some undercut her price, but

60 State vs Ndebele (2011).

61 Based on fieldnotes: 210724 and 210907.

she offers reliability and can charge a little higher. Rival vendors are linked into different chains and Nomvula has switched supplier a couple of times. As much as the vendors in Batloung compete they also talk and are keen to recruit others to their chain. She is however now back with her initial supplier, though that's more about family politics than profit margins; there are arguments with her cousin when she switches supplier. Occasionally, clients defect to another vendor, usually after defaulting on payments.

Increasingly, Nomvula's business is less door to door and more WhatsApp messages. Now she only visits Batloung once a month and otherwise relies on messaging. Clients pay with EFT, PEPMoney, and other money transfer systems. She's also picked up clients in different townships who have been referred to her from Batloung. She deals with these clients by phone or WhatsApp and has never met them. She charges them R200. The rational for the extra is less to do with her costs but because there are fewer rival suppliers in those townships.

Given the risks, Nomvula takes precautions. Her clients do not know her real name, to them she is Nonku. When a potential client rings, she expects them to tell her that they got her number from one of her existing clients. It's a form of verification. If they only say that they want to buy electricity she doesn't know what they are talking about. She doesn't sell to neighbours, and they don't know about this business.

She used these precautions when she began the business. Then it felt a lot riskier. Now, she laughingly explains, that even police officers are buying from her. If she was caught, she's confident she'd be able to bribe her way out; "South Africa is corrupt!" she exclaims.

When I asked Nomvula if she worries about Eskom losing revenue, she agreed it was a problem but countered with the justification that "we are all hungry!" Moreover, it was clear to her that Eskom was involved in the racket themselves. There must, she reasoned, be people in Eskom involved. She then qualified her concern about Eskom being defrauded, but "not that much" because "the people at the top are eating alone, they don't think about us."

Nomvula is right about the nonchalance with which ghost electricity coupons are increasingly sold. Adverts for "Affordable Prepaid Electricity" can be found on township Facebook pages offering, for example, two thousand units for R450, payable by eWallet or CashSend.[62] So that a new customer knows the deal is legitimate, they will send you a picture of the printed coupon, complete with your meter number, but with some of the twenty digits obscured until you've made payment.

[62] At 2022 Eskom tariffs, when this offer was on Facebook pages, R450 bought electricity worth around R4,000.

Buying "cheap electricity" is psychologically much easier than getting a township electrician to *tshipa* your meter. You are doing nothing to the meter and can frame what you are doing as buying cheap or discounted electricity. Of course, everybody knows it is wrong, at least in terms of the law of the land. Thus, even if others are buying ghost coupons, it is not something you are going to broadcast. And if, like Nomvula, you are part of the network of distribution, you are going to be discreet.

Over decades a vast clandestine web, created by person-to-person connections, has developed to distribute these fraudulent coupons. Everybody in the system benefits and the entire practice, despite its obvious illegality, can be justified on the grounds that those in charge are in on the game and, indeed, taking more than you are.

Part-time criminals

Jason Ditton (1977) writing on workplace theft observes that those pilfering at work are not full-time criminals. While the number of full-time or professional criminals in any society may be small, the number of part-time criminals can be large. Township electricians mix regular electrical work with fixing illegal connections, bridging meters, and installing T-junctions. The foot soldiers of the ghost coupon distribution chains similarly mix legitimate with illegitimate income generating activities.

The same applies, though on a much larger scale, to their clients. They may be stealing from Eskom or the municipality, but they do not see themselves as criminals. A criminal is someone who carries out cash-in-transit heists or mugs somebody for their phone. Rather, they frame and justify what they are doing and, at least on a moral level, decriminalise this activity.

The first act of justification is to reconfigure the stealing of electricity as other than stealing. Buying "cheap electricity," is one way of doing this. When such reframing is difficult there are excuses. The most compelling is that they cannot otherwise heat their home in winter or cook food for their children and so on. Then there is simply the cost; it's affordable but only if something else is foregone. Why should they make that sacrifice when others are not? To stand aside demonstrates only worldly stupidity. Then there is the question of service. Why should they pay such high prices if they are not receiving a reliable service? Notwithstanding that the poor service is, in part, created by the very actions that they are justifying. Then there are assertions that what they are doing has been given the wink by the authorities, an informal system of tolerated redistribution. Finally, there is the argument that others, higher up the social hierarchy, are getting away with much more.

Any justification is much easier when many are carrying out the act that requires justification. The risk of detection and sanction decreases but so too does the stigma. The increasing numbers of *izinyok*a brings confidence and this further increases the numbers willing to join in. At this point it is not only those who cannot make ends meet, but also those who can afford to pay who join the bandwagon. Once stealing electricity, albeit described otherwise, is ubiquitous, only remarkably moral citizens will resist the temptation. Who doesn't want to save money? Even if you have a regular salary, of say a police officer,[63] saving on your electricity bill means being able to afford something otherwise unaffordable. Not to do so, when everybody else is doing so, is to be a "stupid."

These justifications provide a far better explanation than the contention that a culture of non-payment remains from the struggle against apartheid. There were service payment boycotts in South Africa's townships justified as resistance to apartheid, though as Antina von Schnitzler (2016) points out, to argue that these were entirely aimed at apartheid, rather than linked to the benefits of not paying bills, is to gloss over the realities of everyday life. The argument is, however, wrong for a more pertinent reason; culture is not something that travels through time determining actions in the present. People act within a context which is influenced but not controlled by the past. Township residents well understand that apartheid has fallen. To suggest otherwise is ludicrous. To imagine that people are trapped in a culture created almost four decades ago and are unable to realise that things have changed is both patronising and naive.

The crime that keeps a corrupt elite in power

The SECC has long disappeared from public view, but stealing electricity, whether through fraud, theft or non-payment, is widespread. Despite efforts to persuade, cajole, and enforce payment in the township, stealing electricity has become all but the norm. This norm has its own economic ecology. Just as the different systems of stealing electricity provide *menyetla* for users and suppliers, so too does the mitigation of risk. There is *menyetla* proliferation when those charged with enforcing payment and given "street level authority"[64] to enforce compliance look away for a consideration or provide the necessary Eskom paraphernalia to disguise the bridging of a meter.

Put differently, the stealing of electricity illuminates how the *lex constitutional* does not operate in the township. Or at least has only fleeting power. The state is able, though its agents, unreliable as they are, to clamp down temporarily, as when municipality officials, private security, and police officers mount an operation to remove illegal connections in an informal settlement.

63 The average, total cost to company, remuneration of SAPS employees was R416,000 in the 2020/21 financial year (Business Tech 2021). The minimum wage in 2021 was around R44,000 per annum.

64 Lipsky (1980).

However, this show of lawful authority does not endure; cables are reconnected. The high-profile enforcement of the *lex constitutional* ebbs away and the *lex lokasi* returns.

Yet, the widespread part-time criminality of the township serves a useful purpose for those at the top of South Africa's social and political order. It secures their position, despite engaging in graft on a far larger scale. If township residents cannot log a fault with Eskom when the transformer burns because Eskom will ask them for their meter number, even more so they cannot point to those who have stolen billions through corruption. It is one thing to grumble, or to rhetorically justify your own misdemeanours by reference to those at the top eating alone, it is another to level accusations openly and directly. To do this you must be confident that you stand on firm ground. But few do and this keeps those guilty of far larger crimes secure.

6

A fleeting *monyetla*: the Social Relief of Distress grant

Introduction: R50 out of R350

In May 2020, during South Africa's first COVID-19 epidemic lockdown, President Ramaphosa announced the introduction of the Social Relief of Distress (SRD) grant, intended to relieve the hardship of the lockdown. The grant was for those without work or other income and who were ineligible for other social security grants. The grant was set at R350 per month and came to be known as the "Ramaphosa" or "three-fifty" grant. As the epidemic subsided it was withdrawn but then re-introduced and is now a *de facto* permanent component of South Africa's social security system.[1]

The SRD grant covered what had been a major gap in South Africa's social security system, the long term unemployed. While the country's social security is now comprehensive in scope,[2] the size of the grant provides only limited relief. When introduced in 2020, the food poverty line, the bare minimum required to buy adequate food for a month, was estimated to be R585.[3] The grant remained at R350 until April 2024 when it was increased to R370.[4]

Any large-scale benefit provision provides opportunities for corruption and fraud and the SRD was no exception. Fraudulent claims were made and post office employees in the retail outlets, initially the key distribution mechanism for the grant, were able to use their position to extract bribes from claimants, particularly in townships. While the term bribe was not used, the tellers' involvement in what came to be known as the express system was classic corruption; the misuse of public office for private gain.[5]

1 Unless replaced by a basic income grant scheme or BIG (Khoza 2022).

2 For those with identification documents.

3 Institute for Economic Justice (2021).

4 The increase has not kept pace with inflation. If adjusted in line with CPI the grant would have been approximately R440 in 2024.

5 See the Introduction.

However, the primary focus of this chapter is not on this corruption or fraudulent claims, though these feature in what follows. Rather, it is on how others, whether working with or without post office tellers, created opportunities or *menyetla* for themselves within the chaotic rollout of the SRD grant. Fraudulent claims aside, R50 or 14 per cent of the grant's value emerged as the standard payment for assistance in accessing the grant.

Eventually, the distribution chaos was resolved. This was not through implementing the *lex constitutional* in the form of disciplinary or criminal charges against post office tellers or the effective control of queues. Rather, the chaos and the R50 *menyetla* that it enabled ended with the expansion of collection points for the grant.

South Africa's social security system

South Africa's social security system has two components: social assistance, the transfer of resources via taxation in the form of grants from richer to poorer citizens; and social insurance, in which contributions fund compensation paid out in the event of adverse circumstances.

The social assistance component of social security was reformed following the end of apartheid with payments, subject to means tests, equalised across race groups. Prior to the introduction of the SRD grant, the largest social assistance grants in terms of expenditure were the old age pension for those over sixty, child support grants for children under the age of eighteen, and the disability grant.[6]

There are three social insurance schemes which cover road accidents,[7] occupational injuries and diseases, and unemployment.[8] Compensation for unemployment is through the Unemployment Insurance Fund (UIF). This was originally designed for short-term unemployment and applied to white workers. In the current context of mass unemployment, the UIF, which pays for a maximum of twelve months following retrenchment, is of limited assistance, given the extent of unemployment in South Africa. Hence the value of the introduced SRD grant to millions of unemployed people.

Excluding the SRD grant, there were almost 18 million recipients of social grants in 2020, over 12 million of those being children. In a country where the official or narrow measure of unemployment in the third quarter of 2021 was

6 With total expenditure in the 2020/2021 financial year of R81.6bn, R67.5bn, and R23.6bn respectively (Institute for Economic Justice 2021).

7 Administrated by the Road Accident Fund to which motorists contribute via a levy on fuel.

8 Occupational and unemployment compensation is funded by contributions made by employers and employees.

24.9 per cent and the expanded measure 46.6 per cent,[9] these grants blunt the edge of poverty. Social grants provide the main source of income for almost one quarter of all households.[10] They also have, however, a political dimension. If police roadblocks at township entrances represents physical pinch points where the state is in control, then grants represent a soft, but powerful, hold on the population in the state's otherwise increasingly weak hand. Without the monthly payments many households would sink into unbearable poverty, and the state would lose a key claim to legitimacy.

The Ramaphosa Social Relief of Distress grant

Prior to the introduction of the SRD grant, those under 60 and able to work but unemployed fell outside the country's social security system. Those who had never worked had no UIF contributions to claim against while the scheme does not cover long-term unemployment. As part of the massive support package announced shortly after the first COVID-19 lockdown began in May 2020 the COVID-19 SRD grant[11] was introduced.[12] Administrated by the South African Social Security Agency (SASSA), the grant set at R350 a month initially ran for a year.[13] For eligibility claimants had to have no other income, social grant (excluding child support grants from 1 July 2021),[14] or be entitled to UIF benefits. The restriction on income was later raised from zero to R350 (i.e. parity with the SRD grant) and then to R624 a month.[15] The grant was re-introduced in August 2021. Political considerations likely played a role[16] given that local elections were scheduled for November.

Applications for the grant could be made in several ways. The key information required was the individual's name and South African ID number. Applicants had to state, among a list of eligibility requirements, that they

9 The latter includes those who have given up looking for work and for that reason are statistically excluded from the labour force and, therefore, the narrow definition of unemployment (Stats South Africa 2022).

10 Mahlangu (2022).

11 A social relief of distress grant already existed. This is used for discretional assistance in the form of food parcels, school uniforms, and vouchers. In terms of overall expenditure this grant is marginal. References to the SRD grants in this chapter refer to the COVID-19 SRD.

12 Ramaphosa (2020). Additionally, increases were made, on a temporary basis, to several other social assistance grants.

13 Initially for six months, but then extended by two three-month periods.

14 And grants given to caregivers of the recipient (Zulu 2021).

15 Nkanjeni (2022).

16 As outlined by Brockerhoff (2013:21), "Using social assistance to ensure electoral support is … a phenomenon that can be traced throughout the course of South African history and can be argued to continue to exist today …."

were unemployed and whether they had any income sources. Speaking at the re-introduction of the SRD grant in August 2021, the Minister of Social Development, Lindiwe Zulu (2021), outlined that in the first year of operation (May 2020 – April 2021), R24bn was paid out, putting the SRD grant on par with the disability grant in terms of total expenditure.

Almost 10 million applications were received in the first year of operation, however just over 6 million were approved. Those honest enough to declare an income, however small, were turned down. Many applicants, while not in formal employment, had income from informal work or renting backyard rooms. If this was declared their applications were declined. Some applicants were refused for reasons they were unaware of, such has having unclaimed UIF payments.[17]

Others with regular employment took a chance and successfully applied.[18] Minister Zulu (2021) outlined how in the first year of the SRD grant's operation,

> … there were public servants,[19] businesspeople and children from financially comfortable families who applied for the grant. I really want to plead with members of the public, if you do not need this grant – please refrain from taking away from the people who are truly in need.

When President Ramaphosa reported in September 2021 on the nation's response to the COVID-19 pandemic, he stated that 13 million applications for the re-introduced SRD grant had been received, of which 3.7 million had been declined "mainly because applicants have other identified sources of income or are registered for assistance like UIF and NSFAS [National Student Financial Aid Scheme]."[20] While it's not possible to distinguish between applicants who were turned down for honestly reporting minor income streams or who genuinely didn't know they didn't qualify for the grant and those taking a chance, the figure of 3.7 million suggests that Minister Zulu's plea to the public had little impact.

Nevertheless, the SRD grant was being paid to just under 10 million people, increasing the country's grant recipients from some 18 to 28 million. While the size of the grant limited the impact of the fiscus, the logistics of getting the grant to recipients was enormous.

17 Fieldnotes: 211106. This could happen if dismissed for misconduct, meaning they did not qualify for UIF, but nevertheless UIF payments had been allocated without them being notified. Similar problems occurred with unrealised provident funds that the claimant was not aware were owing to them (Fieldnotes: 211009).

18 Fieldnotes: 210403.

19 Close to 6,000 government employees were identified (Felix 2021).

20 Ramaphosa (2021).

Queues at the post office

The SRD grant was initially run separately to the existing SASSA grant system. Applicants were encouraged to provide bank account details into which the grant could be paid, however if no bank details were provided recipients collected the grant in cash from the South African Post Office (SAPO). Often recipients did not have bank accounts or if they did were reluctant to use them because of the charges that would be incurred. Many had outstanding charges on otherwise abandoned accounts. The result was long queues.

These queues could not be serviced and as a result people were turned away empty handed. The key constraint in this regard was SAPO's limiting of cash delivered daily for the SRD grants. Cash for the SRD grant was ring fenced from other cash used in post offices. This set the number of claimants who could collect the grant from any one office. The allocation of cash was poorly matched to the distribution of claimants. The result was that post offices in townships rarely had enough funds to pay out those queueing, while suburban post offices had excess funds. Claimants would queue at township post offices for hours only to be told that no more grants would be paid that day. Unless the claimant got to the head of the queue by arriving in the early hours of the morning, this frustration was likely to be repeated.[21]

The frustration of being turned away without collecting the grant increased as the express service took hold. This system of jumping the queue, described below, took advantage of the difficulties in accessing the SRD grants. While assisting some claimants, for a fee, to avoid having to queue, the express service disadvantaged claimants attempting to collect their grant by queuing in line given SAPO's rationing of SRD grant cash.

Controlling the line

Throughout the first year of the SRD grant, Kwenzekile post office in Katlehong had to deal with more queueing SRD grant claimants than its daily allowance of 200 SRD grants could service. To have any chance of getting the grant, claimants needed to be in the first 200. In fact, even this didn't guarantee getting the grant as the express system took off, and as those beneficiaries who could afford to bank the money by not claiming immediately, began to collect several months' grants at a time.[22] In one case I was following the recipient accumulated seven months' grant before collecting at Kwenzekile. The numbers attempting to access the SRD grants at Kwenzekile increased

21 Sometimes, due to logistical reasons, no SRD grant cash was delivered and nobody could be paid that day. Fieldnotes: 210429.

22 Fieldnotes: 210619. This indicates that these individuals had other sources of income.

further when the nearest post office, Khumalo, at Sontonga Mall 3 kilometres away, stopped paying out the SRD grant because of threats to staff from claimants who had been turned away.[23]

The difficulty of collecting from Kwenzekile, as with many other township post offices, created opportunities. Those wanting to collect the SRD grant were required to queue separately from other post office users and control of places in this queue was a resource. A group of unemployed youth began to set up camp overnight, burning car tires to keep warm. By camping at the post office door, they were at the head of the queue in the morning and would sell places to those desperate to get their grant that day or who would rather pay R50 than waste several hours, possibly fruitlessly, queueing. With numbers, and effectively now a gang, the youth started to sell multiple places. The fee was paid after the recipient had collected their grant, and the youth would monitor those leaving the post office to ensure they were paid.

Those camping out overnight at Kwenzekile were frequently labelled as *nyaope* boys. This referred to the use by unemployed young men of the crudely refined opiate *nyaope*[24] that is smoked with cannabis. Typically, addicted users neglect personal hygiene, hence another widely used term; "dirty boys." With little or no income, and with an addiction to be funded, they steal incessantly from family and neighbours. As one claimant who collected their grant from Kwenzekile (but refused to pay for a place) put it, while he used his R350 carefully, allocating it primarily to food, those selling places in the queue were using the money to buy drugs.[25] Not surprisingly, their presence created problems for residents in the area with complaints of theft from yards, harassment of women, the use of their outside toilets without permission, and when these were locked, urinating and defecating in surrounding streets.

Attempts were made to bring order to the queue. Attempts by individual claimants to organise the queue on a first-come-first-served basis, so that latecomers could not buy a place at the front, were met with direct or indirect threats from those selling places.[26] After a while, SAPO employed security guards. They started work at 7.30am and would hand out numbers to those in the queue, but by then the *nyaope* boys had already sold places and could still sell their security guard-allocated number.[27] On occasions, the police were

23 Fieldnotes: 210619. This was put down to the nearby presence of a large informal settlement. In early 2021, this post office was closed entirely due to disputes over rent and to date has not been re-opened. See also Modiba (2021).

24 Also known as whoonga or wonga.

25 Fieldnotes: 210619.

26 Fieldnotes: 210619.

27 The latter practice was later prevented when guards signed the ID copy that the claimants brought with them, rather than allocate numbers (Fieldnotes: 210619).

called either by SAPO employees, residents, or frustrated claimants. Their arrival would see order restored, but things would revert once they left.[28]

Controlling the head of the queue by young men at post office branches was widespread and a problem for those working in the post office as well as nearby residents. One post office employee, working at a different branch, angrily wrote on a union WhatsApp group that SAPO had not done anything to protect them; "[Management] must clear up first those dirty boy[s] at gates n in our doorsteps … they [management] failed to protect us since last year May [2020: the introduction of the SRD grant]. *Ho thata guyz re sebetsa ha bohloko* everyday [It's tough guys, we work with difficulty every day]."[29]

At some locations, gangs of youth were replaced by more organised committees of self-appointed "queue marshals." However, these carried on in much the same way by selling places in the queue.[30] The charge for a place at the head of the queue was all but standardised at R50 (per month's grant of R350) nationwide.[31]

Divided claimants

The practice of controlling post office queues whether by *nyaope* boys or self-appointed marshals to sell places revealed divisions among claimants. Some were willing to part with R50 out of their R350. This might be because they were truly desperate and needed the money that day or because they did not depend on the grant and were willing to pay R50 not to queue for hours, possibly unsuccessfully. Paying became more attractive if claimants had banked several months grant. If this was the case, they would be careful not to reveal how much they were collecting.

Much as R50 became a standard charge for a place at the head of the queue at Kwenzekile, those selling places would push to get more if they saw the chance. In township idiom they would *panda* or hustle. If they knew that somebody was collecting several months of the grant, they would try to up the charge, reflecting the always contested nature of resources in the township. Those intent on claiming the full R350 because they valued every

28 Fieldnotes: 210619.

29 SAPO employees (2021a).

30 Sizani (2021).

31 Although there were variations. For example, see the Daily Sun's report (Mgidi 2021), in which the charge for assistance was R100 and that in the Daily Maverick (Sizani 2021) in which the charge was cited at between R50 and R100. Given that R50 was usually levied for each month of a claim, it's possible that reports on the charge being R100 referred to individuals claiming two months' grant. Joining a "friend" in the SRD grant queue in the small Free State town of Fouriesburg was informally set at much less; R10.

rand had to arrive early and hope that the *nyaope* boys did not sell too many places ahead of them.

If claimants had organised and agreed to stand together, they could have simply queued up behind the *nyaope* boys who had no business at the post office[32] and would, when the post office doors opened, have had to make way for the queue behind them. This however did not happen, rather some bought places, acting against their own interests in having to lose R50 of their grant and in doing so put themselves ahead of claimants who needed the grant in full.

Riding for the grant

Since the SRD grant could be claimed at any post office, the mismatch of funds to beneficiaries' locations saw minibus taxi drivers transporting claimants to suburban post offices when not busy with rush hour commuters. The mismatch, and resulting opportunity for taxi drivers and owners, was exacerbated when some township post offices stopped issuing the grant. This could be because of security issues associated with the queue of SRD claimants at a particular office, as with the Khumalo Post Office at Sontonga Mall, or because branch post offices had been destroyed, as happened in January 2020 during the Qwaqwa[33] shutdown protests. The destruction of these post offices saw large numbers of claimants travelling by minibus taxis to nearby Free State towns to draw their grants, adding to the SRD queues there.[34]

Taxi drivers would scout for business at post offices where there were long queues and transport those unable to claim because of cash limits to quieter offices, generally in the suburbs. In Katlehong, the transport charge also settled on R50. This was collected after the claimants had received their cash and before they were transported back to the township. Problems could arise with this system. On one occasion, several claimants picked up from Kwenzekile Post Offices were taken to Steeldale, but had to walk back, some 16 kilometres, after emerging empty handed.[35]

In March 2021, ten months after the grant's introduction, a system of allocating collecting days, using the last three digits of claimants ID numbers, was introduced. This made a significant impact on the queues but ironically could also boost the business of transporting claimants. If a claimant couldn't claim on their allocated day because their local post office had insufficient cash, or no cash arrived at all, they would have to wait at least a week before

32 Other than claiming their own R350 grant once a month.

33 Qwaqwa, the old Basotho homeland located in the Eastern Free State.

34 Fieldnotes: 210421.

35 Fieldnotes: 210619.

their ID number was again scheduled for payment.[36] Those desperate for the money had little choice but to travel elsewhere, sacrificing R50 of their grant.

The express service

The limited cash provided at post offices to pay the SRD grant provided *menyetla* for groups that banded together and took control of the queues. This relied on claimants not being able to access the SRD grant other than by joining the queue to enter through the front door. However, a different *monyetla* was available to SAPO employees working on the SRD tills in post office branches. This came to be known, euphemistically, as the express service since it meant the claimant did not need to queue.

Payment of the grant was verified with a copy of the claimant's ID. A SRD teller could process a claim without the claimant coming into the post office if they had the claimant's ID, or a copy. Usually, they would process these before the doors were opened for the claimants queueing outside.[37] Initially, the recipients were required to sign for the grant when collecting, but this didn't present a significant barrier as it was quickly realised that nobody was checking the signatures.[38] As the express service took hold it reduced the number of grants that could be paid to those queuing given SAPO's rationing of cash for SRD claims. This only made the express service increasingly attractive to claimants as well as strengthening the position of those controlling the head of the queue outside.

Some tellers processed the claims of family or friends though the express system as a favour. However, increasingly, the express services became a business operation for post office employees. The charge, or bribe, though it was not usually described as such, for this service also settled at R50 a month. Tellers were in a position to make this charge for each month's grant as they knew exactly how much was being claimed. The taking of a cut of the R350 grant by tellers falls squarely into the classic definition of corruption. However, to expand the express service, tellers started to work with intermediates. These informal agents of the express system brought clients to the tellers, in the form of ID copies, and after both teller and agent took their cut, gave the remaining money to the client. By establishing themselves in this intermediate position these agents established a *monyetla* for themselves, even though they had no public office to leverage advantage, but worked with a teller who did.

36 Two weeks if they were unable to claim in the last week of the month as no SRD grants were paid out in the first week of the month at post offices.

37 A different method was to alternate processing SRD grants between a claimant from the queue with one from the express service.

38 The requirement for a signature was later dropped.

A dismissible offence

Officials of a union with several thousand members in SAPO were aware of the express system and warned members that taking a bribe was a dismissible offence and a crime through various channels, including a WhatsApp group. Some members responded to this message by pointing out that they did this as a favour for family, with one responding defiantly, "Tell [me] I can't help my sister or brother, dey must queue for de whole day [?] Is impossible. I work there. My family can't queue there for de whole day. I'm gng to help them. I'm talking abt my family here."[39]

Steering well away from the union official's original warning, other workers chipped in with advice for those who said they were assisting family members to avoid the queues. This included processing IDs before opening the office or otherwise avoid those queueing outside seeing that they were processing other people's grants. Above all, "be discrete those people [queueing for the SRD grant] are so clever, they see every movement [and may report you]."[40]

Responding to the official's warning that SAPO's Security and Investigation unit were investigating complaints about these practices, one member boasted how the security guard at their office had tipped them off in the morning that the unit were waiting for staff to arrive [and so had not brought any ID copies with them].[41]

As much as helping family members was used to defend the express system when it was called out, it went far beyond assisting family and union officials were aware of this. One official described how SAPO retail workers were "chasing targets for what they could make in a month [by processing SRD grants through the express system]."[42] Union officials also raised with members the morality of taking money from a person's R350 monthly grant when they were earning twenty-five times that amount.[43] In fact, union leaders were aware that some retail branch managers were involved in the express system. They would be earning at least fifty times more than somebody receiving the SRD grant.[44]

Mike and Palesa: a hard-nosed approach

Mike,[45] a postman, started collaborating with a teller at Mofeng post office on the East Rand. As a postman he had nothing to do with the payment of SRD

39 SAPO employees (2021b).
40 SAPO employees (2021b).
41 SAPO employees (2021b).
42 Union Official A (2021).
43 SAPO employees (2021b).
44 Union Official B (2021).
45 A pseudonym, as are the name of the post offices. Fieldnotes; 200205.

grants, but he had a legitimate reason to enter the Mofeng office to collect parcel slips for his delivery round. He also knew Palesa, one of the office tellers who was responsible for the SRD grants. As a post office employee, Mike would be approached by friends and neighbours for assistance in claiming their grant. They assumed that if he worked for SAPO he could assist them.

Once he realised that his partnership with Palesa could boost his income, he started to actively recruit clients. This included from post office queues on a busy day. With child maintenance to pay and a heavy drinker, Mike was always short of money. When I interviewed him in February 2020, he estimated he was assisting between thirty and forty people each month to access their SRD grants using the express system. He would take their ID books, or copies of them, into Mofeng post office and wait while Palesa processed the claims. Sometimes he would pass the time talking to the supervisor while Palesa was busy. Those in the office knew what was going on.

It was preferable that two months of the grant were claimed at once. This made the taking of Mike and Palesa's respective cuts easier to organise. Of the R700 paid to the beneficiary, Palesa would take R50 and Mike would take R50, handing over R600 to the claimant. If a client pushed for one month's grant, Mike would tell him that no money had yet come into the system for him. His clients, unable to check this information without themselves queuing, would be pleased when Mike told them that two month's grant had come in and that he had R600 for them.

Mike's clients recommended him to others. As his network expanded so too did the risks. He was given a list of ID numbers by one person to process for the grant, some of them were invalid, but Palesa got others onto the system. However, it turned out that one of them was dead. Despite this they went ahead and drew the dead man's initial payment and split the grant, R175 each. They then got cold feet and concocted a story in case there was an investigation.[46]

On occasions, when he was under financial pressure, Mike would keep a claimant's entire grant, after Palesa's deduction, telling them that there was nothing on the system. This was something the claimant would struggle to verify, though in one case that was worrying him, a claimant who Mike had defrauded of two months' grant had found out that the grant had been paid out.[47] Mike knew he was skating on thin ice but saw Palesa as more vulnerable than himself if the fraud was ever investigated.

Mike took a hard-nosed approach to his role in the express system, seeking to maximise what they could get out of it. He was clear that he wasn't helping

[46] That someone claiming to be the person had begged to be paid and had promised to return with his ID book and that Palesa, out of compassion, had allowed him to take the grant.

[47] Via a relative working in another post office who had checked for them.

people out of kindness. It was a service for which they should pay. As he put it, if they didn't like it, they could "sleep overnight at Mofeng."

Thabo and Ntate Radebe: appreciation and a dead letter box

In contrast to Mike, Thabo was not a post office employee. Yet like others he established himself as an express service agent. He also differed from Mike in his approach. He was at pains to stress that what he was doing was helping people and that the R50 was not a charge or fee but was given in gratitude.

Thabo was himself claiming the SRD grant fraudulently as he had regular part-time employment in a youth centre funded by the Provincial Department of Social Development. He had reckoned on two things in his favour when making the application. The centre was managed by a charity, so despite the ultimate source of funding he wasn't a state employee. Also, his monthly salary of R3,500 was below the tax threshold. Based on this, he calculated that the grant approval process would not pick up his income. In this he was correct. He received an SMS telling him to take his ID to a post office.

Mike was familiar with Tshwareng post office. One of his responsibilities at the youth centre was to collect mail from the NGO's Mail Collection Point (MCP) box at Tshwareng. Mail is placed in the box from the inside and the client opens the box from the outside, without having to enter the post office.

He received an SMS to collect his first payment which he did without difficulty. After that there were no SMSs. Unsure as to whether he might be risking things if he went to collect, he approached a teller with whom he had a nodding acquaintance. He had thought up a story to explain why he was asking a favour, but it wasn't needed. As soon as he mentioned that he had been approved for the grant, the teller asked if he had his ID with him and told him to meet him in his lunch hour. When they met, the teller, who he now knew as Ntate Radebe, handed him his ID and the full R350 grant which had been waiting for him in the system. From the money Mike gave Ntate Radebe R50 in appreciation for sorting things out and saving him queueing. Ntate Radebe told him that he was welcome to bring in other claimants' IDs and things went from there. When I interviewed Thabo in January 2021, he was regularly providing Ntate Radebe with twenty-odd claimant IDs for express service.[48]

Initially, they did the handovers outside the post office. This, however, had risks. In some offices those queuing cottoned on and took photos. Thabo had the brainwave of using the MCP as a dead letter box. He had the key to the

[48] This was probably an over-estimation. In a more casual conversation not long after the interview he said he was helping nine or ten people, though this was after SAPO management had put out a warning that it was investigating unauthorised processing of the SRD grant.

box and would place the IDs in the NGOs box which Ntate Radebe would collect from within, process and return along with the claimant's cash paper clipped to their ID copy. As with Mike and Palesa, Thabo and Ntate Radebe moved the claimants onto a two-month collecting cycle. This made the mutual enterprise easier to operate. Both collected R50 from the R700 paid to the claimant for two months of the grant.

Thabo insisted when I interviewed him that Ntate Radebe never took the money directly. Rather, they would meet nearby, and Thabo would give him R50 in appreciation for each claim. Thabo then gave the claimants the remaining R650. They in turn would give Thabo R50 for his trouble. The emphasis that Thabo placed on these financial exchanges underlined his point that what he and Ntate Radebe received were tokens of gratitude for help received.

Ba roba molao, mara ... **[They are breaking the law, but ...]**

One less altruistic reason why Ntate Radebe might have chosen not to take the money directly is that it avoided having cash that he would not be able to explain should SAPO's Security and Investigation unit arrive. However, Thabo's account of the harmonious reciprocation between clients, agent, and teller enabled him to frame the express system as mutual aid based on goodwill, using the Sesotho *maele* or saying, *matsoho a hlatswana* (hands wash each other).

By contrast, Mike's bluntness over his role was an exception to the general way in which the *menyetla* provided by the SRD roll out was euphemised as favours, assistance, and mutual aid. Even the *nyaope* boys who intimidated and if necessary threatened claimants to control the queue generally attempted, however thinly, to disguise this as holding places.[49]

The introduction of the SRD grant raised a minefield of moral questions. Minister Zulu focused on fraudulent claims by those who were not in dire need. However, this apparently easy judgement was blurred by the initial rule that only those who had no other form of income whatsoever could claim. This excluded those who declared occasional casual work or rent from backyard rooms, even if this did not clear the poverty line. The effect was that dishonesty was rewarded and honesty penalised.

Far away from the poverty that pervades the township, the SRD grant was portrayed as a leg-up to prosperity by President Ramaphosa in his February 2022 State of the Nation Address in which he announced a further extension of the grant. His speech optimistically stated that "some people used the [grant] money to start business." He went on to cite cases in which recipients had

[49] Fieldnotes: 210619.

saved their grant and were now operating successful enterprises, including an ice cream store employing four people opened by a Soweto resident.[50] Not surprisingly, the president's speech was ridiculed in the township. For a start, it was pointed out, how could the recipient have saved the grant if they had no other form of income? And as a follow up; if you used the grant to buy stock – more realistically sweets or cigarettes to sell than an ice cream parlour startup – should you now declare the profit and disqualify yourself from future payments? This criticism of presidential fantasies was valid, but it also served as criticism of the grant's inadequacy and was a reaction to the implicit moral judgement passed on those unable to convert the R350 into budding businesses.

My interview with Mike was facilitated by another postman, Biza, not involved in the express system, but a workmate and friend of Mike and who sat in on the interview. Afterwards, Biza and I talked over Mike's unashamed confession that he had stolen some grants outright. Biza made a distinction between those who cheated applicants of their grant and the R50 payment. Cheating somebody was not acceptable, it was robbing somebody who needs the money to feed their family. But the latter was an agreement and legitimate. The person doesn't want to wait in the queue and agrees to pay R50. It's not legal, but it's OK. As he put it: *Ba roba molao, mara* … [They are breaking the law, but …].[51]

Bounded *ubuntu*

While we might frame the issue of the R50 charge/token of appreciation as a moral one, morality is contextual. The morality that accompanies the *lex constitutional* is one of privilege in which moral choices are made from a position of relative financial comfort. The morality that accompanies the *lex lokasi* is one forged in far more difficult circumstances.

Taking R50 from claimants was an opportunity to pursue. Some of those taking R50 had little more than the claimants themselves. Others had considerably more, such as retail post office workers. The point is not about fairness but about grasping *menyetla* when they arise. In the township, striving to be fair will not win you praise. It will see you left behind as others take advantage of what you turned down.

Taking opportunities as they come, irrespective of the impact on others, echoes Edward Banfield's concept of "amoral familism" in which individuals "maximise the material, short-run advantages of the nuclear family; assuming that all others will do likewise."[52] The context of Banfield's research in the

50 Ramaphosa (2022).
51 Fieldnotes: 210221.
52 Banfield (1958:83).

southern Italy of the 1950s differs from that of post-apartheid South African townships. The extended African family means that many relatives must be considered, as illustrated by the quote above from a post office teller being unable to refuse requests from relatives to assist accessing the SRD grant. The argument made by SAPO employees over the need to assist family members, while undoubtably in part cover for assisting others who were not family, is valid. Not to have helped them would have been regarded as a moral afront within the family. Yet, Banfield's assumption of transparency over resources within the nuclear family rarely operates within township families, as described in Chapter 3.

Further, Banfield linked amoral familism with what he termed political incapacity; the failure of the community to mobilise for development. For example, not rallying around to improve local schools or volunteering to teach extra classes for students, despite education being the route to success. Political incapacity, framed in this way, is certainly applicable to the township, but it would be wrong to assume that cooperation is not taking place. Many of the opportunities exploited in the SRD rollout were the result of cooperation. The *nyaope* boys banded together and, in a more sophisticated way, so did SAPO tellers and their agents. The difference was that their objectives were limited to their own benefit. At times it was disguised as mutual aid and concern for others, but in outcome it was self-help for some at the expense of others. Putting aside the moral affront of taking money from the poorest in society, these practices were entrepreneurial. An opportunity was identified and exploited through teamwork and innovation.

If *ubuntu* is understood as considering the well-being of the whole community, then the *menyetla* around the SRD grant is bounded *ubuntu* in which a confederation of agents works together for their collective interests to the detriment of others. Control of the queues by youth extracted payment for a bogus service, but it also illustrated the limited *ubuntu* within township residents. Claimants who did not need the grant urgently were willing to pay and jump ahead of those who needed every rand. The express service illustrates how employed Africans took advantage of unemployed Africans even though they were part of the same community. Mutual aid at the expense of others.

Conclusion: *Menyetla* and social order

In August 2020 SASSA permitted SRD grant recipients to change their initial payment election from SAPO to a bank account. They also appealed for recipients not to go to post offices unless they received an SMS notification that their grant was ready for collection. Neither of these measures did much to reduce the queues. It was not till March 2021 that a system of allocating collecting days for the grant was introduced. This made an impact on the queues but did not close the *menyetla* completely. With the re-introduction of the grant in August 2021, eligible claimants holding SASSA cards (for example those colleting child support grants) could draw the SRD grant from bank ATMs. A month later, claimants without a SASSA card could collect the grant at Pick n Pay or Boxer stores, further reducing pressure on queues. The number of retail outlets was increased in March 2022 with the addition of Checkers, USave, and Shoprite supermarkets.[53] By May 2022, SAPO had withdrawn from the distribution of the SRD grant[54] and the *menyetla* were closed.

The rushed and badly managed introduction of the SRD grant in May 2020 resulted in an ecosystem of corruption and *menyetla* fuelled by the R50 assistance "charge" or, to euphemise, "appreciation." Beyond fraudulent claims, the opportunities were largely the result of SAPO's inability to service claimants collecting the grant in cash from post offices. A key opportunity was for tellers to operate the express system, in what was conventional corruption, albeit much of it at arms' length through their partnerships with informal agents acting as middlemen and scouting for clients. The express system, by reducing the cash available for those in the queues outside post offices, assisted those who turned the queues into their own *monyetla*. Finally, there were spin-off opportunities from the long queues and limited cash available, as with taxi drivers who transported grant recipients to quieter post offices where SRD cash was on hand.

One thing this matrix of corruption and *menyetla* illustrates is the limited social order or cohesion in the *kasi*. SRD claimants could have established a fair queuing system in their own neighbourhoods, but this didn't happen. Rather, some took advantage of the opportunities presented.

If SAPO had been able to efficiently manage the distribution of cash to its retail outlets many of the *menyetla* described in this chapter would not have arisen. Further, if SAPO's Security and Investigations division had been on the ball, some of these *menyetla* would have been curbed. Despite the scare that the notice of investigations caused among post office employees operating the express system in early 2021, there were few disciplinary cases and no criminal proceedings. Mike, Palesa, and Ntate Radebe were never called to account, nor was Thabo's fraudulent claim ever rumbled. By mid-2023 union officials knew of only one dismissal for involvement in the express system[55] with two cases still pending.[56]

53 Maleke (2022).

54 Far from assisting in SAPO's turnaround strategy, it turned out to be a financial drain with the costs of administrating the grant, including the cost of transporting the required cash, double the administrative fee received (Illidge 2022).

55 A branch manager was caught with many ID copies in her possession and was dismissed after a disciplinary hearing.

56 Union official B (2023).

What closed the *menyetla* was the use of supermarkets as pay points. The increased number of outlets and the more ordered and supervised queues, being inside stores which themselves are often within shopping malls, contributed to greater fairness in the form of first-come-first-served service and all but eliminated the R50 charge/appreciation. The closure of this *monyetla* illustrates the often-precarious nature of *menyetla* which must be taken while they can. The *lex lokasi* operates in the township, but only because there is incentive, opportunity, and the *lex constitutional* is weak. The closure of one *monyetla* strengthens the *lex constitutional*, but it is only marginal. One *monyetla* may close, but others will open. It is not the details of specific *menyetla*, fascinating as they are, on which we should focus, but the forces that shape the social order in which *menyetla* are a way of life.

7

Mangobers: riding the Metrorail for free

Introduction

THE SOUTH African Metrorail was built to provide cheap transport in large urban areas. There are four systems in the country[1] with some 470 stations and over 2,200 kilometres of track. Other than the Eastern Cape lines, the system operates electric trains powered from overhead cables. The lines follow the geography of apartheid, running between townships and historically white urban areas: industrial estates, suburbs, and town centres. The trains are used by township residents commuting to and from work, college students, those going to shop in "town," and job seekers. Or at least this will be the case when the system is rebuilt following its destruction in 2020.

The Metrorail's destruction was the result of a three-part tragedy of corruption, fare evasion, and looting during the COVID-19 lockdown. Corruption at the Passenger Rail Authority of South Africa (PRASA) that runs Metrorail, was carried out by what Jacques Pauw describes as the PRASA Nostra.[2] This looting of PRASA from above has been documented by the Public Protector, the Commission of Enquiry into State Capture, or Zondo Commission, the Auditor General, the National Treasury, and others and shows no sign of letting up.[3] This chapter, however, concentrates on fare evasion or, in township lingo, riding *mangober*. The lockdown looting is the subject of a later chapter.

Fare evasion is a long running problem on the Metrorail. In August 1996, fifteen people were killed in a stampede at the Tembisa Township Metrorail Station, northeast of Johannesburg, when security staff used electric prods as they attempted to prevent *mangobers* from accessing trains.[4] Reports at the time linked non-payment with the politically inspired boycotts against

1 Gauteng, Durban, the Eastern Cape with one line in Gqeberha (formerly Port Elizabeth) and one in East London, and the Western Cape.

2 Pauw (2022).

3 Mashego (2025).

4 News24 (2001).

apartheid and the resulting culture of non-payment.[5] While struggles against apartheid did establish norms of non-payment, more than a quarter of a century later the explanation has run out of line.

Metrorail

PRASA is a state owned enterprise (SOE) with the government as sole shareholder. In addition to Metrorail, PRASA runs train services between South Africa's major cities,[6] and two long-distance bus companies, City to City and TransLux. PRASA's purpose is to "deliver high quality passenger services in a safe and secure environment ...."[7]

The Metrorail is, however, neither fast, flexible, reliable, or safe.[8] Frustrations over delayed and cancelled services result in angry commuters attacking train drivers and burning carriages. In February 2001, some 6,000 commuters at Pretoria Station, frustrated by cancellations, stormed the station and set it alight.[9] Travelling during rush hour is a harrowing experience with carriages packed tight and passengers hanging onto the sides of carriages. When a train pulls into a station, there is no waiting for those exiting to alight first, but a scrum as passengers, pushed on by those behind them, struggle to board and alight simultaneously.[10]

People ride the Metrorail because it is cheap. Tickets can be bought for a single or return journey or as a weekly or monthly pass. Passes are heavily discounted and cost a fraction of travelling by the faster and more flexible minibus (or black) taxis, which, along with limited bus services, are the only mass transport available to township residents.

The Gauteng system is the largest of Metrorail's systems with 200 stations. It stretches from Vereeniging in the south to Soshanguve north of Pretoria and from Carletonville in the west to Springs in the east. Three of these stations – Johannesburg's Park Station, Pretoria Station, and Germiston Station – form key hubs for the network at which multiple lines converge and passengers transfer for onward journeys. The Kwesine–Germiston line, part of the Gauteng Metrorail system, and which features in this chapter, comprises of some 20 kilometres of track with fourteen stations.[11] It connects the township

5 Daley (1996).

6 Including the luxury Blue Train between Cape Town and Pretoria with single, one-way tickets costing between R20,000 and R40,000 in 2021.

7 PRASA 2020:4.

8 De Waal (2012); Rees (2020).

9 McGreal (2001).

10 Fieldnotes: 120421; see also Geffen (2015).

11 Including Germiston. Travelling from Katlehong the line divides at Elsburg into two, the eastern branch has only one station, Kutalo, the western branch has six stations.

of Katlehong to Germiston town centre, through suburbs and industrial areas of the East Rand.

A multitude of hawkers set up at station entrances and on station platforms or ply their wares as they traverse moving trains with sweets, *makwena* (fat cakes), fruit and vegetables packed into plastic bags, peanuts, *dimumu* (iced pops), cool drinks, loose cigarettes, and much more. The occasional evangelist preaches, Bible in hand, to largely indifferent commuters. However, certain train carriages are enthusiastically occupied by women who turn carriages into mobile churches with singing, prayers, and vibrant testimony. During peak travel times, groups of entertainers move from carriage to carriage performing short song and dance routines before hopefully holding out a hat.[12]

Metrofail

Metrorail management has been a catastrophic failure. As outlined by Bekezela Phakathi, "Metrorail has been under pressure because its rail commuter services have been in a serious state of decline caused by decades of underinvestment, outdated technology, the loss of critical skills, deferred maintenance and corruption."[13] More succinctly, Nathan Geffen summed it up as "Metrofail!"[14]

Pauw details how corruption at PRASA was home grown (that is, it did not involve the Indian Gupta brothers) and that it continued despite the efforts of Popo Molefe, as PRASA's board chair, to curtail the looting, with Molefe's direct appeal to the ANC's top leadership for support going unanswered.[15] When the overriding consideration in awarding a contract is the amount that can be syphoned off, it is not surprising if costly mistakes occur. Perhaps the most dramatic of these was PRASA's ordering of long-distance trains from Spain, at a cost of R3.6 billion which were too tall to operate on the South African railway lines.[16] Nor was the theft of public money restricted to contract kickbacks. Some 3,000 PRASA ghost workers, almost 18 per cent of the workforce, were on the payroll of PRASA in 2022.[17]

PRASA management amounted to "everybody doing what they pleased," as Bheki Hadebe, a member of the parliamentary Standing Committee on

Both branches terminate at Germiston and those travelling further must change here.

12 For a more detailed description of riding the train on the Kwesine–Germiston line, see Dickinson (2021b), Chapter 2.

13 Bekezela (2021).

14 Geffen (2015).

15 Pauw (2022:68).

16 SCOPA (2021).

17 Phakathi (2022).

Public Accounts (SCOPA), bluntly put it in 2021.[18] This was papered over by constant promises of a new start. By 2020, PRASA had attempted five turnaround strategies since its inception in 1990. These were accompanied by upbeat assessments of newly appointed CEOs about getting back on track.[19] Rather than turn around the SOE, the "turn-around-about" of turn around plans[20] concertinaed into each other and allowed past mistakes and corrupt transactions to be swept under the carpet.

A well-run urban rail network can provide cheap, efficient, and safe transport for commuters. As Chief Justice Zondo explained in December 2022:

> PRASA is a very important state entity that was established to provide essential transport to the people of SA, particularly poor people. But PRASA has not been able to provide a safe and reliable transport service to poor people in our country, and corruption, maladministration and incompetence have a lot to do with that inability.[21]

The CEO of PRASA between 2008 and 2015, Lucky Montana, invented fake job offers to bounce the board into increasing his salary.[22] Daniel Mthimkhulu, PRASA's head of engineering whose career was championed by Montana, faked his academic qualifications.[23] But if PRASA management was taking chances, so too were many of its passengers.

Fare evasion

Public transport systems are financed through a combination of passenger fares and government subsidies.[24] The amount contributed by passengers in this funding mix, the farebox recovery, varies. A few systems, such as Hong Kong's Mass Transit Railway and the London Underground or Tube have positive farebox recover; ticket revenue exceeds running costs.[25] However, most public transport systems rely on government subsidies to cover some of their running expenses. PRASA's financial statements do not disaggregate between its component entities, so its farebox recovery cannot be calculated

[18] SCOPA (2021).

[19] See Barron (2020) for "the tide has turned," or SCOPA (2021) for "better days ahead."

[20] The term is quoted in Chipkin (2013).

[21] Bengu (2022).

[22] Mvumvu (2020).

[23] Mthimkhulu was sentenced to fifteen years imprisonment in September 2024 for fraud (Njilo 2024). Montana became a Member of Parliament for the uMkhonto we Sizwe Party in August 2024.

[24] Along with minor contributions from advertising, rental income, and other sources.

[25] Wikipedia (N.D.a).

for Metrorail alone. For PRASA as a group, however, fare revenue in the 2019/20 financial year amounted to approximately R2 billion, while operating costs were R13.4 billion, a farebox recovery of 15 per cent.

PRASA low farebox recovery is due in part to fare evasion. Fare evasion, fare dodging, or free loading is a problem for public transport systems around the world.[26] To travel without a ticket passengers must get past systems designed to enforce their purchase, such as turnstiles, and avoid ticket inspections. Other forms of fare evasion are overriding (travelling beyond the validity of a ticket), failing to validate a genuine ticket (allowing it to be used again), and the use of counterfeit tickets.[27]

What distinguishes fare evasion on the Metrorail from other public transport systems around the world is scale. Fare evasion is hard to measure,[28] so evasion rates should be seen as approximate. In Bogota's TransMilenio system evasion is estimated at 15 per cent, on Melbourne's public transport 12 per cent, and on the Paris Metro five per cent. By contrast, in 2018, the acting provincial manager of Metrorail for Gauteng explained that "The last time we had a stop-and-check operation [about which more below] only about five per cent of the full train which takes about 1,800 people had tickets."[29] Or, put differently, a fare evasion rate of 95 per cent.

Fare enforcement

With a fare evasion rate of 95 per cent, it would likely be cheaper to make travel free and save on ticketing and enforcement expenses. Instead, however, Metrorail made increasingly desperate attempts to ensure passengers purchased tickets.

To get onto the platform or out of the station you need to show a valid ticket. Only some of the larger stations in the Gauteng system had automatic ticket readers. Most stations had manual turnstiles that an operator monitored and could lock closed if a passenger didn't show a valid ticket. The easiest way to get past the turnstiles was to find an alternative way onto the platform. Tracks from adjacent streets leading to the end of Metrorail platforms started to appear. Alternatively, a more direct route for the agile was to climb over station fences.[30] A different approach could be taken if you knew one of

26 Barabino, Lai, and Olivo (2020).

27 Barabino *et al.* (2020:34). In 2003, Metrorail announced a crackdown on the use of fraudulent tickets being printed and sold by syndicates as well as passengers altering the date on their tickets (IOL 2003).

28 Barabino, *et al.* (2020:28).

29 Regter (2018).

30 Fieldnotes: 170209.

the turnstile operators who would let you through flashing an invalid ticket, something more likely at your home station in the township.[31]

Getting out of the station at your destination required similar tactics. This was difficult at the larger, better controlled stations, particularly the system's hubs.[32] The solution was to alight at a prior station, if this was not too far from your eventual destination. *Mangobers* travelling from Katlehong alight at President Station, some 500 metres short of Germiston Station. The station is known, informally, as the *mangobers'* station. At President, throngs of passengers disembark in the morning rush hour and an eccentric hawker greets those alighting; "Welcome to President Station! Welcome to the station of *mangobers*! Welcome kings and queens of *mangobers*! Welcome!" The crowd smiles and laughs at the hawker's teasing and stream out of the station with nobody showing a ticket.[33]

Metrorail employs inspectors to check tickets on the trains. Typically, they operate as a team, one group enter the first carriage of the train, the other the last. They then work towards the centre asking passengers to show their tickets. Once the two teams met, they alight and board another train, though sometimes they will make a return sweep to check the tickets of those who had just boarded.

Inspecting tickets on the trains can be difficult, especially if they are packed tight during rush hour.[34] It can also be risky once the number of passengers riding *mangober* grows. The previously mentioned stop and check operations were a response to these difficulties. Busy trains would be stopped in the morning rush hour at stations with facilities necessary for the operation.[35] Scores of security guards were on hand to support the inspectors. Passengers without seats were told to leave the train and stand on the station platform. Inspectors then entered the train and checked the tickets of those seated. Those without tickets joined those standing on the platform. Those on the platform with tickets were then invited, via the station PA system, to re-board the train, showing their ticket as they did so. The invitation turned to teasing once those with tickets re-boardered, those remaining on the platform were urged not to delay as they would be late for work.[36]

31 If you were lucky, you might also know somebody at your destination station (Fieldnotes: 151122). Turning a blind eye to the invalid ticket is a favour for which some reciprocity is expected.

32 Though even at Germiston, when security was withdrawn (see below) *mangobers* used tracks leading from the end of platforms to surrounding streets.

33 Fieldnotes: 150926; 151122; and 160115.

34 De Waal (2012).

35 On the Kwesine–Germiston line, this took place at Katlehong Station, the last of the township stations, or the Wadeville and Elsburg stations. For the Western Cape system see IOL (2016).

36 Fieldnotes: 150926.

Once all ticket holders were on board, the train departed. Those left on the station platform with money were channelled into the station building to purchase a R40 booking fee, Metrorail's no-ticket penalty,[37] and were free to leave the station. Though if they wanted to get to work, they needed to buy a ticket for the remaining journey. Those without the necessary funds were directed into a holding room to await the arrival of a friend or relative who could pay their fine. If this didn't happen they would, in theory, be taken to the nearest police station to be charged.

These stop and check operations were attempts to turn back the tide of fare evasion and reflected the failure of more conventional methods to ensure ticket purchase. An even more desperate measure, the corridor project, was later implemented. For the moment, however, we turn to how those riding *mangober* initially ducked and dived rather than defy Metrorail.

Risking it for R170

It was Donald, Thabo's work mate, who taught him, or rather goaded him, to ride mangober *in 2015.*[38] *"How much," he would ask Thabo "do you pay for that monthly ticket?" Donald knew the answer, but he'd make Thabo tell him. One hundred and seventy rand. Each and every month. To rub the point home Donald would suggest alternative uses that the R170 could be put to. Always things that could be drunk. A case of this or a case of that. It was a below belt tactic of persuasion. Thabo was a casual worker, employed through agencies and on minimum wages. He would be* tjonne *broke the day after payday.*

Thabo boarded the twelve-carriage train after scrambling onto the end of the platform. He got into the sixth carriage. It would give him more time if inspectors boarded. At Pilot Station, the third station and still in Katlehong, people left the train in numbers. Far more than usual. By the time Thabo clocked what was happening the train was moving too fast to jump. An inspection team had boarded. He watched up the train to see when the inspectors would reach his carriage. With passengers depleted, they would have light work; remaining passengers would, for the main, be showing their monthly tickets.

He held his nerve and continued riding. As they approached Wadeville Station, he saw inspectors in carriage five, only one carriage away. He stood up and left the train just in time. Standing on the platform, safe for the moment, he saw that the other group of inspectors, working from the back of the train, were now retracing their steps, sweeping for anyone newly boarded. Carriage seven, he reasoned, would be safe. The group now working in carriage six would turn around as the other group had. As the train started to pick up

37 The penalty had been raised from R20 to R40 in 2005.

38 Fieldnotes: 150919 and 150926.

speed he ran and jumped into the open doors of the train, hoping to make it to President Station without being caught.

Risk and response

The vignette illustrates the way in which risk constitutes a parallel currency to cash in the township. Those in precarious employment working for minimum wages must constantly weigh risks against the benefits of what readers likely consider modest outlays. Less than what you would pay for this book.

The R170 for the monthly Kwesine–Germiston ticket in 2015 was a bargain. Far cheaper than travelling by taxi, but it was still R170. R170 in 2015 rand is equivalent to R247 in 2022. In 2022, the national minimum wage was R23.19 an hour. On the minimum wage, it would take[39] ten hours and forty minutes work to pay for the monthly ticket. It's cheap travel, but also expensive if you're on the minimum wage.

The *mangobers*' risk was managed by staying alert and staying ahead: avoiding stations with tight security, leaving the train if inspectors entered, doubling back down the train after them, or some combination. There were other tricks. Before he started to ride *mangober* himself, Thabo had seen strange things happen when inspectors entered a carriage with the barked command of "tickets!"[40] Men in the middle of an animated discussion abruptly switching to energetic versions of sign language; women rushing to the already crowded church carriage with a newfound joy in Jesus' holy name; men stricken with sudden disabilities.

Such manifestations of affliction could be highly realistic. Ticket inspectors are not permitted to search, but only demand to see tickets. Those instantly disabled by the command of "tickets!" might be unable to understand what the inspector wanted; others would display severe distortion in their movement that were matched only by their determination to produce their ticket. Yet, the harder the disabled person tried, the clearer it becomes that the only thing likely to be achieved was a seizure. He[41] starts to shake with the effort, crying out with exertion, but his hand still can't reach his pocket. If the inspector hasn't moved on by now, the saliva that starts to run down the man's chin settles the matter. The inspector is not going to push things. Perhaps it isn't a performance?[42]

If you aren't willing to go to such extent, then a bribe, cool drink, *tjhotjho*, or *diza* is necessary. On the Kwesine–Germiston line you could usually get

39 Excluding deductions, the Unemployment Insurance Fund employee deduction of 1 per cent is taken from the minimum wage.

40 Fieldnotes: 150926.

41 For women the option of pulling off such stunts are limited and shameful. A man who pulls it off can claim kudos for his performance.

42 Fieldnotes: 150926.

away with R10. A wise *mangober* carried a single R10 note in a pocket or wallet. Anything more would be kept elsewhere. You could show it was all you'd got and likely it would be accepted. Though it's not just about the money, bribery involves a relationship, even if fleeting, and attitude is important, something well described in Raji Matshedisho's (2009a) ethnographic accounts of street-level police corruption. You need to show respect. The transaction must be framed as one of mutual assistance.

On another occasion[43] Thabo, realising that he could not get out via the turnstiles of a station as he had planned, walked down the platform to a gate leading out to the road. The only problem was two security guards. He pleaded with them that he had intended to buy a ticket but there had been a long queue at the ATM. He'd already been warned that he'd be fired if late again. He couldn't be late again. It was a risk he'd taken. He was sorry. He would buy them a cool drink when he returned in the afternoon. They said they wanted something now and not just a promise. So, he said he'd check; maybe he could find something and made a show of searching himself, knowing that there was only fifty cents to find. He eventually proffered this as generously as he could. One of the guards took the fifty cents and told him to "*tsamaya!*"

Procedure versus practice: *menyetla* proliferation

By the rule book, those caught without a ticket had to pay the booking fee, for which they should be issued a receipt. If the booking fee was not paid, then the *mangober* was liable to prosecution. Schedule 1 of the *Legal Succession to the South Africa Transport Services Act* outlines that anybody travelling[44] and who fails to show a valid ticket commits an offence. If found guilty they can be fined or imprisoned.[45]

In practice, things are done differently. During the stop and check operations on the Kwesine–Germiston line, those without the required R40 for the booking fee were detained until they could get somebody to come up with the necessary cash.[46] However, in practice a sliding scale of "fines," without receipts, was applied depending on how long you'd been detained. After an

43 Fieldnotes: 211023.

44 Or is on station premises and who has travelled or intends to travel.

45 *Legal Succession to the South Africa Transport Services* Schedule 1, Section 12(1). The amount of the fine or length of imprisonment is not specified.

46 Assuming that they had the necessary airtime to make a call. Of course, those with airtime would also warn relatives and friends travelling later that the trains were being stopped that morning.

hour it was dropped to R30, another hour R20, and so on until eventually everybody was released.[47]

A similar system operated if passengers were detained for another reason. In July 2011, Thabo was searched by Metrorail security on the train and a *poke* (packet) of cannabis found.[48] He was taken off the train and held at Wadeville station. The security guards asked for R200 otherwise they would take him to the police. He had refused the "fine" which had then been reduced to R100, but he had continued to refuse telling them that they must take him to the police station. Something which he anticipated they weren't keen on doing. In the end, they accepted R20.[49]

Talking to the media about the dramatically named Operation Spider[50] in November 2016, Metrorail's Western Cape's regional manager, Richard Walker, explained that; "Anyone on board a train without a valid ticket is illegal and will face fines, or arrest and prosecution risking a criminal record if found guilty."[51] In practice, at least when Walker wasn't present, there was a different system in operation. This utilised the *lex constitutional*, in the form of legislation prohibiting fare evasion, but in practice operated as the *lex lokasi* in which Metrorail ticket inspectors, security guards, and *mangobers* co-existed. This was regulated by social norms, such as the all-but standard bribe on the Kwesine–Germiston line. These norms were, in effect, the product of negotiations-in-practice that reflected the parties' respective power resources. The ticket inspectors and guards used the law to extract bribes from those without tickets, *mangobers* used their wits to avoid paying bribes or to minimise them when evasion was impossible. At least until through strength of numbers the *mangobers* were able to openly assert riding for free.

The *mangobers* were besting the system. The agents of the system, in the form of guards and inspectors, were besting the systems intended to stop the system being bested. The extraction of bribes from those riding without a ticket, by those employed to prevent fare evasion, illustrates *menyetla* proliferation – opportunities derived by the attempt to counter the underlying, original, *monyetla*.

The corridor project

Automated turnstiles, opened when a valid ticket is scanned, are widely used in transport systems around the world, combined with physical security to

47 A similar system seems to have been in operation on the Western Cape Metrorail, see *GroundUp* (2015).

48 Metrorail's *Conditions of Carriage* state that it may search passengers "upon reasonable suspicion of a crime." Metrorail (N.D.).

49 Fieldnotes: 110725. At the time possession of cannabis was a crime.

50 In fact, simply a series of stop and check operations.

51 IOL (2016).

prevent the machines being bypassed. Metrorail made only limited investments in automation but rather relied on manual turnstiles and/or inspectors to check tickets presented by passengers. Once it was clear that turnstiles, ticket inspectors, and stop and check operations was failing to stem fare evasion, Metrorail introduced its corridor project in 2019. This involved walling in the Metrorail track to "combat fare evasion, high levels of vandalism and illegal trespassing that causes accidents."[52] The head of PRASA's war room, Sipho Sithole, explained that PRASA was planning to spend R6.5 billion over three years to enclose railway lines in urban areas with concrete blocks.[53]

They were wasting money.[54] A wall, some three metres high, had been built on the Kwesine–Germiston line in April 2016.[55] The purpose of the wall was to make it difficult for mangobers to access station platforms other than through turnstiles. It extended for some 5 kilometres within the township. However, there were numerous access points along the line which were never gated, meaning people could still access the line. Nevertheless, given the position of these access points, getting onto the station platforms was more onerous and there was an initial increase in the number of commuters buying tickets and going through the station turnstiles.[56] However, this was not to last. The corridor project, pre-figured on the Kwesine–Germiston line, was a technological response to the social problem of poverty segued into an increasingly established *mangober* norm of fare evasion.

Defiance: The Battle of Kwesine

The growing number of *mangobers* on the Kwesine–Germiston line, and the increasingly poor service provided, saw a gradual shift from *mangobers* being a minority of passengers on the lookout for inspectors to being the majority that came to assume, though custom, the norm of free passage on the Metrorail. This came to a head in October 2017 with the Battle of Kwesine. Given the inconvenient location of the planned, but ungated, gaps in the corridor wall, more convenient gaps appeared under cover of darkness. These breaches gave *mangobers* easy access to the station platforms. It took a while for Metrorail to

52 PRASA (2020:38).

53 De Villiers (2019).

54 Though if the real objective of a project is to syphon off funds through tenders, then this is achieved however pointless the project.

55 At least one other wall was scheduled to be built prior to the announced national corridor project. This one, at a cost of R3 million for 24 kilometres, was due to be built in 2017 and was the first part of a planned R68 million walling project on the Western Cape Langa–Bontheuwel–Nyanga triangle route. However, the *GroundUp* reporter who went to investigate in 2021 found "no sign of construction." Postman (2017).

56 Fieldnotes: 160416; 160717; 161001; and 161105.

respond. On a Monday morning five guards arrived, their job to stand guard at the breaches. They were easily pushed aside by *mangobers*. There were more guards the next day, some with firearms. The situation became increasingly tense. Insults flew and the *mangobers* rallied around the justification that "The Guptas are stealing money! We are owed something! We're taking it here!"

Stones started to fly and shots were fired into the air by a panicked guard. This infuriated the *mangobers* who surged forward. The guards broke and ran. Some to the station offices, others down the track. On the third day the guards, knowing they were beaten, changed tack, stood aside, and allowed people though the gaps. The *mangobers* had won.

The Battle of Kwesine brought to a head a conflict between *mangobers* and Metrorail. It could be argued that the battle fits into Peter Alexander's (2010:37) influential argument that a rebellion of the poor is underway in South Africa's townships.[57] At least when protests "reflect disappointment with the fruits of democracy." The Battle of Kwesine could with this argument be framed as the township underclass at odds with the state, in the form of a state owned enterprise, in a distributional conflict. But the argument holds less weight if the rebellions of the poor are, in Alexander's words, "locally organised protests that place demands on people who hold or benefit from political power …."[58] The public disorder at Kwesine was not asking for anything, it was to maintain the illicit *menyetla* already taken by the *mangobers*.

Not long after the Battle of Kwesine, one of the two branches of the Kwesine–Germiston line was closed for repairs. The line splits after Elsburg Station. The western branch reaches Germiston Station via President Station, the *mangobers'* station. It was this branch that was closed. While commuters could still travel to Germiston, the Kwesine train wasn't running through President Station. There is no station close to the city centre on the eastern, Kutalo, branch of the line at which Germiston-bound *mangobers* could alight. Their response was to travel to Germiston Station, but instead of attempting to exit via the turnstiles, walk down the railway line, in their hundreds, for some 500 or so metres to reach President Station and from their make their exit.[59]

By this stage the *mangobers* were, like the management of PRASA, doing what they pleased, though not wherever they wanted. The Battle of Kwesine had been won by the *mangobers* in large part because the station was located deep within Katlehong. That it was adjacent to the Kwesine, or Boys', Hostel was an additional advantage, since it was from the grounds of the hostel that gaps had been smashed through the corridor wall. But even after Metrorail had

57 See Chapter 1.

58 Alexander (2010:26).

59 Because President Station is on the Johannesburg–Germiston Metrorail line, in addition to the Germiston–Kwesine line, it remained open while the Germiston–Kwesine line (via President) was closed for repairs (Fieldnotes: 171007).

ceded Kwesine Station, it still held some authority at Germiston Station, one of the Metrorail's major hubs. Here, *mangobers* took the less confrontational approach of walking down the line to President Station rather than attempting to storm the turnstiles of Germiston.

A deteriorating service

Using the Metrorail was never a luxury for township residents. Carriages were crowded and seats few. In summer you were hot and sticky, in winter it was cold. As the service deteriorated, trains would frequently not arrive, passengers would be late for work risking their pay being docked or even dismissal. Trains would stop between stations for indefinite periods without explanation. There were accidents.[60] Passengers came to expect delays and danger on the overcrowded trains.

In July 2019, a winter month in South Africa, the shortage of rolling stock saw Metrorail run half-refurbished carriages on the Kwesine–Germiston line. If you were unable to squeeze into one of the carriages that had glass in the windows, the early morning journey, with the sun not yet risen, was freezing. By then few passengers were buying tickets, but the conditions only increased feelings of entitlement to travel without paying.[61]

As the number of *mangobers* increased, fare-paying passengers questioned why they were one of only a handful of people going through the turnstile with a ticket.[62] You were paying for what others were taking *mahala*. Once such a realisation takes hold a tipping point is reached. There is a limit to doing the right thing. You stop buying tickets. Then nobody is buying them.

Others switched to minibus taxis. It meant paying two, three, or even four times as much to get to work, and there is not the slightest chance of riding *mangober* in a taxi, but at least you get to work on time. Given the expense, some low-paid workers mixed and matched transport. They would take a taxi to work in the morning to be sure of arriving on time, but ride back *mangober* in the afternoon when delays had less consequence.[63]

The Metrorail became the transport of those unable to afford better; an inferior means of getting around. This was to be a factor in the looting of Metrorail during the COVID-19 lockdown described in a later chapter.

60 At the scene of an accident, the priority for PRASA staff is to check whether those injured have valid tickets. Only those with tickets will be able to claim compensation (Fieldnotes: 180203).

61 Fieldnotes: 190713.

62 Fieldnotes: 171214.

63 And attempts at fare enforcement less effective as delays do not jeopardise *mangobers* employment by arriving late (Fieldnotes: 181215).

A distraction from corruption?

It could be argued that a focus on the *menyetla* of township commuters riding *mangober* deflects attention from the corruption of the PRASA Nostra that in financial terms constitute crimes many orders of magnitude greater. Certainly, PRASA downplays corruption while highlighting fare evasion. Both are addressed in PRASA's 2020–22 corporate plan, but in different ways. The documented evidence of corruption in reports by the Public Protector, Auditor General, and National Treasury (the Zondo Commission was yet to report) is described as "allegations".[64] The response to these allegations was the turgid reassurance that:

> PRASA is committed to preventing fraud and corruption and to creating an anti-fraud culture. To achieve this, PRASA will comply with the relevant requirements of the Public Finance Management Act (PFMA), 1999 (Act No. 1 of 1999) (as amended by Act No. 29 of 1999) and the principles of corporate governance.[65]

Which in practice translates as "we are not going to actually do very much." By contrast, the problem of fare evasion was presented as real and pressing. Costly responses, including the corridor project, were reported to be underway or on the way.[66]

The focus on fare evasion in this chapter does not deny the impact of corruption on the demise of the Metrorail. However, one should not be set off against the other. Corruption was out of control and so was fare evasion.

A social struggle or individual advantage?

Riding *mangober* could be framed as a social struggle. In the context of non-payment for water and electricity services, Antina von Schnitzler, describes how the cat and mouse installation of meters and consumer counter measures to bypass or otherwise defeat pay-for-services systems constitutes techno-politics; "Low-intensity battles … take shape on terrains not immediately apprehensible as political …."[67] In other words, non-payment for services can be understood as a distributional struggle, albeit convoluted. An intermediated class conflict in which the poor gain from the rich by fiddling a state owned enterprise that is subsidised through taxation.[68] In some countries there have been collectively

64 PRASA (2020:67).

65 PRASA (2020:83).

66 PRASA (2020:55–65).

67 von Schnitzler (2016:200).

68 And along the same lines or reasoning, the corruption at PRASA is also a distributional struggle though with the lines less clearly defined. Here, a new managerial

organised fare evasion campaigns, either in protest at fare increases as in Chile in 2019,[69] or as long-term campaigns for free public transport as in Sweden.[70] By contrast however, riding *mangober* in South Africa, while practised on a massive scale, was neither collective nor strategic.[71]

Thirty years into democracy, fare evasion cannot be pinned to anti-apartheid struggles. Yet, neither is it resistance to corruption in PRASA. While it constitutes a *de facto* distributional struggle, this is not consciously pursued. Rather, the agency of the *mangobers* is the individualised clawing of advantage at public expense.

Conclusion: The *lex lokasi* on wheels

Even the small gains of *mangobers* from fare evasion must be shared with PRASA employees and contracted security guards in the form of bribes. In effect, these constitute an informal tax, or in economic terminology rent, on the *monyetla*. Something that stabilises, rather than prevents, fare dodging. Put another way, much of the Metrorail has moved from the *lex constitutional* to the *lex lokasi* even if it is the *lex constitutional*, in the legal requirement to pay fares, which allows *menyetla* proliferation as the trains travelled through suburbs and town centres.

Initially, *mangobers* rode stealthily, seeking to minimise the bribes they had to pay. However, as their numbers increased the *lex constitutional* was openly defied, as events on the Kwesine–Katlehong line illustrate. At this point, the need to pay bribes ended, as did fare revenue. This illustrates how social feedback mechanisms have cascading consequences when social actors respond to opportunities in increasing numbers. A dynamic that needs to be incorporated into any understanding South Africa's entropic trajectory. What starts at the margins can, if unchecked, set in motion escalating consequences. If the country is collapsing from the periphery into the centre, this has been prefigured on the Metrorail. While major stations remain under the control of PRASA and the company's *Conditions of Carriage,* on the tracks and in minor stations this authority has all but vanished, replaced by the *lex lokasi.*

---

class, largely African, is extracting from the rich (which includes themselves) by stealing from a state subsidised enterprise.

69 Bartlett (2019).

70 Flegenheimer (2014).

71 Organised campaigns in South Africa, notably #UniteBehind (N.D.), have focused on petitions and legal action to address corruption and service deterioration.

8

Lockdown liquor: the sale of alcohol during COVID-19 prohibition

Alcohol in South Africa

THE WORLD Health Organisation reports that 70 per cent of South Africans aged fifteen and older say they do not drink alcohol.[1] You might find this hard to believe on a township weekend. The WHO estimates the per capita South African consumption for those fifteen years and older is 9.3 litres of pure alcohol per year, compared to the global average of 6.4 litres per year. Among those who do drink, the average consumption in 2016 was 29.9 litres, with males drinking more than twice as much as females (37.5 and 13.7 litres respectively). The WHO goes on to report that South Africa is a country with one of the riskiest drinking cultures. Almost one in two men and one in five women who drink, binge drink; that is, consume large amounts of alcohol over a short period. Binge drinking is a significant factor in violence, road accidents, and disease.

In South Africa, liquor legally refers to any drink with more than 1 per cent alcohol, not only distilled spirits.[2] I use the terms alcohol and liquor interchangeably for all alcoholic drinks. Alcohol is widely used in South Africa for recreational and social purposes. Drinking is a major feature of township life. It is an important social lubricant and pastime, particularly for men. Indeed, drinking together is the primary form of socialisation for many township men. The most consumed drink is beer. This is typically sold in 750ml quarts or 1-litre bottles, though a range of other sized bottles and cans are available, especially for higher-end premium brands. Spirits, which in South Africa are 43 per cent alcohol, are often drunk alongside beer. Home-brewed sorghum beer, *umqombothi,* is an essential aspect of traditional rituals and celebrations, though it is also sold commercially. A range of other home-brewed

1 WHO (2018).

2 *Liquor Act* 1989 and *Liquor Act* 2003. In lay definitions, Sorghum beer or *umqombothi*, especially when home brewed, is generally excluded from the category of liquor.

concoctions, the official term used for non-sorghum home-brewed alcoholic drinks,[3] are made, particularly in poorer communities. Women drink, though less publicly, predominantly cider, cooler mixes, and wine.

Historically, colonial legislation restricted the sale of "Western" or "European" liquor, that is malt beer, wine, and spirits rather than sorghum beer, to Africans.[4] From 1928 municipal authorities had the option to impose a legal monopoly on the sale of sorghum beer in townships. While not all municipalities opted to sell sorghum beer, many did set up municipal (sorghum) beer halls. As described in Chapter 2, this provided a major source of income for township administration. Where municipalities exercised their rights to a monopoly, the brewing and selling of alcohol in shebeens, unlicensed drinking establishments, was prohibited. *Klopjags* (police raids) were carried out, often relying on informers, cracking down on illicit brewing.[5] Such brewing was generally done by women, the "shebeen queens" of the township. From 1962, municipalities were also permitted to sell European liquor in townships. At this point the black market in European liquor was so extensive that as Anne Mager outlines, "Every respectable white[6] wine-farmer, distiller and brewer was implicated."[7] This illegal trade continued after 1962 with South Africa Breweries (SAB) in particular bypassing the municipal monopoly on alcohol sales in townships by suppling shebeens.[8] By 1979, shebeens accounted for approximately one-third of SAB's beer sales.[9] In the early 1980s, attempts to legalise shebeens began, supported by SAB, though with limited success.[10]

In the usual terminology applied to contemporary drinking venues in South African townships, a licensed venue is a tavern while unlicensed venues are shebeens. The most informal shebeens, especially those that brew their own alcohol, have a range of names in local dialects including *spot* and *chafpozi*.[11] Additionally, people sell beer and/or concoctions from their homes, often alongside illegal (untaxed) *loose draw* (individual cigarettes), as well as a limited selection of food items. The Department of Trade and Industry (DTI) estimates that there are some 230,000 liquor outlets in South Africa.[12] Depending on how such outlets are defined, this may be an underestimation.

3 See for example, Section 123, "Prohibited concoctions and drinks", of the *Gauteng Liquor Act* 2003.
4 Rogerson and Hart (1986).
5 Interview with former township manager, 6 September 2019.
6 Race not colour.
7 Mager (1999:372).
8 Mager (1999:385–6).
9 Rogerson and Hart (1986).
10 Rogerson and Hart (1986).
11 The township term *chafpozi* implies a hidden location.
12 Department of Trade and Industry (2016).

Charman *et al.* (2020), in a study of seven neighbourhoods in Tembisa Township, with a population of around 40,000, identified 577 liquor-selling outlets of which over 400 were home-sellers, rather than taverns or shebeens.[13]

The current legislative regime regarding alcohol is complex. The *Liquor Act* of 2003 regulates large scale production[14] and distribution of alcohol. However, small scale manufacture and retailing of alcohol is regulated at the provincial level.[15] Where provinces have yet to promulgate regulations, the *Liquor Act* of 1989 continues to apply, sometimes and confusingly in conjunction with provincial legislation.[16] The complexity of applying for licences to retail alcohol as a tavern or bottle store[17] are onerous and include having the area re-zoned for business use, obtaining police and community consent, and bringing the venue up to the required standards. As Charman *et al.* outline, "the great majority of township entrepreneurs have neither the financial means nor the legal skills to navigate through this web of legislation …."[18] As a result, many township liquor outlets remain unlicensed, a situation that Charman *et al.* refer to as "enforced informality."[19]

Where do these unlicensed outlets get their stock? The situation is not that different from the black market of yesteryear. The presence of licensed township taverns allows brewers, distillers, and distributors to legally sell to these venues, which then sell on to shebeens and other unlicensed venues. This allows global corporates in the brewing business – South African Breweries (SAB), owned by Anheuser-Busch (with an 87 per cent share of the South African beer market[20]); Distell; Heineken; and Diageo – to sell profitably into the township without having to take responsibility for "the consequences of informalisation or harmful drinking."[21]

Enforced informality also means that unlicensed sellers of alcohol are vulnerable to arbitrary law enforcement. In response, shebeen owners have adopted, "covert strategies to manage the risks of closure, fines, temporary

13 A crude extrapolation of Charman *et al.'s* (2020) findings produces a figure of 850,000 liquor outlets for South Africa with a population of 60 million in 2022. Even if the figure is halved, it is still more than twice the DTI's estimation.

14 A macro manufacturer is one that produces 100 million litres of malt beer, or 500 million litres of sorghum beer, or 4 million litres of wine, or 2 million litres of spirits per year (Department of Industry 2004).

15 Based on Schedule 5 of the South African Constitution in which the issuing of liquor licences is a provincial responsibility.

16 The DTI (2016) Section 2.6.

17 i.e. an off-licence selling alcohol for consumption off the premises.

18 Charman *et al.* (2020:198).

19 Charman *et al.* (2020:195).

20 Followed by Heineken with 12 per cent (Statista 2019a).

21 Charman *et al.* (2020:198).

imprisonment and bribes demanded by the police."[22] Where the police seek or accept a bribe and/or confiscate stock for their personal benefit they are operating outside of any formal policing strategy. Where police apply above board legal sanction, this may be the result of police officers responding to a target-based policing approach from their superiors[23] in which Matshedisho suggests the police, "remove 'safety' from the concept of community policing and replace it with statistics."[24]

Defiant drinking

During the COVID-19 pandemic there were four periods when the sale and transport of alcohol was prohibited. In total these lasted over 160 days during 2020 and 2021.[25] Outside these periods of complete prohibition there were restrictions on opening hours for on- and off-sales of alcohol.[26] The primary justification for prohibition was to free up ICU beds for COVID-19 patients given the role of alcohol in accident and violent trauma. Some of the restrictions were illogical in terms of the transmission of COVID-19, such as permitting drinkers to sit in taverns, but not to buy off-sales to drink at home over weekends. The lockdown prohibitions intensified the already widespread illegal distribution and sale of alcohol in the township.

The initial show of strength by the police and army enforcing the first lockdown was not sustained. While state agencies were able to control pinch points, such as roadblocks at townships entrances,[27] after the first few weeks there was little restriction on movement within the township and the lockdown regulations were widely ignored. However, while the township might ignore the plethora of lockdown regulations, the corporate players of the alcohol industry could not openly defy the imposed prohibition. This presented both opportunities and risk in what was now an entirely black market. The price, and therefore profit, from selling alcohol rose. At the same time, with sales from licensed venues displaced to unlicensed ones, including COVID-19 assisted start-ups, there was greater scope for arbitrary law enforcement and thus risk to those selling liquor illegally.

22 Herrick and Charman (2013:25).

23 Faull (2013).

24 Matshedisho (2009b:35).

25 Between: 26 March 2020 and 1 June 2020; 13 July 2020 and 17 August 2020; 28 December 2020 and 2 February 2021; and 28 June 2021 and 25 July 2021.

26 Government of South Africa (N.D.).

27 Generally, township entrances are few with the apartheid policy of restricted entrances to facilitate control largely unchanged.

As with the shebeen queens of apartheid, the township responded with determined if disguised defiance.[28] Towards the end of the fourth prohibition period, which had lasted four weeks, the message in a Katlehong *chafpozi*, where patrons were drinking a home brewed concoction for lack of an alternative, was that "Ramaphosa *wa bora rona!*" (Ramaphosa is boring/irritating us!).[29] Not everybody shared this view on prohibition. Some, especially women, welcomed it given the amount of money spent by men on alcohol that could be used for other purposes, and the problems of drunkenness. However, the focus here is on how prohibition was defied in the townships.

Ways of drinking

Aside from the looting of closed liquor stores,[30] there were three main ways in which drinking was able to continue during periods of prohibition.[31]

First, there was the selling of tavern stock to unlicensed outlets. This was a continuation of the practice in which unlicensed venues were supplied before lockdown, though the stock that the taverns would have normally sold directly to customers was now also released into this line of sales. Since the four lockdown prohibition periods were announced without warning how much stock was held by a tavern was a matter of luck. However, the breweries, with their own stockpiles building up during prohibition periods, quickly restocked taverns once each period ended. The stop-go pattern to the prohibition meant that this source of alcohol was available on four occasions.

Second, clandestine black-market networks for distributing alcohol quickly expanded. Much of this was for spirits and liqueurs given the transport required for any significant volume of beer or cider and the danger of roadblocks outside the township. This distribution relied on stolen stock, stock sold out the back door of warehouses, depots and bottle stores, alcohol smuggled into South

28 As did many people in the suburbs who also bought liquor on the black market, drank wine in teacups in restaurants, and *in extremis* brewed their own concoctions using recipes from the internet. By and large, however, richer households had less need to resort to the black market or home brewing as they keep some alcohol in the home. Most drinkers with resources stocked up after the first prohibition period, correctly anticipating that it might be re-imposed. Having a personal stockpile of alcohol in the townships, outside of affluent sections, is impossible. Alcohol is for drinking, not storing, and if the owner doesn't drink it, somebody else will.

29 Fieldnotes: 210724.

30 Madubela (2021).

31 There was also switching from alcohol to cannabis as a recreational drug, especially as the price of alcohol rose, and the drinking of methylated spirits (containing methanol rather than ethanol). While cannabis smoking was widespread, the drinking of methylated spirits was limited (Fieldnotes: 200524). It's generally understood that the practice is dangerous and this method of achieving intoxication is largely shunned.

Africa from neighbouring countries, and the production and distribution of illegal, untaxed, domestically produced brands of alcohol.

Third, there was the brewing of sorghum beer and concoctions. Although the purchase of the key ingredients of sorghum beer was also prohibited,[32] this simply meant that alternative concoctions were brewed since any starch can be used as the basis for fermentation. The two most brewed drinks in the townships, collectively known as *rwaza* and by a host of different names,[33] are *gemere*, flavoured with ginger,[34] and *pinapole*, made with pineapple. The scale of prohibition brewing is illustrated by an article in South Africa's financial newspaper *Business Day* by reporter Lisa Steyn, "Of pineapples and potatoes: prices flex amid the pandemic."[35] The sale of pineapples at Johannesburg fresh produce market increased from 10,000 on the first day of the first lockdown (27 March 2020) to 90,000 by late April. As Steyn shrewdly noted, the increased sales of pineapples was not a hankering for Hawaiian pizza, but that "the right combination of pineapple, sugar and yeast can result in an alcoholic brew with a kick – something consumers are craving amid prohibition."[36] At one point, the Shoprite supermarket chain restricted customers to a maximum of five pineapples each.[37] Which is more than you need for a Hawaiian pizza.

Nthombi: entrepreneurship[38]

There is a cardboard notice, written with a koki pen, fixed to Nthombi and S'bu's front gate.[39] It lists items and prices of what they sell to neighbours. A cheap brand of wors, Russian sausages, atchar by the tub, boiled eggs R2 each, and sachets of Grandpa headache powder.

32 Though permits were issued for limited purchases of these ingredients for funerals or other recognised traditional ceremonies.

33 I have recorded the following, contemporary, names for home-brewed alcohol in South African townships, excluding the names for sorghum beer brewed for traditional ceremonies. There are undoubtedly many more as often names are specific to a single township: Mbamba, Pinapole, Gemere (alcoholic version), Spayon, Sanpopo, Shampopo, Seyantheria, Senantoto, Bomba, Skrephatotse, Qamokgela, Seroko, Mokoko, Takanyesa, Ntakonyesa, Makgazumane, Skokiaan, Seqhaqhabolo. Very few of these have written sources, spelling is therefore my own and generally phonetic.

34 A non-alcoholic version of *gemere* is a common drink at township funerals and over the Christmas period.

35 Steyn (2020).

36 Steyn (2020).

37 *Business Day* (2020).

38 Based on Fieldnotes: 200801; 200808; 200814; 210130; and 210724.

39 Based on Fieldnotes: 200801; 200808; 200814; 210130; and 210724.

Before moving in with S'bu, Nthombi had worked as a saleswoman for Ackerman's store in Germiston. When that job ended, she bought clothes in Jo'burg CBD and sold them door to door in the township. When she moved in with S'bu, a vat 'n sit *arrangement with* lobolo *ongoing and their first child on the way, it made sense for her to be at home, selling from the kitchen, while S'bu went to his job as a warehouse supervisor. Initially, S'bu wasn't keen on the business, it meant people knocking on the back door day and night wanting this and wanting that. If somebody wants Grandpa to sooth a raging headache, they want it now, whatever the hour.*

However, it is not only the listed items that can be bought if you knock on the back door. Nthombi is an enterprising woman and understands the importance of business diversification when operating in competitive markets. And the kasi *is as competitive as it comes. There is nothing stopping a neighbour starting to sell boiled eggs for the same price six doors down, and why would somebody walk another six houses if they can get the same thing at the same price next door? You could lower the price, but then your profit disappears.*

Despite not having a liquor licence, Nthombi arranged for deliveries of sorghum beer from National Sorghum Breweries (NSB). They deliver 20L drums and she sells it at R10 a litre, poured into customers' bottles in the kitchen. She can squeeze twenty-two 1-litre "scoops" *from each drum and make almost 100 per cent mark-up. This line of business ended with the liquor ban, but other opportunities opened.*

They were needed. S'bu was laid off in the first week of the lockdown, after which he changed his mind about Nthombi's business. Now he welcomed each knock on the door. Nthombi took to brewing sorghum beer herself. There are few women in the townships who don't know the basics of brewing given the traditional importance of umqombothi. *However, with the key brewing ingredients prohibited, getting hold of King Korn or a similar product became expensive and then all but impossible. She hesitated over brewing* gemere *or* pinapole. *It was, she felt, a step down. A drink for those who cannot afford anything better. Sorghum beer – in effect the traditional African brew of* umqombothi *– has dignity. Only a few doors from Nthombi and S'bu's place, Nelly runs a long-established spot selling a range of concoctions. Broken men hang out in her back yard keeping each other company. Some drink till they can only sway and stagger when they get to their feet.*

Instead, Nthombi started to sell what liquor she could source. She knew the nearby tavern owner and early in the first lockdown bought four cases for R20 a quart bottle. She was able to sell each quart for R30 and then, as prices rose, R35 a bottle. It was good money. The business grew. At one point they had eight cases in the house. But the tavern owner, knowing the price his stock was being sold by Ntombi, raised his price to R30 then R35. Beyond R40 and sometimes R45 the market for quarts stalled. People switched to alternatives. So did Nthombi.

She asked friends and relatives and bought whatever she could: King Arthur whiskey-flavoured vodka in 100ml sachets; Soldier Whiskey, which hails from Mozambique; and Cormard Quality Label Pure Gin which is very unlikely to be pure and lacks any of the legally required information on the label. All went out the back door with a markup in the region of 100 per cent.

Throughout the lockdown prohibitions both Nthombi and S'bu were nervous about being bust. This was most likely if the police stopped somebody on the street with bottles. They would give them a choice; tell them where they had bought it or be taken into the station and face prosecution themselves. Nthombi and S'bu insisted that people brought a bag with them when buying. A school bag, not a carrier bag. This became standard for sales of alcohol in the township. A wag coined a meme on the matter: "Shebeens must be selling stationary nowadays. I see people going in and out with school bags!"

They would get jittery if a police van came down the street, cases of beer are impossible hide. The fear of being bust was not just about the bribe that they would have to pay, but also the indignity. Nobody wants the police in their house, searching the rooms, exposing their secrets. It's not a nice experience. It's going to scare the children and the whole street will be talking about it. And likely if it happens once it will happen again. They will be back. Not the same cops. They will tell colleagues, who will arrive after you've had time to restock. "Teamwork" on the police's part as Nthombi put it.

"Why take the risk?" I asked Nthombi and got the answer I expected. "Money, money, money!" They had to eat. They would say the same thing, in a slightly different format, to the cops if they were ever busted. They were selling to feed the family. Nobody in the house was working. It would assist in negotiating the bribe. Though the amount would also depend on what stock they were caught with. How much did they think they would have to cough up if they were caught with eight cases? S'bu thought something between R500 and R1,000. Raising it would be difficult at short notice. Perhaps, if the police could see they were struggling they would take less. But they might get impatient, thinking they were being strung along, follow procedure and book them in at the station. A case would be opened. Then there would need to be a bigger bribe to avoid a court case that would drag on and on. It would be better to borrow and pay the bribe on the spot. Either way, their stock would be taken, but "not back to the station!" It would be passed over to someone to sell, likely a relative of one of the police officers.

Lockdown liquor markets

The townships defied prohibition in different ways.[40] Some sold beer obtained from nearby taverns, others brewed for sale, yet others bought a range of spirits for resale, and some combined two or sometimes three of these methods. These drinks of defiance had distinct supply chains but were sold into a single market. The sale price of lockdown liquor in this black market was readily available to consumers.[41] In the Katlehong street that this chapter is based on, information was rapidly communicated among consumers. Differences in price between outlets could be gained without having to walk more than a couple of hundred metres. Information on availability and prices further afield was shared across the townships using WhatsApp messages and calls.

Prices moved upwards incrementally after the first prohibition period was introduced. Prior to this, a quart of "brown" beer[42] retailed from between R15 and R18 in the township. It rose over the course of a few weeks to settle at around R40 a quart, a price which became more or less standard. In this first prohibition period there was an uneven process of price increases, sometimes two outlets in the same street might be selling at a R5 difference. These differentials were however closed once the standard R40 price was reached. In subsequent lockdowns the price moved immediately to the R40 standard following announcements of another prohibition period. While higher prices were sometimes asked, R40 appeared to be a psychological barrier and township drinkers balked at paying beyond this and rather switched to alternatives.[43] In line with the rise in the price of beer, recognised brands of spirits sold for between R300 and R400 a bottle,[44] around twice their normal retail price.

When President Ramaphosa announced that prohibition was to be lifted at a "family meeting," as his Sunday night addresses to the nation came to be known, prices of lockdown liquor fell back to normal commercial levels. Once a family meeting was announced during prohibition, informal retailers had to make a call over whether the president would or would not lift alcohol restrictions. If prohibition continued, their stock would retain its value, and they could continue selling at prohibition prices. If prohibition was lifted,

40 This section is based on Fieldnotes: 200404; 200418; 200524; 200627; 200718; 200725; 2000801; 200814; 200815; 210130; and 210724.

41 In a rural township of Mashaeng, Free State, the lockdown price of quarts approximated those of the Gauteng urban townships, however the price of concoctions was slightly lower, possibly reflecting a more established home-brewing culture in these locations.

42 See Chapter 3 for more on the significance of beer brands in the township.

43 Between periods of complete prohibition, higher prices operated over weekends if sales were not permitted, but at a rate between the legal sales price and that of complete prohibition.

44 750ml bottles or "straights."

their stock would instantaneously halve in value. They would end up having to sell stock at cost price or even below.[45]

The price of concoctions or *rwaza* also increased. In part this can be explained by the increased costs of the raw materials. The previously mentioned *Business Day* article reported how the wholesale price of pineapples increased with demand; from R12.50 a kilo at the end of March 2020 to R22.5 a kilo a month later, an 80 per cent increase. But since alternative core ingredients for home brewing increased by considerably less, the price increase of concoctions was shadowing those of black-market quarts. In the first lockdown the price of a 2-litre *scoop* of *rwaza* in Katlehong rose from R16 to R18, then to R25, finally reaching R30, a price increase of almost 90 per cent.

An economic explanation would be that *rwaza*, a drink of desperation – whether of poverty, or the impact of a supply side shock such as prohibition – kicked in as a substitute for beer and cider as the price of these rose. However, those selling *rwaza* never referred to the cost of alternatives, though they were well aware of them, but rather talked about "risk."[46]

Gideon: risk and benefit

Gideon started his spot or, as he prefers his to call it, his joint, after he was dismissed from his job as a shelf packer.[47] *Setting up his joint wasn't planned. Friends came around and hung out. It became a regular thing. He started stocking his fridge with quarts to sell. It was Patrick, owner of the tavern a few doors away, who suggested Gideon should buy regularly. He would give him a discount. Patrick didn't see Gideon as competition. In fact, it was quite the opposite, it was a way of increasing his sales. His tavern was filled to capacity, and he had no room to expand seating with every part of the yard needed to store cases of beer delivered by SAB in a huge lorry that blocks the street while cases of beer are offloaded, and crates of empty bottles returned. By selling to spots in surrounding streets Patrick was growing his business. They were in effect satellite outlets.*

Gideon might be selling beer at a markup, but social relationships were important. Sometimes, if things were going well, Gideon would put a straight down for a group of drinkers-cum-friends. A gift to say thank you to those drinking his beer. And in return, if a group bought a straight to share, Gideon would help himself to a glass without needing to ask. It was give and take.

45 This problem was compounded if consumers also thought that prohibition would be lifted since they were then reluctant to pay lockdown prices when regular prices were likely only one or two days away.

46 In one overheard public questioning of the price being asked by Nthombi the questioner was told to take the matter up with Ramaphosa.

47 This section is based on Fieldnotes: 200808; 200814; 200822; and 210123.

Sometimes customers would club together to buy skop *(sheep's head), man's food, and eat it with pap cooked in Gideon's kitchen. There were rarely women at Gideon's place. Indeed, for many of Gideon's chums, his place provides a refuge from domestic worries. A men's fellowship lubricated with liquor. Such an approach to business is not uncommon in the township. Car washes, almost as ubiquitous as spots, are another example: it's a business, albeit one that's not likely to expand, but it's also a place where young men and sometimes their girlfriends hang out with a sound system playing and a* braai *on weekend afternoons.*

But as much as it might feel like a social club, Gideon's joint made money. Before the prohibitions he was clearing around thirty cases (each of 12 quarts) a week. He bought the cases from Patrick for R160. He sold each bottle for R18, a mark-up of 35 per cent. Along with sales of (untaxed) loose draw, *selling the odd* straight *and along with rent from two backyard rooms, he could manage. In fact, though he kept no accounts, he said he was making more money than he had as a shelf packer and, to boot, he was his own boss, running the place as he pleased.*

Prohibition presented opportunity to make more money. Patrick was keen to shift his otherwise unsellable stock through spots. He began by selling to Gideon at R250 a case or just under R21 a quart. This was still more than what Patrick would have been able to sell outside of prohibition. Gideon sold at R40 a quart, a 92 per cent margin on what he paid. And the number of customers increased. He made serious money.

The downside was the risk. As an unlicensed venue, there was always the possibility of police arriving and asking for the permit to sell alcohol that they knew you didn't have. Nobody expected that this would be done by the book. It would be a matter of negotiating a bribe and saying goodbye to your stock. What made it worse was that once on the police's radar they would return.

Like Nthombi and S'bu at the other end of the street, the biggest risk in Gideon's view was the police stopping somebody in the street with bottles. They would want to know where it had come from. So, there were no exceptions to the rule that a bag must be brought for off-sales. If Gideon saw a police car in the street he would stop selling for a while, telling the prospective purchaser to come back later. Those who did purchase off sales should not hang around, even to greet people they might know. You should "buy and go!"

Another risk was a neighbour reporting them, especially if the place was noisy with patrons drinking late into the night. Gideon kept on good terms with his neighbours and made sure that they weren't disturbed by his chums-cum-customers. Without somebody informing on him, even if there was a group sitting in the tiny front yard of the house, the spot would be hidden in plain sight. As long as there weren't bottles of alcohol prominently displayed, there was nothing to say that the group of men weren't simply getting through a lockdown afternoon or evening together.

It was different with Sindiswa's place that opened across the road from Gideon's spot. She was a recently arrived backyard tenant and only started selling alcohol during prohibition. Drinking spilled out into the yard and went on late into the night. Possibly one of the neighbours complained, or perhaps a passing patrol realised what was happening. The police raided and confiscated her stock. She carried on selling after the raid, but kept her stock in a neighbouring house, in case the police returned. The neighbour had been unemployed for years and welcomed the opportunity that his warehousing provided, recognised with the odd *mahala* quart for himself.

Patrick also ran a risk in selling to Gideon and other outlets. While he had a liquor licence, he was not permitted to sell or transport alcohol under the lockdown regulations. He was careful about who he sold to and how the transaction took place. His tavern and Gideon's spot were only a few houses apart, but under prohibition their transactions took place in a different section of the township. Patrick brought the beer from the tavern in his *bakkie* and Gideon hired transport from a friend to bring it back to almost the same place it had come from half an hour earlier.

The *kasi* as a risk society

Risk operates as a parallel currency to cash in the *kasi*. There is no agreed exchange rate between risk and cash, though there is an expectation of proportionality. However, what is proportional is subjective and, further, it's impossible to isolate risk in the matrix of factors that set the price of alcohol during prohibition. Risk was a reason for higher prices, but also an excuse to increase margins. Customers were often sceptical as to whether the risk being run by those selling alcohol justified the prices charged. Gideon would, sensing resentment, sometimes mollify regular customers by giving them a R5 a quart discount.

Resentment was, however, most apparent when legality restored supply and prices to normal levels and customers reflected on how much they had been paying. Gideon's customers pointed to the two additional rooms that Gideon built in his back yard. It was obvious to everybody that he had done well out of prohibition.

The lockdown provided opportunity to profit alongside risks. Those taking the *monyetla* did so at the expense of customers willing to pay double or more to drink. Much of this activity was clothed in the language of mutual aid. Those who took to brewing concoctions would explain that they were just doing it to help neighbours after Ramaphosa had left them high and dry. But much as they might stress their embeddedness in the community, they also had a good prohibition. The return to retailing normality meant a drop in income and some sellers privately expressed the wish for the bans to be re-instated.

The risk, whether selling home brew or black-market liquor, came from police officers. With prohibition, the risk increased; you were selling without a licence and breaking lockdown rules. The police were especially vigilant during the first week or so of each prohibition period. Then things settled down and by keeping a low profile you could, with luck, avoid being bust.

Given lockdown regulations, the police were legally entitled to confiscate stock and charge those selling alcohol. In practice, they would take advantage of the lockdown regulations, particularly prohibition, to pursue their own *menyetla* by confiscating stock for resale and extracting bribes in return for not pursing prosecution. Instead of enforcing the law, they acted as klepto-parasites, in which one animal steals food collected by another. Such stealing from the endeavours of others is thinly justified as law enforcement tempered by mercy in not pursuing criminal sanctions.

Whether the risks run by those selling lockdown liquor justified the inflated prices is impossible to calculate. Despite the indeterminacy of the quantity of risk, it operates as a parallel currency in the township alongside rands and cents. Indeed, the *kasi* is a risk society. Not in the sense developed by Unrich Beck (1992) and Anthony Giddens (1999) of societies needing to balance the risks of their own (technological) creation against social benefit, but in a much simpler sense. To survive or to get ahead in the township means taking risks: the laws, rules, and regulations of the *lex constitutional* must be broken.

In the shadow of big money

Prohibition exacerbated the complex array of conflicts within the township. Some township residents scored and climbed ahead in the constant competition of the *kasi*. However, these conflicts, while real enough, took place in the shadow of the far bigger systematic bypassing of South Africa's laws orchestrated by the major brewing and distilling companies.

This commercial network that has long penetrated into the township is based on a confluence of interests. At the apex, major corporations involved in brewing, distilling, and distribution can shift volumes beyond what is lawfully possible, but without risk to themselves. Instead, it is the township owners of liquor licences who multiply corporates' sales by selling stock on to unlicensed outlets that take the risk along with the licensed outlets themselves.

The realities on the ground illustrated the limited reach of the rule of law whether in prohibition or not. Those seeking to regulate the consumption of alcohol are up against a confederacy of major corporates and myriad township residents willing to take risk for the money that can be made.

Despite this, the established *de facto* distribution system, operating in parallel to the putative regulatory framework, was rattled by the lockdown prohibitions. As described, the impact of prohibition on the corporates was less than it would have been if they played by the book; taverns were restocked after each prohibition period despite them not being legally permitted to have sold stock in the interim. The corporates did, nevertheless, lose out because of the overall reduction in alcohol consumed and as illicit brands and home brewing took off. Nevertheless, protests of the corporates[48] should be placed in the context of their decades-long complicity in selling alcohol indirectly to unlicensed outlets.

Conclusion: *Menyetla* proliferation, risk, and regulation

This chapter illustrates how the *lex constitutional,* when weak in practice, provides opportunity for *menyetla*, whether through unlawfully selling alcohol (from township spots selling concoctions through to the open secret of multinational brewers distributing through unlicensed outlets) or through the klepto-parasitism of law enforcement officers' street level extortion. These *menyetla* are not restricted to the COVID-19 epidemic that the chapter has focused on. However, COVID-19 regulations, all but imaginary in their intended application, paradoxically accentuated, albeit unevenly, these opportunities. The chapter also illustrates how *menyetla* are accompanied by risk created by the limited writ of the *lex constitutional* in the township.

The Department of Trade and Industry's (DTI)[49] *Final Liquor Policy Paper* of 2016, acknowledges the failure of previous legislation to transform the industry. It notes that, "On the whole, the South African liquor [industry] is currently still predominantly white-owned owing to a large extent to the fact that its past regulatory regime has led to high concentrated ownership patterns and subsequent high barriers to entry."[50] It also notes how these disparities have resulted in "many unlicensed liquor outlets operat[ing] and continu[ing] to operate to date."[51]

What the DTI's paper does not address is the social facts of the township and liquor. The thrust of the DTI's recommendations is to increase regulations on the sale of alcohol. This will only further cement enforced informality and the resulting *menyetla*, turning entrepreneurial township residents into criminals and providing opportunities for their extortion. It will do nothing to prevent the harm wrought by alcohol in the township. This approach to policy making also reveals a lack of understanding that the state's writ is limited in the township. To enforce policy that restricts economic activity, whether the sale of alcohol or any other business, requires that the *lex constitutional* is operating. If there is to be regulation and moderation of alcohol mis/use in the township, it will need more than the proclamation of statutes.

48 SAB sought an order declaring that the lockdown liquor ban was unlawful (Mabuza 2022).

49 Now the Department of Trade, Industry and Competition.

50 The DTI (2016: Section 4.2.1); see also Damons (2022).

51 The DTI (2016: Section 1.1).

9

Therapeutic fraud: medical aid scams

MOST SOUTH African readers will be members of a medical aid scheme providing access to private healthcare. There are a wide range of schemes available offering different levels of benefits which are paid for by members' monthly contributions. "Day-to-day" medication and treatment benefits smooth what would otherwise be payments made by the member directly. Schemes also provide cover for more serious health problems requiring hospitalisation, operations, or other major expenses. Having medical aid means not having to use South Africa's public healthcare system characterised by long queues, rundown facilities, limited treatment, and indifferent service.

Medical aid membership is not cheap, even for the most basic schemes. Under 20 per cent of the population can afford the comfort and convenience that private health cover provides. The rise of an African middle class in post-apartheid South Africa has diversified the racial profile of scheme membership. However, there are township residents who have medical aid despite their salaries not being close to professional levels. This is because they work for private or public organisations that require membership as a condition of service. In public sector organisations there has been significant growth in medical aid membership, even as the percentage of the population with membership has changed little over the last twenty years.

For medical aid to be affordable for non-professional workers, the employer must subsidise monthly contributions. Yet, even with subsidisation and when employees are on cheaper schemes, contributions nevertheless represent a significant deduction from pay packets.

Contributions cover a capped day-to-day set of benefits as well as possible major expenses, including the statutorily required prescribed minimum benefits that must be offered by medical aids, as well as the administrative costs of the scheme. Membership may not look like good value when you are told midway through the year that you now need to pay for whatever it is you are collecting from the pharmacy as you have reached your day-to-day limit, but you are still going to have premiums deducted for the rest of the year. There are, however, ways of besting medical aid.

Medical aid schemes

South Africa spends around 9 per cent of GDP on health, around half of this expenditure is in the private health system which services a minority of the population.[1] In 2020, 72 per cent of South Africa's 60 million citizens normally consulted a public healthcare facility when ill.[2] Payment for private healthcare is either out of pocket, health insurance, or through a medical aid scheme. Out of pocket is what it says: you pay from your own resources. Health insurance provides limited health cover. It is not subject to medical aid regulations and offers cheaper premiums for less comprehensive cover. Just over 1 million people have such insurance.[3]

Some 9 million people are covered by medical aid schemes. These require monthly contributions by the main member and, where the scheme is linked to employment, the employer. The main or principal member of a medical aid pays additional contributions to enrol dependents (nominated members) onto the scheme. In 2020, there were some seventy-five medical aid schemes operating with a wide range of benefit plans available, though all are legally required to include the list of prescribed minimum benefits for a range of conditions.[4]

Schemes can be open or restricted/closed. Open schemes allow anyone to join, restricted or closed schemes are limited to individuals meeting certain criteria, typically employment with an organisation that the closed medical aid covers. Where a closed medical aid is for the benefit of employees it is generally a condition of service that the employee must be a member of a medical aid scheme. Open schemes had 4.9 million members and restricted schemes 4 million in 2020.[5] Administering medical aid claims is complex and medical aid schemes often outsource this management function to medical aid administrators.

Medical aid benefit plans specify, over and above prescribed minimum benefits, what healthcare expenditure will be paid to the healthcare provider or reimbursed to the member if they pay the provider directly. Essentially, the greater the contributions paid, the more comprehensive the benefits provided. This applies to the range of healthcare services covered, the limits to payment per item (since healthcare providers charge at different rates), and overall annual limits for each category of healthcare covered.

1 Which, additionally, carry a lower burden of disease given socio-economic circumstances (Rispel *et al.* 2016).

2 Maluleke (2021).

3 Council for Medical Schemes (2022:4–5).

4 This requirement remains in place, despite a process begun in 2015 by the Council for Medical Schemes to allow these to be dropped and schemes to offer much cheaper (but less comprehensive) medical aid options (Kahn 2022).

5 Council for Medical Schemes (2021a: Annexure Z).

Between 2000 and 2020, the membership of medical aid schemes fluctuated between 15 and 18 per cent of the population.[6] However, in the context of a growing population, membership of medical aid schemes has, in absolute numbers, grown over the period from 6.7 million to 8.9 million.[7]

Given that medical aid membership is based on the ability to pay, membership is dramatically skewed by race. In 2022, 15.8 per cent of the population were members (main and nominated beneficiaries who typically are family members) of a medical aid scheme, but this differs by race. Of whites, 73 per cent were covered; Indians 52 per cent; coloureds 17 per cent; and Africans 10 per cent.[8] However, in absolute numbers, in 2018 there were more Africans with medical aid (4.6 million) than whites (3.2 million), coloureds (860,000), and Indians (736,000).[9]

The most significant new medical aid scheme in the last twenty years is the Government Employees Medical Scheme (GEMS) established in 2006, providing medical aid cover for government employees. In 2020, GEMS had 1.9 million beneficiaries and was the second largest scheme in the country and the largest restricted scheme. In addition to GEMS, there are medical aid schemes for several state institutions and enterprises. These include the South African Police Service, local government employees, Transnet, SAPO, and the South African Broadcasting Corporation, with a combined total of some 800,000 beneficiaries.[10]

Medical aid fraud

Fraud is a problem for medical aid schemes.[11] In 2020, South African medical aid schemes spent R30m on fraud investigations and recovered R252m.[12] Fraud is primarily detected though statistical analysis of claims and by members acting as whistle blowers. The actual scale of fraud in the medical aid industry is estimated to be much higher, between 5 and 15 per cent.[13] For an industry that paid out R178bn in claims in 2020,[14] this translates to between R9bn and

6 Council for Medical Schemes (2021a:9); Business Tech (2019).

7 Council for Medical Schemes (2021a:9).

8 Statista (2019b).

9 The total of 9.4 million (Stats South Africa 2019) is higher than that given by the Council for Medical Schemes for 2018 at 8.92 million.

10 Council for Medical Schemes (2021a: Annexure A).

11 As are waste, resulting from the overuse of medical services or accidental over-billing, and abuse in which reimbursement is paid for services that are not medically necessary (Association of Certified Fraud Examiners SA 2018).

12 Council for Medical Schemes (2021b:73).

13 Mothudi (2018).

14 Down from R185bn in 2019 because of the COVID-19 pandemic which saw members defer elective procedures (Council for Medical Schemes 2021b:15).

R27bn. It is impossible to know the true figure, as Dr Hleli Nhlapo, Deputy Chairperson of the Board of Healthcare Funders, put it, estimations of private healthcare fraud are “all thumb suck, the truth is we don’t know.”[15]

The additional cost of fraud has, however, been described as “killing the goose that lays the golden egg”[16] since it contributes to driving up the cost of medical aid membership to unaffordable levels. The CEO of Discovery Health, the largest medical aid scheme in the country, has described it as a threat to the future of the healthcare industry.[17]

Tsholofelo Legotlo and Ashley Mutezo (2018) identify a wide range of ways in which medical aid schemes can be defrauded. Providers can defraud medical aid schemes by: making false claims for services which were not rendered; “up-coding”[18] in order to claim for a more expensive service than actually provided; inflate the services provided (such as the time taken); deliberately provide unnecessary medical services; duplicate claims; and miss-code an item to something that medical aid will pay for.[19]

Members can defraud the schemes by: card farming (i.e. allowing another person, not covered by the medical aid, to claim for a service under the member’s name) and by not disclosing pre-existing medical conditions (when joining a scheme).[20] Some fraud relies on cooperation between members and service providers, such as “cash back” schemes, in which unnecessary treatment is knowingly provided and the medical aid payment split between provider and member. There can also be fraudulent relationships between providers, such as independent health professionals and private hospitals. Legotlo and Mutezo also identify fraud committed by medical aid scheme employees and by brokers. Brokers in the medical aid industry provide consumers with advice about joining a medical aid scheme and are paid on a commission basis when they sign up members.

Medical aid and tight budgets

The affordability of medical aid becomes a problem when membership is a condition of service and the monthly deduction a burden. It is not possible for medical aid schemes to provide the most basic healthcare cover for less

[15] Reported in Bateman (2015).

[16] Mosiah (2018:15).

[17] Broomberg (2018).

[18] Medical aids code every service along with the amount that the scheme will fund.

[19] Such as pharmacies which stock items which are not covered by medical aid schemes.

[20] Generally, waiting periods apply to pre-existing conditions for new scheme members.

than R1,000 a month. In part because of prescribed minimum benefits,[21] though the underlying problem is the rising cost of medical care. Medical aid can only provide what members' contributions, averaged over time and with administration costs subtracted, is able to cover.

Recognising the difficulty that lower paid workers with compulsory medical aid cover face, some closed schemes operate a sliding scale of payments based on income. Generally, this makes only a marginal difference. MEDiPOS, a medical aid scheme for SAPO's employees, has three options or plans. The cheapest has four payment levels depending on the employee's salary. In 2022, this option cost R1,410 per month for the principal member earning at or below R8,185 a month and R1,752 per month for those earning R14,986 and above. Taking the maximum amount for the lowest payment level and the minimum for the maximum level (on the same, cheapest, option), an 83 per cent higher salary sees medical aid contributions increase by only 24 per cent. SAPO subsidises medical aid payments by 70 per cent, which means that, as a percentage of monthly income, medical aid contributions deducted from the employee's gross salary amount to five per cent for somebody earning R8,185 a month and 3.5 per cent for somebody earning R14,986 on the lowest cost scheme available.

However, these figures are for the principal member only. Unless the employee has no dependents, or does not put them on their medical aid, they need to pay additional contributions to cover family members. Thus, if a SAPO employee wanted to include their spouse and two children on the cheapest option available, the cost in 2022, taking into account SAPO's 70 per cent subsidy, would be between R1,013 and R1,296 a month, depending on their salary level. This translates to between 12.4 per cent of gross salary for the lower paid worker and 8.6 per cent for the higher paid.[22]

For the cheapest option available in the MEDiPOS scheme, the 2022 annual day-to-day expenditure limit, which includes consultations with a GP and specialists as well as medication, was R2,880 for the principal member. After this limit has been reached, further expenses are not covered. The member must then pay out of pocket or use the public health system. Alternatively, if the member doesn't use this day-to-day allowance, it is forfeited.

In comparison with higher income earners, those on lower incomes are paying a higher percentage of their salary for less benefit.[23] You pay for

21 Theunissen and Child (2021).

22 MEDiPOS (2022). The contribution of a principal member's adult dependents is slightly discounted, child dependents at around a third of the principal member's contribution.

23 MEDiPOS's top end scheme, which is a flat rate for all income levels, costs R7,233 per month, effectively R2,170 with a 70 per cent subsidy, for the principal member. This gives a larger annual day-to-day limit of R8,450 for the principal member

what you get, but the scheme is better value if you can afford the higher options. Someone on a higher income, while complaining about the cost of medical aid, likely appreciates it for insuring them against possible future serious health problems. However, for those on low incomes, the focus is on day-to-day payments.

If this is the exclusive focus, then it's poor value. A principal member on MEDiPOS's cheapest scheme earning R8,185 or less a month has R5,076 deducted from their salary a year in medical aid contributions, but can only access R2,880 in day-to-day benefits over the same period. This calculation ignores what that can be accessed via the medical aid in the form of specific benefits not included in the day-to-day limits and the uncertain future possibility of hospitalisation or major illness. But the simple comparison of deductions versus day-to-day expenditure limit is the approach taken by those on low incomes and tight budgets.

Those on lower income levels who are required to have medical aid as a condition of service may appreciate the benefits they can claim and do not want to rely on public healthcare but still do not see their membership as good value. As outlined by the Association of Certified Fraud Examiners of South Africa's Health Care Forum, "The truth is that a large percentage of healthcare policy holders see their monthly contributions as a grudge purchase."[24]

If deductions for medical aid are viewed as a grudge purchase, it is hardly surprising if members seek to maximise benefits. Thinking about medical aid as long-term insurance for ill-health later in life is not a priority if you're broke at the end of the month. It is now a short step to fraudulently maximising benefits from what is a remote and resented scheme.

Card farming

If medical aid is a condition of service, this is only for the employee, not their dependents. But if an employee is struggling to afford the medical aid deductions, what do they do about dependents? If they include them,

---

(MEDiPOS 2022). Comparing a member on the top end scheme with one on the cheapest scheme at the lowest income bracket, the top end member is paying 114 per cent more in terms of contributions, but their annual day-to-day limit is 193 per cent higher.

24 Association of Certified Fraud Examiners SA, Health Care Forum (2018:12). Unions under pressure from their members, seek to renegotiate medical aid for their members, calling for "affordable medical aid for all" (DEPACU 2017). Put otherwise, the demand is for greater subsidisation. One response to these demands by organisations with closed medical aids has been to allow employees to join other, open, medical aids. This provides choice but does not solve the bottom-line constraint of medical aid unaffordability for those on low incomes.

deductions from their wage package will be even higher. The easiest way out of this dilemma is to card farm; the member's card is used to fund treatment of others who are not registered beneficiaries.

Card farming requires a relationship with the healthcare provider, who must not check too carefully who is presenting the card. It is not hard to find a township doctor or pharmacist who will, for example, treat a medical aid member's wife/girlfriend or children using the man's card.[25] When a sick child is brought for treatment, collaborating with card farming is easy to justify. The doctor or pharmacist is, after all, assisting the family member of a patient who otherwise cannot afford private care. The alternative is that the child must be taken to a public clinic where likely they will have to wait for much of the day and possibly only receive basic treatment.

Overlooking that the child is not covered by the medical aid of the main member constitutes a good deed. But there is also the awkwardness of refusal and lost income if the member's card is taken elsewhere. The chances of fraudulent card use being detected are limited, unless the claims become outlandish and are picked up statistically by the medical aid scheme. Even if detected, penalties are likely to be limited. As outlined by Katlego Mothudi, Managing Director of the Board of Healthcare Funders, "Factors that contribute to the challenges in fraud detection and mitigation include the sheer volume of medical aid claims; the lack of information sharing and pooling of resources between industry players, and the lack of meaningful prosecution and stringent sanctions for fraudsters."[26]

Tooth bling

Once day-to-day benefits are maxed for the year, those wanting to further stretch the value of their medical aid need to diversify their fiddles. Cosmetically desirable gold teeth, paid for by medical aid, illustrates how members and providers work together to defraud medical aid schemes. This is not to provide healthcare, but to meet fashion trends and status symbols in the *kasi*.

Gold teeth, inlays, and decorative studs constitute tooth bling. Such decoration is not only fashionable but also signifies status. Once, when talking to someone who I'd first known as a casual worker but was now in a permanent position, I was told how different things were for him. He capped a long list of achievements that his increased income had permitted by pointing to his teeth and saying, "Look! I've got gold!"

25 A useful indicator of whether they would consider putting uncovered family members on the account of the principal member is their willingness to routinely issue sick notes, post-dated if necessary, with only perfunctory examination, or no examination at all (Fieldnotes: 201219).

26 Mothudi (2018:14).

The alternative to private dentistry, whether for routine, essential, or cosmetic treatment, is the public health service. This is rudimentary. There is a shortage of dental health professionals working in the public sector and treatment is often limited to extractions. Dr Bulele Vava, chairperson of the Public Oral Health Forum, has described public dental healthcare as "dental butcheries as opposed to oral healthcare centres."[27] Given this, many township residents without access to private healthcare opt for self-extraction. Once teeth have been lost, very few of those without medical aid can afford implants. Rather, they adapt by avoiding difficult to eat food. Eventually, as more teeth go, the only option becomes the extraction of all remaining teeth and dentures. While teeth extraction is free in the public health system, payment is required for dentures.[28]

Medical aid membership, only possible for many township residents through employment in the public sector, is extensively used to fraudulently fund decorative gold teeth bling.[29] Indeed, gold teeth in the township likely indicate membership of a medical aid, or a connection with somebody willing to farm their card for that purpose.

Three gold teeth and two medical aids

When Dumi was employed by the municipality there were benefits, including medical aid. Initially, he had nothing but praise for the scheme.[30] *True, he could see it was a hefty deduction from his salary, but the advantages were obvious. If he was sick, he didn't have to get up early to join the queue at the clinic. Rather, he'd go to Dr Ikameng's surgery. Nobody ordered him about or gave confusing instructions as to where he must go next. After he'd completed the forms, the receptionist had asked him to take a seat, "the doctor will be with you shortly Mr Sefalafala." Dr Ikameng listened to his symptoms. He took Dumi's pulse and listened to his chest. He wrote out a prescription along with a sick note for three days. Dumi didn't have to pay anything.*

Compare that with his neighbour Crispen's account of his latest visit to the clinic for his three-monthly HIV-check-up. After waiting two hours, he got to see the nurse. She was busy talking to her friend who was drinking a cup of tea. Crispen's nurse was paying more attention to what her friend was saying

27 Quoted in Mehlwana (2021).

28 The cost for a set of dentures provided following free extraction in a public health care clinic in the Free State in 2016 was R2,800 (R3,500 in 2022 prices) (Fieldnotes: 161206). This is far cheaper than a single dental implant which cost tens of thousands of rand, but not far off twice the monthly state pension.

29 Gumede (2021).

30 This composite case study is based on Fieldnotes: 161203; 161217; 161224; 191026; 210109; and 210130.

than to Crispen. The needle jab had been painful. So, painful that Crispen had whelped. The nurse told him not to be a cry-baby. By evening his arm was bruised, swollen and painful. It took over a week before the pain receded.

However, Dumi's enthusiasm for his medical aid began to fade. Nice as it was to get treatment for free, he was paying more in deductions than he was claiming. Besides, he had set his heart on gold. A workmate had told Dumi which dentist to go to. Dumi told the receptionist, Palesa, that he was on medical aid and wanted a gold tooth. She made an appointment. Dumi pointed to the tooth he wanted blinging to Dr Shumba. It didn't cost him a cent.

It was Palesa who suggested he should bring in a friend. The medical aid would cover the costs, if he waited a while. It paid for dental treatment every six months. He should phone her directly to make the appointment. She was, Dumi realised, on commission, and he followed suit. His friend Mike wanted gold. They agreed that Mike would pay Dumi R600. Everybody got a bit of the action, Dr Shumba, Palesa, Dumi, and Mike.

After Mike, he rang Palesa about a tooth for his sister Dieketso. Palesa wasn't so keen. She said something about investigations. But Dumi persisted, Dieketso had been nagging him for months and he'd promised. Palesa checked his medical aid. Could he change schemes? In fact, Dumi had been thinking of doing just that as he felt he was paying too much. He didn't want to downgrade his current scheme. Word was that they would check your claims. It was better to move to a new scheme. The new scheme signed him up in a flash.

When he went to make the appointment for Dieketso, Palesa told him that there was a slight change to how things were being done in the practice. Dr Shumba was now asking for a co-payment of R200 in cash. To this Dumi agreed, he didn't want to let Dieketso down.

Needs and wants

There is financial gain in getting gold into people's mouths for the dentist, for anyone acting as an agent bringing in customers on commission, and for those farming out cards for consideration. In Dumi's case, Dr Shumba scored financially on all three teeth; Palesa with two on which she could claim commission from Dr Shumba; Dumi gained financially from the tooth in Mike's mouth, but lost money on Dieketso's. This pyramid of transactions constitutes nested *menyetla*, the health professional at the fraud's peak, followed by agents working on commission such as Palesa, then card farmers turned occasional broker such as Dumi, and finally those who get the gold in their mouth.

Since displaying gold is for cosmetic reasons and not medical need, fraudulently claiming for tooth bling challenges an explanation of medical aid fraud as driven by economic need. That challenge rests however on a reductionist view of human want associated with Maslow's hierarchy of needs.[31] Wants are culturally determined and if tooth bling is how status is conferred in the *kasi*, then that is what you want. Bling doesn't count as a need in terms of rational policy making. But the poor strive to be human as much as everybody else. It's a very unusual person who does not put effort into signalling their material status, whether through clothes, cars, phones, houses, jewellery, travel destinations, or tooth bling. All of these have dimensions beyond pure functionality and beyond this functionality they are not necessary. But because we are humans living in societies which determine what symbolises standing and status, we want them.

None of that makes the unnecessary fitting of cosmetic gold teeth on a medical aid any less fraudulent. But it does provide insight into how, when there is opportunity to gain, people take it. Dumi was inducted into the practice by a co-worker who was ahead of him in understanding how to defraud the medical aid, but Dumi caught on fast. When it comes to *menyetla* it is not a matter of what is right or wrong, it's a battle of wits in the never-ending struggle over who gets what. We will return to the top of this pyramid later, but for now note that the *kasi* is a training ground for individual agency and struggle. Everything is contested. How could it be otherwise when so many are competing in such restricted circumstances for economic advantage and social status?

Bigger fish: cashback for rehab

Scoring gold is a win, but there are bigger fish to catch in the medical aid pond. In 2019 MEDiPOS, a restricted scheme for SAPO employees, noted with concern an operational deficit of R73.6 million in 2018, more than double than recorded in the previous two years. While its reserves remained above the required minimum, the minutes of the scheme's 2019 AGM outlined that this was unsustainable. Of particular concern was the "substantial increase in hospital admissions for mental health disease and excessive claims from allied health professionals in relation to these mental health admissions."[32]

The scheme's 2018 benefits allowed for claims of up to R56,000 for admission into psychiatric institutions per family per year, and R32,000 for substance and alcohol abuse treatment, subject to pre-authorisation and approval.[33] It was noted in the AGM minutes that investigation and recovery initiatives were ongoing.

31 Dickinson (2015).
32 MEDiPOS (2019:4).
33 MEDiPOS (2018).

In early 2018 Themba Tshabalala received a call from a number he didn't know.[34] *It was Oupa who'd got his number from Stoba, Themba's co-worker. Themba was a member of MEDiPOS, was that correct? Oupa asked. It was. Oupa explained he was a broker and that Themba was entitled to three-weeks' rehab. Everything would be taken care of while he stayed there and there was a cashback system. We should not confuse Oupa's brokering with medical aid brokers who advise people on which medical aid would be best for them to join. It would be better to think of Oupa as a fixer.*

On the admission date, Oupa drove Themba to Better Being, a private psychiatric hospital. On the way he told him to think of the problems he was struggling with at home or at work. If necessary, he was to bua maaka *(tell fibs) to the psychologist and other doctors. But Themba didn't need to lie, he reeled off some of his problems: there was a fight over the family house; he and his sister were hardly on speaking terms; he was struggling to pay off loans ... he could go on.*

Themba explained all this to Dr Magashula at their first consultation. She listened and told him that he smoked cannabis. They had taken a blood sample when he was admitted, so he didn't deny it. Rather, he said he only smoked occasionally. Dr Magashula looked at him, smiled, and wrote down something in her notes. Themba was on the standard three-week programme at Better Being. The timetable ran over three pages of the booklet he was issued on admission. As well as the timetable the booklet listed Better Being's rules that patients had to keep during their stay. This was followed by a page outlining that Better Being did not engage in or tolerate any kind of fraud. That was the biggest maaka *of all. Better Being was a scam from top to bottom. A few patients had been admitted for genuine problems, but Oupa and other brokers had been busy. Most patients, generally employed by one state owned enterprise or another, had come for the cashback treatment. Not that it was said openly. If anybody broached the subject, they were immediately hushed.*

Rather, they got on with the programme. Pills in the morning and pills at night. They slept like logs, and their appetite went through the roof. Soon Themba was putting on weight. Barring the occasional tiff over what to watch on the TV everybody was happy, the anti-depressant and anti-anxiety pills saw to that. The pills also dropped their libido, the rule of no romance or sex was surprisingly easy to manage.

But it wasn't all pills and regular meals. Between their six o'clock start and ten o'clock bedtime there were one-on-one consultations with the psychologist, social worker, and dietician, individual counselling sessions, group discussions on anger, conflict management workshops, talks about boundaries, massages

[34] This section draws on Fieldnotes: 180310; 180407; 180414; 180425; 180428; 180616; 180721; 180825; 190112; 190713; 210102; 210306; and 210313.

from the physio, exercise twice a day, and art classes in the gardens. Absolutely no alcohol and no zol *allowed.*

After each session, patient and health professional would co-sign in the booklet. Themba never missed a session and always made sure his book was signed. He was a model patient. At his final sessions with the different health professionals, he was asked for his bank account details. Once discharged, with a three-month prescription for anti-anxiety pills, and back at work, he could talk openly with others who had been at Better Being. The talk was all about cashback. In the end Themba received five payments, ranging between R2,000 to R4,000 deposited into his account. He sent Oupa R500. It wasn't necessary but he wanted to say "thank you." It was also an investment, he wanted Oupa to keep him in mind for next year.

Therapeutic fraud?

It's true that Better Being was a scam from top to bottom, but it's worth asking whether Themba's stay at Better Being was fraud, therapy, or both?

Clearly it was fraud. That was obvious from when Themba took Oupa's first call. What stands out is how many people were in on the scam. Fraud was central to the business of Better Being, and to the health professionals who attended to Themba. Oupa took a cut as a fixer, and Themba received cash backs. Compared to gold teeth, this fraud involved a far larger syndicate. The fraud over rehab had a significant impact on the MEDiPOS finances and it moved to plug the gap, largely by restricting the psychiatric hospitals where members could claim treatment.[35]

Themba went to Better Being for the cashback. It was the sole reason he took three weeks leave. Yet, his attendance was also therapeutic. He took Better Being's programme seriously and it did him good. He stopped smoking *zol*, at least for a year or two, he drank less, he made an effort to eat better (though it is difficult in the township), he learned skills to deal better with interpersonal relations, he practised techniques to reduce stress when he felt himself start to tense. As I totted up these benefits, it struck me that Better Being provided something akin to a German spa treatment, albeit chemically supercharged. In Germany, a three-week stay in a spa resort is an approved form of treatment aimed at preventative and restorative health and will be funded every three years under the German healthcare insurance system.[36] Those attending a spa go back rejuvenated into the environment that necessitated

35 MEDiPOS was put under curatorship in February 2023, primarily because of the failure of SAPO, itself put into business rescue in July 2023, to pay medical aid contributions to the scheme (Kahn 2024b).

36 Contanze (2018).

restoration. So too those who went to Better Being, after three weeks they returned to the same environment they came from and the same stresses.

Notwithstanding strong attachment of township residents to their *kasi*, township life is toxic. A never-ending carousel of demands which can't be met. Tension within families and between neighbours. Those who work face long, crowded commutes. Those without work scrape by on grants and what they can hustle from others. There is constant noise, crowded housing, few parks and, beyond dirt football pitches, limited sporting or leisure facilities. Alcohol and cannabis are the most accessible form of relaxation. All this is especially damaging for men since *kasi* culture requires them to accept it without complaint.

Three weeks at Better Being dissolved much of Themba's stress. They might have drugged him to the eyeballs with prescribed pills, but he was de-toxified from the *kasi*. It was fraud, but it was also therapeutic.

The middle class joins in the looting

Medical aid fraud illustrates how middle-class professionals work with medical aid members to defraud schemes. How does this fit into the *kasi* and looting from below? The so-called Section 59 Investigation provides a vantage point to view this question. This investigation, begun in 2019, stemmed from complaints made to the Council for Medical Schemes, a statutory body charged with overseeing the private healthcare industry,[37] by healthcare providers alleging that "they were being treated unfairly by medical aid schemes based on race and ethnicity."[38] The name of the report refers to Section 59 of the *Medical Schemes Act* which regulates how medical aid schemes may challenge claims from providers where they suspect fraud, waste, or abuse, "FWA" in the industry jargon.[39]

The core and controversial finding of the investigation's interim report of January 2021 (the final report is still pending as of May 2024[40]) was that the

37 This includes, *inter alia*, protecting the interests of medical aid schemes and their members; monitoring schemes finances; controlling and coordinating the functioning of medical schemes; and collecting information on private health care in South Africa (Council for Medical Schemes N.D.).

38 Ngcukaitobi *et al.* (2021: Section 1).

39 The Act requires medical aid schemes to, *inter alia*, raise any billing issue with providers within thirty days to allow for correction, and provides for medical aids to "claw back" from future claims made by the provider where it is deemed the provider's claim was invalid.

40 When the Council for Medical Schemes (2024) issued a notice stating that "The CMS and the Panel wish to assure all stakeholders and interested parties that the final report is close to completion and will be released and published as soon as possible."

methods used by the two medical aid schemes and medical aid administrator investigated[41] to detect FWA were not racially biased, but the outcome of these investigations constituted unfair racial discrimination.[42] Statistical evidence showed that "black practitioners were 1.4 times more likely to be classified as having committed FWA than those identified as not black."[43] This the enquiry found to be discriminatory.

If this sounds counterintuitive – fair procedures leading to unfair outcomes – that's because it is. The finding was achieved by working backwards from the Constitution's prohibiting of discriminatory outcomes on the grounds of race: if there is a different profile statistically linked to race then it must be discriminatory. But race is not the only social stratification that should be considered. Something the enquiry team fail to do in the report. Does the colour of your skin make you more or less likely to conduct FWA? Obviously not. Could other demographic and historic characteristics result in differential levels of FWA by providers? Let's see.

Individuals will band together based on shared economic interest or, in Weberian sociological terminology, class. Class, one form of social stratification or division, is defined in many different ways. Karl Marx and Max Weber, two key sociologists, use the term class differently. For Marx, an individual's class position is determined by their ownership, or lack, of the means of production, that is the core economic assets of an economy. For most people this class position remains the same from birth to death. Few people can break class barriers defined in this way, exceptions include self-made men and women who have come from humble backgrounds, and those who tumble the other way.

Weber by contrast defines a person's class in terms of their economic interest. Interest is a much more flexible and multi-potential status than ownership of the means of production. A person may simultaneously belong to several Weberian classes, depending on their varied economic resources and holdings. These are not confined to the ownership of the means of production but include, *inter alia*, skills, connections, experience, and so on. Additionally, this range of Weberian class positions can change over a person's life as they transition, for example, from child to student, to employee, to manager, to pensioner. Interests can rapidly arise and then dissipate around economic opportunities. These are the ongoing struggles between people over the

41 The two schemes were Discovery and GEMS, while the administrator was Medscheme.

42 Ngcukaitobi *et al.* (2021: Section 29.2).

43 Ngcukaitobi *et al.* (2021: Section 13.1). The investigated medical aids/administrator disagreed with the statistical level found by the investigation's own analysis but still produced results which showed black providers were more likely to be found having committed FWA than white providers.

distribution of economic resources. Thus, the Weberian concept of class is far more flexible in application than that of Marx. It does not rival Marx's conception in terms of the depth of social structure, but it does capture the immediate and changing struggles over distribution with interests changing and new coalitions – or Weberian classes – forming and re-forming.

In explaining why there is a statistical difference in the levels of medical aid fraud between white and black medical professions, we can look at the creation of two Weberian classes or interest groups in post-apartheid South Africa.

First, black health professionals. A class/interest group which has expanded with the opening up of previously whites-only medical schools[44] to black students. This group is ambitious and under pressure to demonstrate personal success while being subject to black tax (that is, demands from the extended family, particularly for Africans in a country with mass unemployment far higher among Africans than other racial groups). They are also without the generational advantages of earlier cohorts of predominantly white health professionals that had stronger family finances, social capital, and professional networks already established. While individuals differ, taken as a group, the incentive to earn extra, to euphemise FWA, is stronger among black health professionals than white health professionals.

The second interest group is that of township residents, largely Africans, in relatively low-paying but permanent employment who have become members of a medical aid as a condition of their employment. Many are struggling to manage financially and view medical aid as a grudge purchase. Some of them seek to maximise what they can get out of their medical aid by way of fraud.

In Weberian terms, classes based on a particular economic interest defend or advance that interest in alliance and/or opposition to other classes. Health professionals and medical aid members are linked by their respective positions as health service providers and members of medical aid schemes. Medical aid fraud provides an opportunity for health professionals to advance their interests in alliance with medical aid members. Something that can be understood as a joint venture *monyetla*.

The statistics with which the Section 59 Committee has been wrestling don't show that black medical professionals commit FWA and white ones don't. But that, taking black and white health professionals as a whole – the former has a statistically higher rate of FWA than the latter. While the statistical evidence correlates higher FWA to black (i.e. African, coloured, and Indian) health practitioners, this provides only a superficial explanation. It is not skin colour but how two Weberian classes (both predominantly African) have, given

44 Or at least overwhelmingly white as a few black students were admitted into otherwise white universities, something requiring permission from the Minister of Education.

their social positions within the post-apartheid period, greater incentive, and are under greater pressure, to take the fraudulent routes available.

Bounded *ubuntu* and joint venture *menyetla*

Race is, however, an important factor in the relationship between black health professionals and township residents with medical aid when it comes to fraud.[45] Sometimes the fraudulent transaction is direct, as when a doctor claims for writing a sick note at the request of a healthy patient, or a pharmacy miss-codes purchases on a member's medical aid so that they can purchase uncovered items. In other situations, the relationship may be mediated by brokers, not, as previously noted, official medical aid brokers, but fixers. Dumi was a broker, albeit briefly, when he farmed his card out for other people's gold teeth. Others are brokers on an ongoing basis. Palesa worked on commission for Dr Shumba while Oupa touted for business among state employees with medical aid.

But whether cooperation between the two groups is direct or mediated, race facilitates the relationship. The South African reality is that people are more at ease with people of their own race. It is far easier for an African medical aid member to broach the possibility of cashback with an African healthcare professional than with one of a different race. The typical stereotype of whites in the township is that they follow the rules, but that Africans are approachable. It's a perception that's important and it eases broaching subjects that both sides know are beneficial but not kosher.

These arrangements between African health professionals and African township residents with medical aid are typically framed as mutual aid; *matsoho a hlatswana*, one person helping another. Such behaviour can, as previously argued, be seen as bounded *ubuntu*.

Ubuntu, the African philosophical concept that a person is a person because of other people, is a staple of South African discourse – raised when people show, or fail to show, *ubuntu* by their actions. A person may display *ubuntu* by helping others. Somebody who acts selfishly or malevolently does not possess *ubuntu*. *Ubuntu* concerns the relationships between people that stem from their good characteristics, and which rendered imperfectly into English can be translated as solidarity.

The relationship between health professional and medical aid member when jointly conducting fraud together is one of mutual aid – one helps the other. This solidarity is however bounded because they are not the only parties

45 And by extension the same applies to white-to-white interactions and similarly for any race group in a society where race is salient. The point made is how racial congruency facilitates fraud in a context where objective social conditions create greater pressure on one race group to engage in fraud.

involved; their mutual benefit is at the expense of a wider body of people – the scheme's members, since costs are passed on to them via higher monthly premiums. Enough bounded *ubuntu* and the scheme collapses.

To attribute fraud to race is wrong. But to refuse to see race as a factor within the dynamics of South African's *lex lokasi* is naive. The extension of unaffordable medical aid to a significant number of township residents and the emergence of an African middle class subject to black tax in a hyper materialist society creates the incentive for taking the *monyetla* of medical aid fraud. This is facilitated by racial homogeneity. What is also illustrated is how *menyetla* are extending beyond the township to become part of the daily life of all South Africans.

Conclusion: Class collaboration as bounded *ubuntu*

Private medical aid coverage has expanded post 1994 among civil servants and employees of state-owned enterprises. This allows employees and family members to use private healthcare and skip long queues and indifferent service in the public healthcare system. It is, however, frequently a benefit that the employee can ill afford. Combined with short-term financial time horizons, the temptation is to maximise benefits using fraudulent *menyetla* that membership of the scheme brings into reach.

However, most medical aid fraud requires cooperation between scheme members and healthcare providers: township and suburban confederates in clandestine joint ventures. This amounts to bounded *ubuntu,* since it constitutes mutual aid, but it is bounded because the benefits shared are obtained for participants at the expense of collective provision. The class collaboration between township and suburban residents, necessary for these *menyetla* to operate, which racial affinity assists, illustrates how taking *menyetla* is not only a feature of the scrabble to survive but also about scrambling to get ahead.

10

The lockdown looting of the Metrorail

Introduction: From blocking to looting

THIS CHAPTER assesses the destruction of the Metrorail in an orgy of looting during the COVID-19 lockdowns of 2020. The account focuses, as with other chapters, on Katlehong Township, though the Metrorail looting was widespread. As described in Chapter 7, by 2020 the service on the Kwesine–Germiston line, which runs from Katlehong to Germiston, was only used by those unable to afford more reliable transport. Yet while the value of the line was diminished, it remained important for those with low-paying jobs as well as job seekers.

In 2018, two years before the 2020 looting, the line was closed for several weeks due to a protest by township residents pursuing a local grievance. The result was that trains only ran to Katlehong Station at the northern end of the township some 7 kilometres north of Kwesine, the last station on the line. This resulted in many township residents using more expensive transport. The effect of the 2020 looting was a quantum leap in impact over the 2018 shutdown. The railway was not blocked in protest but taken in theft, the cessation of services was not a matter of weeks but years.[1]

A key question the chapter grapples with is how the Metrorail could be looted in plain sight. This requires more than pointing to the incompetence and corruption of PRASA's management, outlined in Chapter 7. There were a range of actors who stood to gain from the looting, seizing the short-term *monyetla* presented, while others lost out in the longer term as cheap transport ended. A third category were those who, metaphorically, folded their arms while the looting proceeded.

1 R50 billion has been allocated for rebuilding and recapitalising the Metrorail (Mkentane 2023). A limited service on the Germiston–Kwesine line, from Germiston to Lindela station, resumed in October 2024 and a service along the full line is scheduled to start in April 2025.

The Metrorail as bargaining chip

In September 2018, the Kwesine–Germiston line within Katlehong Township was closed for several weeks due to protests by residents of Ncala Section.[2] This was just shy of a year after the Battle of Kwesine of October 2017 in which *mangobers* forced their way past security to ride the trains without tickets. The Kwesine–Germiston line runs from Germiston town centre to Katlehong Township, through suburbs and industrial areas. The township is some 12 kilometres from north to south, but from west to east varies between 3 and 6 kilometres. From Germiston the line enters the townships northern tip with Katlehong Station, there are then two further stations, Lindela and Pilot, before the last station of the line, Kwesine, which lies approximately halfway down the townships north–south axis.

Several Katlehong housing sections were electrified in the 1980s with credit or monthly read electricity meters, the bills for which many residents were ignoring. This included Ncala Section that the Metrorail passes alongside. Attempts by Eskom, which supplies electricity to Katlehong,[3] to install pre-paid meters in Ncala[4] resulted in protests, amounting to a local insurrection of several week's duration with streets blocked and vehicles torched.[5] Just as the Battle of Kwesine illustrates the limited reach of the *lex constitutional* inside the township, so too the Ncala insurrection. Similarly, very little filtered out of the township with reports of the Ncala protest-cum-insurrection getting no further than the local free newspaper, the *Kathorus Mail*.

As with the introduction of pre-paid meters in Soweto, described in Chapter 5, the resistance in Ncala was because installation would make it harder to avoid paying for electricity. When Eskom cut off power to the entire section to enforce the installation of pre-paid meters, protesters upped their own position by stopping the Metrorail.[6] Stones were thrown at trains and the line obstructed, resulting in trains from Germiston terminating at Katlehong Station.

The blocking of roads is a common aspect of protest in South Africa.[7] Though to be effective, the road must be a major artery and must be close to the settlement whose aggrieved residents are protesting. To protest beyond the township means projecting power into areas where the *lex constitutional* still

[2] This was a repeat of much the same situation that occurred in March 2015 in which the same issue resulted in the line being blocked by the same community for the same reason.

[3] Rather than through a municipality which sells on electricity from Eskom at a profit.

[4] See Chapter 5 for issues around the installation of pre-paid electricity meters.

[5] Damane (2018).

[6] Voter registration centres were also prevented from operating during an Independent Electoral Commission weekend registration drive in 2018.

[7] MunicipalIQ (2021).

holds sway. Police will be under pressure to clear protesters blocking major routes, and this is far easier if the blockade is some distance from the township or informal settlement, the power base of such protests. By disrupting traffic, the impact of the protest is increased. The smoke from burning tires closing a national road is far more effective than those burning in township streets. Nobody, other than the residents affected, really cares about the latter. In the same way, blocking the Metrorail inconvenienced few outside the township.[8] It was a dramatic move that achieved next to nothing in furthering Ncala residents' power to resist the installation of pre-paid meters. But it did inconvenience those still using the trains.

There was anger from those who now had to travel by taxi. For somebody living near Kwesine Station they now had to fork out the taxi fare to Germiston, R600 a month, or three times the monthly Metrorail fare.[9] And if they had been travelling *mangober*, as most were by late 2018, the R600 a month was infinitely more expensive than the free ride to which they had become accustomed. The taxi fare was a sizeable deduction from low wage employment; the national minimum wage in 2022 was approximately R3,600.

In Monise, close to Kwesine Station, residents were worked up about the *dom* (stupid) leaders of the insurrection in Ncala. It was pointed out that they were forgetting that people were riding the trains without paying. The protesters were also *dom* in not understanding that pre-paid meters could be bridged, just as other township residents were doing. The Ncala leaders were fighting an unnecessary battle and making their problem other people's problem.

From the perspective of the suburb, these arguments have an absurd dimension. That one section of the township was being criticised for disrupting the lives of others because the former wanted to continue stealing electricity has some logic. However, the criticism in other sections was not that Ncala residents should be paying for electricity, but that they could accept pre-paid meters and continue stealing electricity. This made their protest pointless and, to boot, was preventing people from continuing to travel *mangober* on the trains.

The Ncala protesters failed to take this criticism on board. Attempting to further escalate their protest they marched to the taxi rank on Sontonga Road intending to shut down the remaining major commuter route from the southern half of the township to Germiston and beyond.[10] There was little sympathy from other township sections and barely concealed glee when the marchers

8 If anything, Metrorail now reduced its operational costs on a line for which almost no passengers were paying fares in 2018.

9 The fare structure of taxi travel, and the time to transfer, made it impractical to travel by taxi to the township's northern tip and then transfer to the Metrorail at Katlehong Station.

10 The two other routes running north–south through the township and therefore to Germiston, Masakhane, and Kgotso streets, also ran through barricaded areas.

were faced down by taxi drivers, who were rumoured to have guns, and then dispersed by metro police with rubber bullets.[11]

The tension generated by the Ncala insurrection is important to note. The influential Rebellion of the Poor thesis[12] proposes a binary model of struggle. It frames township protests as collective struggles with the township on one side and political authority on the other. This conflict was more complex. The Metrorail was used as a bargaining chip by a community in conflict with Eskom, an entirely different state-owned enterprise, but the inconvenience did not affect Eskom nor anybody else outside the township. It was other township residents who only differed from the protesters in that they did not live in a section of the township with credit meters. And even this difference melted away when it came to the cause of their protest – it was pointless as electricity can be stolen whether you have a credit or pre-paid meter.

This local township insurrection is a microcosm of South Africa's entropic trajectory, with the *lex lokasi* increasingly the *de facto* social (dis)order of the country. In this chaotic kaleidoscope of conflict, it is the poor that lose. This is further illustrated by the looting of the Kwesine–Germiston Metrorail line in 2020 during the COVID-19 lockdowns.

Vandalism, theft, and looting

To vandalise is to maliciously destroy property. The term is used extensively in South Africa to describe the destruction of public infrastructure. This, however, fails to identify that the reason for most damage is theft. Pure vandalism does occur, as with the torching of carriages by commuters angry at been stranded.[13] However, the term is used well beyond such theft-less destruction. What is often described as vandalism is in fact theft causing direct and indirect damage. The direct damage is what is stolen. The indirect damage is the disruption and degrading of services that results and the knock-on effects on budgets, the economy, and the lives of citizens.

Looting refers to wide scale theft, typically during war or civil disturbances. The dismantling of the Metrorail infrastructure during the COVID-19 lockdown was often described as vandalism in media reports but given that the damage was a result of theft on an industrial scale, the term looting is more accurate. To call theft (or looting) vandalism does not euphemise what happened: theft and vandalism are recognised as morally wrong and criminal acts. However, the term vandalism suggests that it is the work of a mindless minority. But theft is not mindless and to use the term vandalism diverts

11 Fieldnotes: 180310 and 180317.

12 See Chapter 7.

13 See Chapter 7.

attention from the failure of the 1994 transformation project and the entropic trajectory that the country is headed on.

The Metrorail was not the only infrastructure looted during the COVID-19 lockdown. Over 1,700 schools were reported by the Minister for Basic Education to have been "vandalised" during the lockdown.[14] What follows, however, focuses on how the Metrorail was looted.

The lockdown looting of Metrorail

Theft and damage of rail infrastructure was already a major problem before the COVID-19 lockdowns began in mid-March 2020. Transnet, a state-owned enterprise that owns South Africa's long distance railways, ports, and pipelines and is responsible for freight rail services, described cable theft as having reached "epidemic proportions" with some 350 kilometres of cable stolen in the financial year up to March 2020.[15] In October 2019, the PRASA-run central Metrorail commuter line in Cape Town was suspended due to "vandalism and cable theft."[16] As the then Minister of Transport, Fikile Mbalula, observed, the outsourcing of security by PRASA was not working, despite having cost R700 million in the 2018/19 financial year. Several of the security contracts had been found by the Public Protector (2015) to have been improperly awarded, or as PRASA's spokesperson, Makhosini Mgitywa, explained in more candid terms, "Some of the security contracts were really a feeding scheme for the companies and some of the people inside PRASA."[17]

In October 2019, PRASA's board cancelled contracts with twenty security companies.[18] This left the Metrorail lines and stations unguarded, a decision that Mkhuleko Hlengwa, chair of Parliament's Standing Committee on Public Accounts (SCOPA), later described as "reckless, irresponsible, and inconsistent with financial management."[19] When the COVID-19 lockdown was implemented, Metrorail operations were cancelled and the electrified overhead cables switched off, making them easy to steal.

The combined result of withdrawn security and electricity switched off created an opportunity for Metrorail's physical assets to be stolen. This proceeded on a massive scale. Overhead cables were cut down, high mast lights at the stations toppled to strip the cables within, platforms were dug up for the wiring underneath, roofs stripped of sheeting, and offices ransacked.

14 Times Live (2020).

15 Ash (2020a).

16 Open Secrets (2021). The problem was compounded when in the absence of security informal settlements were established on the lines (Washinyira 2021).

17 Ash (2020b).

18 Washinyira (2021); Ash (2020b).

19 Washinyira (2023).

Some stations were all but demolished with roofing, doors, window frames, and even the bricks of the walls removed.[20]

It was only major stations, along with those sections of Metrorail lines shared with Transnet, which continued to operate during the lockdown, that escaped the looting. In a graphic illustration of how the writ of the *lex constitutional* gives way to the *lex lokasi*, Kwesine Station was stripped bare despite being in view of Katlehong South Police Station, with looters removing cables and roofing in broad daylight.[21] SAPS's response to the looting was generally limited to driving up and switching on their sirens, giving looters time to escape. Only in September 2020 was "an intelligence-driven plan aimed at protecting [PRASA's] assets" launched by the Minister of Transport.[22] By then the horse had bolted. It was an expensive horse; the damage to Metrorail assets has been estimated at R4 billion,[23] while the total cost of recapitalising PRASA's operations to return to pre-COVID-19 levels of operations has been estimated at R120 billion.[24]

Agency: winners, losers, and folded arms

The wholesale destruction of a major piece of urban infrastructure, without a finger being lifted to protect it, is a remarkable thing. While the withdrawal of security contracts, the cutting of electricity, and the disrepair that the Metrorail service had fallen into provides the context for the looting, the following analysis outlines the roles played by a range of actors, categorised as winners, losers, and those whose stood by and did nothing.

Winners

Those who gained immediately and directly from the looting were the looters themselves and those who bought the stripped material from them, for the most part scrap yards. Some of the material could be used by the looters themselves, such as the roofing sheets that were taken from stations.[25] Most of what was stolen was, however, sold as scrap for cash. This resulted in knock-on effects in the surrounding areas. This being lockdown it provided a boost to the illicit liquor trade described in Chapter 8 as well as generally supplementing household expenditure. This windfall injection into the local

20 Fieldnotes: 200814; 200815; 200910; and 210123. Lebakeng (2022).

21 Fieldnotes: 200814; 200815; 200910; and 210123.

22 Mkentane (2020).

23 Tshwane (2021) and Patel (2022).

24 Mkentane (2024).

25 Used to build *mekhukhu* (shacks typically made of corrugated iron).

economy was neither equitably nor equally distributed, but it was still a benefit … for as long as the looting lasted.

Once the lockdown was eased, and employers resumed operations, township residents again needed transport to reach their workplaces beyond the township. Mass commuting resumed, but without the Metrorail which was now inoperable on most lines. Alternative forms of transport benefited from the Metrorail's stripping. Particularly so the decentralised minibus taxis industry which was well positioned to transport township residents needing to get to work, to town, to college, or to labour agencies in search of employment.

And there is the benefit from contracts to rebuild Metrorail. When contracts are feeding schemes, the greater the damage the bigger the opportunities.

Losers

Since the system had been shut down as part of the COVID-19 lockdown, there were no losers until the lines were to be re-opened. Once the lockdown was lifted it became clear that there were losers. This included the working poor and students who had saved on travel costs by using the Metrorail as cheap transport, or if riding *mangober*, for free. For those on low wages, higher transport costs meant less available for other items of household expenditure.

Also affected were job seekers. Picking up casual labouring jobs means waiting outside factory gates or at established informal hire spots, the "men at the side of the road" job market. That means travelling from the township to industrial areas or suburbs. Those seeking longer-term employment must get to the offices of employment agencies. In the past, employment was a matter of being tipped off by a working relative, friend, or neighbour that a company was hiring. Few companies now recruit low and semi-skilled workers directly, but use agencies, many reconfigured labour brokers. For those without specialised skills, it is best to wait at the agent's office for when workers are required at short notice. That way they stand a chance of getting their foot in the employment door. But unless someone keeps paying for your taxi fares that's all but impossible; from the Kwesine Station area it's 14 kilometres to the agency offices in the Wadeville industrial area and 18 kilometres to those in Germiston.

The hawkers who used to operate at stations and on the trains lost their markets. Likely, some hawking trade was transferred to the taxi ranks, though if so, those who had made a living on the Metrorail now had to find a way of joining what was an already catered trade and one without on-board sales opportunities.

Some losers were not immediately apparent. One unforeseen consequence of the Metrorail's destruction was the loss of an important form of transport for striking workers. Historically, the Metrorail had been used by strikers to reach companies that were still working to bring workers out to join the strike. With a CCMA "strike certificate,"[26] strikers are permitted to travel for free on the Metrorail.[27] The loss of this assistance to strikers was noticeable in the steel sector strike of October 2021.[28]

There were also losers beyond the *kasi*. PRASA as a public entity and the government, the sole shareholder, and through them the public, lost out. There was also the loss of whatever fares were still being paid. Still harder to calculate is the overall loss to the economy of the destruction of a mass urban transport system in a country where the enduring spatial legacies of apartheid require township residents to commute long distances to work.

Join or lose

It was possible to be on both the winning and losing sides of this looting balance sheet. Low-paid workers laid off during the COVID-19 lockdown or the unemployed could make something by joining the looting. It was only later, after the lockdown was lifted but with the Metrorail no longer available, that they would move to the debit side, now paying more for transport.

In the long-term it was the poorest residents of the township who lost out. In the short-term, looters and others such as scrap metal merchants and illegal liquor outlets were winners. In the longer run the main beneficiary is likely taxi owners.

However, even assuming informed rational economic decision making, a profit and loss calculation does not determine whether an individual should participate in the looting. As with fare evasion on the Metrorail, described in Chapter 7, once riding *mangober* became the norm you were a fool not to follow suit. Of course, in the end enough fare evasion will collapse a transport system, but if it's going to collapse, one individual paying or not paying for their journey isn't going to change anything. The same dynamic, only proceeding at a far faster pace, operated during the looting of the Metrorail. Either you joined the looting and got something while it was still for the taking, or you missed out. Either way the Metrorail was going to be looted.

Folded arms

Why wasn't the looting of the Metrorail prevented? That the guards were withdrawn is the obvious answer. Indeed, the ending of the security contracts not only left the Metrorail infrastructure vulnerable but also created a vanguard of looters. The retrenched guards who had been responsible for guarding the infrastructure knew what was valuable, and how it could be stolen. They were

26 In fact, a "certificate of non-resolution" but which is generally referred to as a strike certificate.

27 Dickinson (2021b:156).

28 Fieldnotes: 211009.

now unemployed and with the economy coming to a shuddering lockdown halt had almost no chance of re-employment. Similar fears were expressed by the acting Chief Financial Officer of PRASA over the aborted plan to employ community guards on twelve-month contracts in late 2020. He questioned what would happen at the end of the twelve-month period and raised the risk of a "sudden increase in theft and vandalism."[29]

However, the explanation that the looting was a result of the absence of security alone is shallow. The PRASA-hired security companies are not the only group responsible for preventing crime; South African Police Service (SAPS), the Metro police, in the case of the Kwesine–Germiston line the EMPD, and Community Policing Forums (CPFs) are also responsible. Yet they did nothing, even when, as with Kwesine Station, SAPS officers could see the looting taking place from their office windows. Why then did they fold their arms while the looting took place?

The mandate of the SAPS is outlined in Section 205 of the Constitution. The objectives of policing are to: prevent, combat, and investigate crime; maintain public order; protect and secure the inhabitants of the Republic and their property; and uphold and enforce the law. That's clear enough, but in practice, the actions of police on the ground are not aligned to their constitutional mandate. Station commanders are evaluated on managerial targets while on the ground the police frequently operate very differently from either their constitutional mandate or management-set targets.[30] Within this paradigm, PRASA was responsible for its security, not SAPS. Supporting this black letter approach to responsibilities is that policemen are frequently also taxi owners; the destruction of the Metrorail was in their interests.

But if law enforcement bodies did not see reason to prevent the looting, should they not have been pressurised to act? Local councillors, supported by ward committees, in areas close to the Metrorail lines could have raised the alarm, yet they stayed silent. As with SAPS and EMPD, they did not see it as their responsibility to protect PRASA's property. Strictly speaking that is correct, but it ignores councillors' roles as representatives of their constituents, many of whom would subsequently suffer with the Metrorail out of action.

However, outside of election campaigns, township councillors are largely detached from their constituencies. Typically, the first thing a newly elected township councillor does is purchase a smart, new car. There is no way they would be using the trains. Their attention is now focused on family, other relatives, *macoms* (party comrades), and *dinyatsi* (boy/girlfriends), something graphically illustrated by the miss-distribution of food parcels by councillors

29 Tshwane (2021).

30 Vigneswaran and Hornberger (2009). See Chapter 8 for how the police operate in the township regarding illegal alcohol sales.

early in the COVID-19 shutdown[31] that came to be known as food parcels *tsa bosiu* (of the night).[32]

But if failed by their elected representatives, why didn't those who relied on the Metrorail organise themselves? Part of the answer is that community members were both perpetrators and victims of the looting. Those looting, or benefiting indirectly from the windfall it provided, who were perpetrators and those who would later suffer lived side by side. Indeed, they could be one and the same person.

If you did report what was happening, you would be reporting neighbours and there is no guarantee that your report to law enforcement, who might be a police officer who owns taxis and was quite happy to see the Metrorail looted, would remain confidential. There are consequences for reporting on neighbours in township communities.

But if not individually, could there not have been a collective response against the looting? Local communities in the Kwesine Station area do occasionally make decisions at mass community meetings. These are usually around the terms and conditions of renting out rooms to tenants to assist in minimising landlord–tenant disputes.[33] Nobody called a meeting over the looting of the Metrorail.

Nor was there any attempt by the range of informal security groupings of residents that are present in the area. These are often ephemeral and fractious. To defend the Metrorail offered no benefit to such groups, only risks. Indeed, to mount a defence of the stations and lines would not only have been dangerous but also foolish. Who were you risking your neck for? For PRASA. Was PRASA paying you? No. *Wa bona!* (You see! [You are a fool!]).

There was also the question as to the value of the Metrorail given its now run-down state. This was illustrated to me when after the July 2021 unrest, the subject of the following chapter, I interviewed township residents who had defended Hlahatsi Mall in Katlehong, without police assistance, and at considerable personal risk. When I asked them why they hadn't done the same for the Metrorail a year earlier, the reason given was that the Metrorail wasn't worth defending, it was already *snax* (nasty or bad), unlike the mall which was valuable to the community.

It is undeniable that the Metrorail was run down and unreliable. For those with resources to use other means of transport it could be seen as not worth saving. But that was not the case for poorer township residents. In May 2021 the local councillor for a ward adjoining Kwesine Station held a public meeting to listen to constituency concerns (the elections were approaching). There were

31 Fieldnotes: 200418.

32 Fieldnotes: 200509.

33 Fieldnotes: 180714 and 211016.

two priorities put forward by those attending: to fix the sewage system which frequently floods into streets and to get the Metrorail line running again.[34]

Conclusion: the dynamics of destruction

Chapter 7 looked at how *mangobers* rode the Metrorail without paying. *Mangobers* avoided paying fares one journey at time. This chapter has described how the Germiston–Kwesine line was disrupted by Ncala protesters in their dispute with Eskom, and the far wider 2020 dismantling of the Metrorail's infrastructure during the COVID-19 lockdown. Despite differences, there is one feature common to the three situations. Individuals in pursuing their own interests impose costs on the wider community with collective provision being undermined or destroyed.

With fair evasion and looting, the outcomes are for the most part asynchronous. The benefits were short term, the costs long term. In the case of *mangobers*, fare evasion reduced the resources available to provide a safe and efficient transport system, while the looting boosted incomes for a few months but closed the line for years.

A second feature, illustrated by the 2020 looting, is that the state failed to protect the long-term collective benefit of cheap urban transport. Those who stood by as looting proceeded were the board and management of PRASA, the South African Police and EMPD services, and municipal councillors. Since PRASA management and board were also looting (from above rather than below) and some police officers have interests in the taxi industry, there was a matrix of participating and inaction by these state factions. This was mirrored within the communities; while some community members looted, others failed to defend collective assets.

This matrix of individual action and collective inaction can be seen in all three situations and is the essence of the *lex lokasi*; contested interests that produce an ongoing social order without collective consideration. The outcome is not the result of consensus over the collective good, but action and inaction guided by individual gain which results in public detriment.

A third feature, at least of the *mangobers* and the looters, is that once a tipping point is reached, not taking advantage of *menyetla* is to lose out.[35] When PRASA's security contracts were cancelled and the power to the overhead cables switched off during the COVID-19 lockdown, looting started in earnest. Looters could gain in the short term yet lose long term. But if you thought long term, you missed out short and long term. The Metrorail would be dismantled whether you joined in or not.

34 Fieldnotes: 210508.

35 Jansen (2023:170) makes the same point about corruption, "not being 'in' on the corruption means not benefiting from what is available."

This dynamic of join in or lose out occurred because of the cancellation of PRASA's security contracts and because the electricity was switched off, but the context of the looting extends beyond these circumstances. The wider context is the failure of the 1994 democratic transformation of society, the dimming of hope for the future, and the increasingly limited reach of the *lex constitutional* as it gives way to the *lex lokasi*.

11

The July Unrest: looting, agency, and legal fetishism

Palpable fear

In July 2021 a wave of looting, targeting shopping malls and retail distribution centres, erupted across KwaZulu Natal and Gauteng provinces[1] following the imprisonment of former President Jacob Zuma. The death toll reached 350, many trampled underfoot as looting crowds panicked, some killed by community members defending their neighbourhoods. The economic damage was eventually estimated at R50 billion.[2] The July Unrest, as it came to be known, was on a far larger scale than the looting of the Metrorail during the COVID-19 lockdown of 2020. Whereas the looting of the Metrorail went largely unnoticed in the media,[3] the July Unrest convulsed the nation.

News24 journalists documented this in their book *Eight Days in July*.[4] Burning tires, rocks, and hijacked lorries blocked major roads in KwaZulu Natal on Friday 9 July, the day after Zuma's incarceration. The government's initial response was to play down events, but by Monday 12 July there was palpable fear that social order was teetering. Supply chains were disrupted and there was panic buying. My abiding memory of that morning is two elderly ladies driving at dangerously high speed out of a suburban shopping centre, the back seat of their car piled high with loaves of bread.

That afternoon I joined a citizen's crisis committee in Sophiatown,[5] a predominantly coloured neighbourhood next to my own, to defend the local shopping centre. Describing it as a committee implies a level of structure that was absent. It was based around those who took the initiative and took a stand.

1 MunicipalIQ (2021).

2 Ginindza (2021).

3 Apart from *GroundUp*.

4 Hunter *et al.* (2021).

5 The suburb in Johannesburg was the subject of forced removals in the 1950s and renamed Triomf (Afrikaans: Triumph) as a working-class white suburb. The name was reversed back to Sophiatown in 1997 and is once again a racially mixed area. The classic account of the old Sophiatown and its removal is *Naught for Your Comfort* by Trevor Huddleston (1956).

Some people knew each other. Some didn't. We were one of perhaps thousands of such groups that formed around the country as it became apparent that the police were unable or unwilling to defend shopping malls. These were the main target of the unrest, but the fear was that it would not end with the malls.

In Sophiatown, rumours had it that "Zuma's people" would arrive in minibus taxis. They were on the road. They would storm the shopping centre with the help of a crowd of assembled would-be-looters. Zuma's people never did reach Sophiatown, and no looters were able to mobilise. A small group of local youth were sent home on Monday afternoon. From then on citizen patrols, armed with an eclectic range of weapons,[6] controlled the surrounding streets and prevented any crowd formation. With hindsight, it was the Monday afternoon dispersal that was the committee's most significant act. The most likely threat to the centre came from unemployed youth who lived in the nearby run-down blocks of flats. Their timely dispersal nipped the problem in the bud.

A pyramid of agency

The July Unrest was triggered by competition between two ANC factions: those of former president Zuma and the current president Ramaphosa. Zuma's incarceration for contempt of court after he defied the Zondo Commission of Inquiry[7] triggered the unrest. It was an attempt by supporters of the former president to make the country ungovernable and shift the balance of power in their favour.

Shopping malls provided a force multiplier for Zuma's people. Crowds assembled in anticipation of looting provided what the government-commissioned report into the unrest described, referring to hostel dwellers who were mobilised to join the looting, as a "surge capacity."[8] However, it was often organised criminals who were first to enter a besieged mall, once security guards had retreated. Their targets were the Automated Telling Machines (ATMs). The Banking Association of South Africa estimated that R120 million in cash was stolen from ATMs and safes during the unrest.[9] After the ATMs it was a free for all.

Some looters arrived in high-end luxury vehicles to load up electronic appliances,[10] but for the most part the crowds that surged through the gates

[6] Including licenced firearms which provided reassurance and resolve on the Monday night when anything seemed possible.

[7] After a week-long standoff at his Nkandla rural home, in KwaZulu Natal. He was imprisoned for fifteen months for contempt of the Constitutional Court but released early.

[8] Africa *et al.* (2021:120).

[9] defenceWeb (2021). Of 1,200 ATMs damaged, 256 were broken into and thirty-six were physically removed.

[10] Africa *et al.* (2021:121).

of malls were the poor. In Katlehong, Thabo Mashinini,[11] employed to dig trenches for an internet fibre company, took part in the looting of Sam Ntuli Mall. Looters had broken into the mall early in the morning of Monday 12 July. Katlehong South Police Station is only 2 kilometres away, but the police were nowhere.[12] There were gun shots. Looters warning looters. It wasn't till Monday afternoon that Thabo screwed up courage to join.

He went, a school bag over his shoulder, entering the mall through damaged gates. By then the shops had already been worked over. Electrical goods had long gone. In Shoprite there was stock spilled onto the floor as people had grabbed in haste. He picked up tins of fish and cartons of juice, returned home to hide his haul and went back for more. What Thabo didn't calculate was that with the serious criminals having departed, the police were starting to react. They would arrive at a mall in the process of being looted and fire off rubber bullets, chase looters, and make arrests. This was too little too late, but easier and less risky than facing down a mob intent on storming a mall.

Kept overnight in the cells, Thabo appeared the next morning at Palm Ridge Magistrate's Court. Bail was set at R500, but he spent two weeks in Boksburg prison before a relative put up the cash. At work he was fired for absconding.[13] *A neighbour, Sello Mofokeng,*[14] *did better. He headed to Sontonga Mall anticipating that the place would fall and was among the first in when the gates were forced open by the crowd. He secured a fridge which he first stored in a nearby house then paid a friend who had a* bakkie *to bring it to his backyard room.*

Thabo and Sello stole. In terms of the *lex constitutional*, they are thieves, albeit part-time and not career criminals. Yet, neither saw themselves doing anything wrong. There was an opportunity, and they took it. Thabo regarded his second, not his first, visit to Sam Ntuli Mall as his mistake.

Thabo and Sello were the base of a fleeting pyramid of agency as different groups took their chances: members of an ANC faction, career criminals, and township looters. At the pyramid's peak were those who kicked off the unrest with the political objective of making the country ungovernable and restoring

11 Fieldnotes: 210814 and 211106.

12 The same police station that allowed the looting of Kwesine Metrorail station in full view of their building, see Chapter 10.

13 If a person is incarcerated they have good reason for their absence and should not be dismissed for absconding. However, the mood was otherwise at the time and dismissal of those found to be involved in the looting widespread. Given that he was dismissed for absconding, he was not entitled to Unemployment Insurance Fund (UIF) payments. When he tried to register for the R350 SRD grant he was turned down on the grounds that he had UIF payments owning. When I interviewed him in November 2021, he was unemployed and unable to claim from either bureaucracy (Fieldnotes: 211106). After a series of postponements, he was sentenced and fined R3,000 (Fieldnotes: 221211).

14 Fieldnotes: 210617.

Jacob Zuma to power. There were career criminals who assisted and used the surge capacity of looters to overrun shopping malls targeting ATMs. Rank and file looters, whether arriving on foot or in luxury cars, formed the base of the pyramid, taking what they could. A further set of agents that grasped a *monyetla* were those who did not loot, but received or bought looted goods at knock-down prices from friends and neighbours. Immediately after the July Unrest new shoes and clothing were being worn everywhere in Katlehong, even when most people in those communities that I visited had not themselves taken part in the looting.[15] The dividing line between the levels of this pyramid of agency is not always clear cut, it was not a formal arrangement, but a configuration or confederacy that emerged. Each group acting in its own interests within different contexts of opportunity, resources, and risk.

On another side: Citizens' defence groups

Unlike the looting of the Metrorail in 2020 when nobody intervened there was a response to the July Unrest. Citizen crisis committees or community defence groups emerged. These groups acted as firebreaks that contained and limited unrest. They had no part in the factional fight for control of the ruling party and hence the country, but their actions played a decisive role in shifting the balance of power between ANC factions and defeating the insurrection. The insurrection stalled when the looting failed to spread beyond the townships and city centres of KwaZulu-Natal and Gauteng.

Those who kicked off the July Unrest sought to destabilise the country, using the surge capacity of those who were willing to take advantage of an opportunity. The community defence groups sought to maintain order and to protect property. In Sophiatown, the shopping centre was defended as the front line against a tsunami of disorder that briefly threatened to overwhelm the country. The government was paralysed and the police incapable or unwilling to act. However, the locals of the Sophiatown Crisis Committee defended the centre because it was where they and their neighbours, most without cars, bought groceries, fast food, booze, and their medications, drew cash, and collected their pension at the end of the month. It was something worth defending.

Richer suburbs in Johannesburg, my own included, had even more to defend, but here citizen groups did not emerge. These suburbs were insulated from the unrest through geographical distance and the protection of private security. It was in lower middle-class and working-class neighbourhoods with less private security and in closer proximity to poor neighbourhoods that defence committees typically emerged.[16]

15 Fieldnotes: 210717; 210724; and 210807.

16 Effectively, these committees acted as a buffer between poor communities where malls were looted and richer suburbs. My own suburb of Westdene is distinctly

In Sophiatown, the crisis committee consisted of those willing to patrol the streets.[17] Word spread largely through existing community WhatsApp groups. The perceived threat held the patrollers together with personal and political differences largely put aside. It was stressed that the patrols were for "the community," there was to be "no politics" and that all were welcome to join on the basis of "All Stations! All Nations!"[18]

It was the malls and shops in the inner city and townships that were attacked and looted. In most cases these were undefended, the police absent, and security guards evacuated. There were however exceptions. In Soweto the Maponya Mall was defended by citizens as was the Motse wa Lijane Mall in Hlahatsi Section of Katlehong. Hlahatsi Mall, as it is known, was the only mall in the adjacent townships of Thokoza, Katlehong, and Vosloorus, collectively Kathorus, not to be looted during the unrest. Its distance from the so-called surge capacity of hostels and informal settlements assisted, but this was not the critical factor; it was people. In fact, to begin with just two people, Pule Motsieloa and Tshepo Nobunga, who independently began to mobilise the mall's defence on the evening of Sunday 11 July.[19] Nobunga's father was a hawker with a stall outside the mall.[20] On Sunday he had packed up early, Zuma's people were coming.

---

wealthier than bordering Sophiatown. The Sophiatown patrols effectively shielded Westdene from potential looters coming from the south and east.

17 Active patrollers were mainly men, the majority coloured and Indian along with a scattering of Africans and whites. Many of the prominent coloured and Indian patrollers were devout Muslims.

18 Like the coalition of agents that conducted the looting, the citizens defence groups were also temporary. Attempts to maintain the momentum developed by Sophiatown's crisis committee and set up a permanent safety and development structure for the neighbourhood disintegrated within weeks. The initiative was for three overlapping groups. One would continue with security patrols, one would promote local economic development to tackle the high rate of youth unemployment in the community, and the third would follow up with the municipality in terms of street lighting, water leaks etc. I was nominated as chair of the overall steering committee (one reason being that coming from a neighbouring suburb I was not party to local disputes and antagonisms). However, I stepped down once it became evident that the personal and political disputes that had been set aside during the unrest remained and that local leaders were unable to adapt to the discipline of collective decision making.

19 Interview with Pule Motsieloa and Tshepo Nobunga, 11 August 2021. The account that follows is based on this interview, follow up questions, informal discussions with other residents of Katlehong, and the one substantive media article on the defence of the mall by the Marxist Workers Party (2021).

20 In the townships practically all shopping malls, most built from 2000 onwards, are surrounded by informal hawkers who operate on whatever space can be found,

Both men anticipated what would happen, the xenophobic riots of 2019 had seen the mall attacked as looting spread beyond foreign-owned business. For both men, it was clear from what was circulating on social media from KwaZulu Natal that malls would be the primary target. As with Sophiatown, Hlahatsi Mall was worth defending. It saved the cost of going into town to buy groceries, there were ATMs to draw cash, and pensioners collected their grants there at the end of the month.

Motsieloa knocked on neighbours' doors, two joined him. He knew the guards at the mall and persuaded them that they join together and defend the mall from the outside. Once the mall is besieged it would be as good as surrendered. By standing outside they would show they were not afraid.

One of Motsieloa's neighbours was a member of the local security initiative. This assisted with spreading the message and the group's two-way radios were to be important over the coming two weeks. However, this standing security initiative was neither first nor central to the mall's defence. An indication of the group's ability to stand up to a crowd is that it only patrolled during the week. Weekends were seen as too dangerous, particularly around taverns and shebeens.

Independently, Nobunga also rallied neighbours. Both groups, at different sides of the mall, faced down would-be-looters. Sometimes it was a standoff; defenders and looters willing the other to back down. At other times there were arguments. Some of those intending to loot were locals, the two sides knew each other.

Sunday night was tense. They had no support from either SAPS or the Metro cops of the EMPD. It got worse. On Monday morning, Letsoho Mall, less than a kilometre to the east, had fallen after all-night assaults. Once it was looted a mob moved towards Hlahatsi Mall. By Tuesday the patrollers had increased in number but there was one time, in the early hours of Tuesday morning, when only warning shots fired into the night sky prevented the defenders, stationed at picket lines in the streets around the mall, from being overrun. There was a second attempt later on Tuesday morning to storm the mall with several hundred people advancing while singing zabalaza *(struggle) songs. Again, they were faced down.*

As each mall around them was overrun, the pressure on Hlahatsi Mall increased. But the tide now flowed in their favour and more locals joined the defenders, including some who had initially been set on looting. A core of some 250 defenders now controlled the area. A kitchen was established, and meals brought to the picket lines. Roads were barricaded and vehicles

---

attracted by the customers drawn to the mall. Customers will shop at both the formal and informal businesses, depending on what goods or services they require.

wanting to use the main street past the mall had to pass through a garage forecourt that the defenders used as a checkpoint.[21]

In Sophiatown, the threat and the fear dissipated after Monday night. Not only because we controlled the streets, but because of the impact of community groups across the country preventing the conflagration from spreading. It took longer at Hlahatsi, as the only mall still standing in Kathorus, and the defenders only stood down after two weeks.

Agency

The July Unrest happened because of social inequality and security shortcomings, but what should be accounted for is the agency of those involved. Several groupings that played important roles on the ground in the July Unrest can be identified: the ANC faction seeking to destabilise the country, criminal elements who took the opportunity to steal millions, the township poor who took the opportunity to steal something, the not so poor who joined in,[22] and the citizens' groups who defended their local shopping malls and centres. The police were of course a significant player in the July Unrest, initially by their failure to respond.

In what follows I look at the agency of the township poor who surged into the malls. This aligns with the central subject of this book, how township residents seize *menyetla*. However, I also examine the agency of the citizens' committees since it was these who put aside the constraints of South Africa's Constitution, its *lex constitutional*, and, in action rather than words, responded to the unrest without assistance from the state.

Agency is an almost inexhaustible resource and almost infinitely flexible, but there is no guarantee that it will succeed. It may be channelled into successful long-term strategies or thrown into hopeless, dead-end gambits. Agency is built one person at a time and if each person pursues only their own interests, society is in perpetual conflict. Social order is about how that agency-driven conflict is channelled and controlled, for better or worse.

If the July Unrest marks a moment in which the agency of many marginalised citizens shifted, openly if temporarily, from asking to taking, then it

21 The garage remained open, under the protection of the defenders. As a checkpoint it had the advantage of being illuminated and fitted with security cameras. Those driving through were asked if they consented to having their car checked. If they refused, they were blocked in by defenders' vehicles and told they would have to wait for the police to arrive.

22 The most high-profile looter in this category was the so-called "Woolies Looter," Mbuso Moloi, who looted from a Durban branch of the upmarket supermarket, Woolworth, taking his haul away in his Mercedes-Benz C300 Coupé (Nkosikhona Duma 2023).

also marks a moment in which other citizens mobilised to collectively defend what they had.

Not the smoke that calls, but the hand that takes

The dominant narrative explaining unrest in post-apartheid South Africa has been that of service delivery protests in which localised protests, riots, and insurrections are an extension of the politics of petitions. As described by Karl von Holdt *et al.* (2011), it is the smoke that calls. It calls, through disruption, for the authorities to intervene and provide for the community. Much as it involves protest, disruption, damage, and violence, it is the politics of petition. However, during the July Unrest, significant sections of the country's marginalised population, concentrated in urban townships, shifted from petitioning to helping themselves. The direction of their agency shifted from asking to taking. Looting is taking for yourself.

That doesn't mean that service delivery protests won't continue, they will if those who are targeted by the protesters still have resources to dole out concessions. If these can be given, then militancy is kept in check. But as such opportunities diminish, the vector of agency shifts. The July Unrest serves to illustrate the dangers of unfilled promises. It was a spike of violence triggered by political infighting within the ANC. In not much over a week it had largely dissipated. It should not, however, be seen as an isolated incident. The xenophobic riots that periodically erupt in South Africa also provide opportunity to loot in the township. In July 2021, instead of targeting foreign-owned *spaza* shops, attention was largely focused on shopping malls and centres.

The July looters were not protesting, nor rebelling, but helping themselves. The citizens of the so-called surge capacity of the July Unrest were acting in their own interests, even if their actions served the interests of others. Their acts were criminal, but, again, they were part-time criminals[23] rather than career criminals, opportunistically taking advantage where they could. This book has described illicit opportunities taken by township residents. For the most part this has been done without openly challenging authority or law. July 2021 was different in that for a week or so, opportunity was taken not *sub rosa* but in full view.

The looters were attempting, however incoherently, to get something of what had been promised. A better life. Seeing little hope for this within a constitutional framework, they helped themselves. Such actions when practised at scale are destructive and unsustainable. But the choice is to participate in

23 Ditton (1977).

this destruction of the future, but get something for now, or to stand aside and get nothing while the destruction goes ahead anyway.

Breaking the law to save order

The defence of property enforces the constitutional right that "Nobody may be deprived of property except in terms of law …."[24] At the same time, the need to defend property, as with the citizens' committees of July, exposes South Africa's key fault line: its continued inequality. Those who defended malls in July 2021 were motivated for different reasons. Some did it out of principle, to take a stand against lawlessness; some did it out of fear that an unstoppable cataclysm of violence would follow; some to prevent their own community's facilities being ransacked and set alight; and sometimes, as with later defenders of Hlahatsi Mall, it was, "if you can't beat them join them." Irrespective of the reason, they were defending social order. But the irony is that this was only possible by breaking the law.

The most effective instrument of community defence was restricting movement. This limited crowd formation at potential looting targets. If a crowd does begin to assemble, then before it becomes too large to handle it can be dissipated by engagement, backed up with a show of strength. However, once a large enough crowd intent on looting has assembled, defending is far more difficult and dangerous.

The last line of community defence for a mall is to physically confront and face down what is now an advancing mob that likely outnumbers defenders. Unless the defenders have firearms, they must yield the mall. At one point during the defence of Hlahatsi Mall it was only warning shots that prevented the defenders being overwhelmed. In Sophiatown, operating initially in an atmosphere of fear and uncertainty, it would have been far harder to initiate the shopping centre's defence without firearms to stiffen resolve.

Defending the malls therefore denied others their constitutional rights of movement and assembly. Theoretically, they could be legally justified: the South African Constitution permits the restriction of rights in terms of laws of general application (that is they apply to everybody equally)[25] and the implementing of a state of emergency, which curtails rights, declared by parliament.[26] But it was not under these provisions that the defenders of July operated. They were filling in where the state had failed. They operated without legal authority, setting up roadblocks, questioning and searching people, detaining those suspected of a crime and enforcing the COVID-19 night-time curfew with press-ups or other *ad hoc* punishments for transgressors.

24 Section 26(1) of the Constitution.

25 Section 36 of the Constitution.

26 Section 37 of the Constitution.

In other words, the defenders took the law into their own hands. The approach can be morally justified, yet it was beyond what the law permits. In the absence of law enforcement, citizens took on a policing function without oversight, other than what leadership on the ground provided.

The potential for this to go beyond denying movement and assembly is obvious. The most problematic situations proved to be adjoining, different, racially homogeneous communities, notably the Indian township of Phoenix in Durban and its adjacent informal settlements populated largely by Africans. At least thirty people, most Africans, were killed by Indian residents in and around Phoenix. Racial conflict played out in the context of looting along with fear and ill-discipline among community defenders. Phoenix highlights the problem of racially linked inequality as well as police inertia.

Significant media attention focused on the killings in Phoenix and the South African Human Rights Commission, a Chapter 9 Institution,[27] held hearings into this aspect of the July Unrest. The racial nature of the killings triggered outrage, though as Nhlanhla Mkhwanazi, the head of the KwaZulu Natal police, testified, the Phoenix killings accounted for a little more than 10 per cent of deaths in the province. In his testimony he outlined how "the majority of deaths in the province were a result of looters scrambling for goods and being crushed in the process or fighting among each other for stolen goods."[28]

Conclusion: Legal fetishism and the Constitution

This chapter has framed the July Unrest as the triumph of short-term gain over long-term benefit that the previous chapter on the looting of the Metrorail presented in microcosm. In doing so, it has illustrated the importance of agency in understanding events and the complex relationship between agency and law.

Public analysis of the July Unrest has highlighted two factors. First, the country's persistent inequality and the limited hope held by those left behind since the advent of democracy. The second is the inability of the state's security apparatus to respond to the crisis. Both factors are important, yet taking either as the starting point for analysis leads to the circular argument that the solution is a functioning state. The argument is circular because the solution proposed is the problem identified: the lack of a functioning state, whether that concerns security or economic development.[29]

Of course, a functioning state would solve the problems that result from the absence of a functioning state. But this it is merely stating the problem.

27 Chapter 9 of the Constitution establishes several bodies to "strengthen constitutional democracy in the Republic." (Section 181)

28 Erasmus (2021).

29 The latter argument is valid irrespective of what role the state should take, or not take, in economic development.

At the very least, the causes of state dysfunctionality need to be identified before they can be addressed.

To parrot the need for a functioning state as the solution to inequality and social disorder amounts to the same platitude as when township residents are accused of mob justice and told that they must not take the law into their own hands, yet there is no working justice system available to them. This insistence on a legal alternative to mob justice, when there isn't one, amounts to legal fetishism. It ascribes to the justice system a functionality that is absent and demonstrates an inability to break from a pre-set, elite-approved paradigm that erroneously posits that the Constitution of 1996 is still functioning.

There are nuances to how this fetish is enacted. It may be admitted that the Constitution is under strain and not working as hoped, but it should, nevertheless, be followed because it is the law of the land. Or it may be argued that its weaknesses can be addressed with constitutional rulings, more laws, and regulations. These nuances amount to the same thing, what is being recommended is the performance of legal processes that do not work. These performances neither provide a functioning justice system nor a mechanism for social transformation. Indeed, the argument that more laws need to be plastered onto already disregarded laws only results in *menyetla* proliferation.[30]

This legal fetishism smothers public discourse over social realities. Stubbornly, debate is required to proceed schizophrenically; to bemoan the inadequacies of the state yet offer only solutions that rest on it being functional. It mistakenly assumes that the constitutional framing of the rule of law can remain in place even after the failure of the post-1994 project of social transformation. It ignores how the law of the township is becoming the norm across the entire country, increasingly displacing the *lex constitutional*.

30 See Chapters 4, 5, and 7.

12

Conclusion: part-time criminals secure corrupt elites

Menyetla: Individual agency, collective collapse

THE *MENYETLA* described in this book demonstrate the agency of township residents who, far from being powerless and waiting for the delivery of constitutional promises, find ways in which to advance their interests. However, this book is no celebration of *menyetla*. Quite the opposite. I have used the term *menyetla* because it carries greater neutrality than the best English translation. But this is neutrality in terms of the *lex lokasi*. The impact of *menyetla* is not neutral but has consequences. A key point developed in the case studies is that *menyetla* provide short-term benefit for individuals, albeit accompanied by risk, but result in damaging long-term consequences for society when practised at scale.

Thus framed, we should reject the idea that *menyetla* should be applauded as challenging South Africa's inequality. By and large, the *menyetla* described *do* constitute distributional struggles within a complex configuration of class and race. But, as much as inequality is the fundamental fault line of South African society, the pursuit of these *menyetla* do not provide a viable response. Chapter 10 described the dramatic, if little reported, destruction of the Metrorail system as short-term gain trumped the long-term value of urban infrastructure serving the poor. The unchecked pursuit of *menyetla* leads not to transformation but disintegration.

The pursuit of *menyetla* reflects a collective action problem in which it is rational to pursue individual short-term interests even when this results in the undermining of social and economic institutions. Individuals, and confederacies, do what they can in the absence of leadership able to marshal progressive collective action. The collective cannot hold because social solidarity is absent.

The R350 *menyetla* opportunities described in Chapter 6 illustrate the limited social cohesion in the township. Residents were unable to establish an equitable queuing system in their own neighbourhoods. Rather, some sought to take advantage of state inefficiencies to extract from the poorest sections of their own communities.

In African idiom, social solidarity and the cohesion it provides is *ubuntu*. It is easy to preach *ubuntu*, but practice is far more difficult. What is widely practised is bounded *ubuntu*, in which members of syndicates help each other at the expense of others. But how can there be solidarity or *ubuntu* if there is not some degree of equality? South Africa's enduring racial inequality, supplemented by increased intra-racial class inequality, provides firm grounds to justify *menyetla*. These concurrent divisions are dramatically illustrated within the township as citizens struggle to survive while others scrabble to get ahead.

Struggling to survive

To draw attention to the short-time horizons that dominate the actions of the poor is uncomfortable, yet impossible to ignore. Banfield's study of a poor Italian village in the 1950s, *The Moral Basis of a Backward Society*, is today as politically incorrect as it is penetrating. Banfield's concept of amoral familism in which, outside family relationships, anything that brings advantage is fair game, cannot be directly transplanted into South Africa's post-apartheid township and its urban-African culture. Nevertheless, it provides instructive insights, including the pursuit of short-term goals over long-term considerations.

Few South Africans save for retirement. In 2020, only 1 million of the 5.3 million South Africans over the age of sixty (the general retirement age, in a country where average life expectancy is under sixty-five years) had any private pension. The rest must rely on the meagre state pension.[1] For the poor this is because they don't have disposable income to put away for retirement.

There is, though, one exception. All but the absolutely destitute contribute to a funeral or burial policy. It permits one last splash. Men and women taking their final journey to the grave in a convoy of luxury vehicles that in life they never rode, outside of others' funerals. Burial policies aside, the longest time-horizon considered by most township residents is twelve months: the annual, often collective, saving that enable the *kasi* December-long holiday, or at least part of it, to be spent in style. In this annual cycle, foresight is putting aside money to cover expenses over the long-lean month of January, before the saving starts again.[2]

This might be an uncomfortable observation, but it is entirely understandable. The poor, left without assistance, have limited choice. If we could homogenise all townships residents as poor and struggling to survive, analysis of *menyetla* would be relatively simply.

For those with little and without hope for better, it makes sense to take what can be grasped immediately. It also makes sense to grasp this by whatever

1 BankserveAfrica (2020). The state's old age pension in 2020 was R1,860 per month, compared to the monthly minimum wage that year of R3,500.

2 Dickinson (2015).

means possible, even if there is risk in doing so. There is no guarantee that the opportunity will come again, and an opportunity forgone is an opportunity forsaken. Taking risks to get ahead or keep afloat becomes the norm. It takes an extraordinary internal moral compass to override this logic, for which there will not be praise from peers but contempt for lack of nous.

The willingness with which the township poor grasp *menyetla*, and the insecurity that results, is a product of fatalism. If the transformational promise of 1994 remained credible there would be hope for the future and faith in those driving change. Instead, township talk frequently leads to a multitude of lay and folk explanations as to how events are manipulated by others. What these disparate explanations are correct about is that the narrators are not in control and those who are in control are taking for themselves. Taken in the aggregate, there is nothing conspiratorial about these theories; the peddlers are in control of very little beyond what they can afford at month's end, an annual splurge, and a final show that was unaffordable in life.

Scrambling to get ahead

However, it is not only the poor that take up *menyetla* in the township. The township's African middle class, previously comprised of teachers, administrators, police officers, and nurses as the only professions open to Africans under apartheid, has expanded rapidly. Apartheid's arresting of urbanisation and class differentiation of the African population limited the growth of the African middle class. The ending of these restrictions, along with the opportunities of access to higher education, affirmative action policies, and expanded state employment with the advent of democracy has seen the African middle class expand. Often, formal employment is combined with entrepreneurial activities, as regular salaries are used to start and support businesses.

This emerging entrepreneurial African class, while ahead of their poorer neighbours, is burdened with its own precariousness, a common feature of all newly emerging middle classes, who start with little but seek much, what Saul Alinsky described, in the American context, as the "Have-a-Little, Want Mores."[3] All the more so in a society with a hyper-materialist definition of success. Wealth must be displayed even though there is little inherited social or economic capital and financial foundations are precarious.

This scramble to get ahead is also a distributional struggle. For rising African entrepreneurs, one waged on two fronts. The first is to capture what whites previously monopolised under apartheid. This struggle is assisted by post-apartheid policies aimed at uplifting the previous disadvantaged, but which in practice have primarily benefited this new black middle-class

[3] Part of his class trinity along with the Haves and the Have-Nots (Alinsky 1989).

fraction of the population. The second front is against customers, clients, and employees in their entrepreneurial endeavours. Here this emerging middle class must tread other Africans underfoot if they are to get ahead, squeezing profits from tight margins.

The exploitation of Africans by the post-1994 entrepreneurial African class is seen, *inter alia*, in the business practices of the black taxi industry, labour broking (and its various reincarnations), residential rentals, and property development. Labour broking provides a clear illustration of this two-front struggle in the scramble to get ahead.

On the one front, African-owned labour broking companies have empowerment credentials giving them privileged access to supply labour to state-owned enterprise or private companies seeking to burnish their own empowerment status. Whites are squeezed on this front, even if they still retain the advantage of inherited economic and social capital. But African entrepreneurs are in competition with each other as they are squeezed by those with whom they contract seeking the cheapest supply of labour. This plays out on the second front; African entrepreneurs must squeeze the workers they employ, since the predominantly white-owned private companies, municipalities, and state-owned enterprises they are contracting with are squeezing them, either to maximise profits or keep to ever tighter budgets. The result is that Africans exploit Africans through systems that maintain precarious, cheap labour.[4]

Frank discussions with members of this African entrepreneurial class surfaces a business philosophy in which they argue that they understand their own race, by which they mean they know the *menyetla* that Africans employees will pursue. To survive as a business, they must give no quarter if they are not themselves to be taken for a ride.[5] Fighting on two fronts to get ahead they must cut corners; using payment systems for the drivers of their taxis that promote reckless driving, exploiting loopholes in labour legislation to hyper exploit casual workers, renting rooms built without planning permission, and evicting without reference to South Africa's eviction laws.

This explains the taking up of *menyetla* by those who, for example, may be able to afford to pay for their electricity, but rather install a T-junction to slash their bills. Those scrambling to succeed take up *menyetla* as part of their attempts to get ahead. What can be saved on electricity can be used to make money elsewhere and, ultimately, establish themselves as somebody who has succeeded.

Medical aid fraud, described in Chapter 9, requires cooperation between scheme members and healthcare providers: a syndicate of township and suburban confederates. This race-facilitated class collaboration between

4 See Chapters 2 and 12 of Dickinson (2021b).

5 Fieldnotes: 230721.

township and suburb illustrates how taking *menyetla* is not only about the scrabble to survive but also scrambling to get ahead.

Coming to the suburb

Chapter 1 outlined how the country's infrastructure is collapsing inwards, from the periphery to the centre. The same applies to practised norms. Since most South African readers reside in the suburbs, the township provides a vantage point to see where we are heading. The *lex lokasi* is entering the suburbs as the *lex constitutional*, up till now the predominant law of the suburb, recedes.

Look no further than your neighbourhood WhatsApp group to see this taking place. The following extract from my own suburb is edited for clarity but still retains the chaotic nature of debate generated on WhatsApp groups, especially when participants are angry, frustrated, and confused. But the drift is clear.

The conversation is about the increasing unreliability of the electrical supply provided by Johannesburg's City Power, a municipal company that resells Eskom electricity. Not only is there regular loadshedding resulting from the national electricity crisis described in Chapter 5, but the ageing infrastructure means unscheduled blackouts for individual houses, streets, or the whole neighbourhood that may not be resolved for days on end.

There are several themes running through the twenty-seven messages reproduced below (in their original order but with some interspaced messages, raising different issues, omitted). What drives the discussion is frustration as participants see the comfort of their previous lifestyles eroded. They share analysis of why this is happening which includes: overloading of the network, lack of maintenance, slow repairs by technicians, illegal connections, and bribery. They also make suggestions as to what they could do to resolve the situation, but frustratingly realise that these are not going to change anything. There is a palpable sense that the law should be kept, but also a reluctant realisation on the part of some that this may no longer be possible. What emerges is a disjointed discussion as to whether they should not also turn to bribery.

There are thirteen suburban residents in the conversation. One, Suburban Resident C, has by far the best understanding of the electricity supply system. It is this resident who offers the only practical solution at the individual level for those who want their power restored quickly; go to the depot and bribe a technician to fix the fault (ahead of others in the queue). The suggestion is met with a range of responses. Suburban Resident A asks, "Is the only viable solution to turn to bribery and commit corruption?" Others are indignant at the suggestion, yet the conversation is a peer education process in which those residents with a greater understanding point out that those who want to get their power restored quickly are going to have to abandon the *lex constitutional*.

The last comment, that of Suburban Resident M, points out what everybody knows; that the problem is not just in their suburb, but across Johannesburg.

If this summary of the conversation makes the point, then you can jump the boxed text.

Suburban WhatsApp Group Discussion, August 2023

[Some houses in the suburb have been without electricity for days and frustration is rising.]

Suburban Resident A: Each person fighting for him/herself does not achieve much. Does anyone have a workable idea to create a group or something with more power?

Suburban Resident B: Is it too much to ask to have our basic needs fill by supplying us with water and power for which we pay no less.

Suburban Resident C: You can also rock up there [the City Power depot] and grab a technician. Option [is] to pay a bribe and get it reconnected.

Suburban Resident A: That should not be a thing!

Suburban Resident C: Unfortunately, that is the reality, almost like there are repairing like shit, taking long on purpose to get paid under the table to fix.

Suburban Resident D: This is criminal and cannot believe this even stated on this group 😠

Suburban Resident E: I can't believe you are condoning bribes!

Suburban Resident C: Also, it's why communes can be illegally connected, and informal settlements gets power with city power cables. Whole thing is corrupt.

Suburban Resident E: So we approve corrupt???

Suburban Resident F: Yes, it is all corrupt, but we need to highlight this and demand proper services for the rates we pay.

Suburban Resident C: No, definitely not [approving corruption], but if residents can't wait to follow normal protocols [for faults to be fixed] that is the only way to speed it up.

Suburban Resident D: This is worrying.

Suburban Resident E: Very. So, we are supporting corruption?

Suburban Resident B: Not knowingly, or willingly, but yes

Suburban Resident A: The point is, we are paying bloody much each month for services, and it happens quite often that these services are not delivered. When we log tickets these are INTENTIONALLY ignored by the city workers. They are quite proud of being able to get paid for repeatedly claiming to have fixed the same issue without even going there. Is the only viable solution to turn to bribery and commit corruption? There must be something else to do, other than sitting and waiting around.

Suburban Resident G: What about we go into the streets and strike?
Suburban Resident A: I really think that is something we should consider.
Suburban Resident H: The only thing these people will understand is when the money is cut off.
Suburban Resident A: Good luck with that. You don't pay, they cut you off and then charge a reconnection fee.
Suburban Resident I: To turn to bribery and corruption would just exacerbate the problem – we would quite literally be digging the very deep hole that we find ourselves in even deeper. As taxpayers and as citizens who pay hard earned blood and sweat money for every unit of electricity that we use (when we have it), it is our right to expect the prompt, efficient, and effective service from CoJ [City of Johannesburg] and those they partner with or employ. Any attempts to extricate bribes for preferential treatment should immediately be reported to our local ward councillors who must then report it to CoJ and they should also monitor what was done about said report and give feedback to their communities.
Suburban Resident A: Ok. This long rant has been fun, but quite frankly it is going nowhere and achieving nothing, so unless anyone has a real actionable idea, I am out of this conversation.
Suburban Resident D: Some people have had no electricity for days and even 13 days … question is how do we help them …
Suburban Resident J: The law is the one thing the [ANC] comrades have not managed to control yet. At least not in its entirety. Someone said earlier that the only way to get them to do anything is by cutting off the money stream. A class action lawsuit for breach of contract could allow us to take action without making us guilty of non-payment. It's obviously not a quick fix, but it may be something to consider.
Suburban Resident C: Unfortunately, they wrote them [laws], compromised long ago, criminals are protected.
Suburban Resident K: Maybe someone can organize a group of protestors to have the response time reduced or even have the problems fixed or, better still, ensure these problems just don't happen!!!
Suburban Resident L: Looking forward to you organising protest.
Suburban Resident M: Listening to the voice messages. We are not the only suburb in Johannesburg having this problem many or most are.

Much as this book has explored *menyetla* in African townships and contrasted this with the *lex constitutional* of the suburb, this division is breaking down. The different *de facto* systems of law operating in township and suburb are increasingly converging. This is not a smooth transition. As illustrated in the case studies there is oscillation between *leges*; between the *lex lokasi* and *lex constitutional*. The former can make use of the latter, the latter is able to temporarily suppress the former. But, taking these oscillations into account, the direction is clear. The *lex lokasi* is on track to become the *de facto* law of the land.

A different track?

Can this trajectory be changed? In theory, yes. In practice, unlikely anytime soon. The best prediction of the future is the past; the best prediction for a deteriorating situation is that it will get worse. The destruction of the Metrorail in 2020 and the July Unrest of 2021 sign the road ahead, though the unfolding destruction is not just physical but also of institutional capacity and social solidarity.

The taking of *menyetla* illustrates that in the township it is the *lex lokasi* that predominates. The transformation project of 1994 has stalled, and a realignment of social forces is stymied by a constitution intended to drive the transformation. Inequality remains the hallmark of South African society and rage smoulders. A problem with believing that you have the best constitution in the world, because it is the most progressive, is that it is difficult to recognise or admit that it increasingly detached from social reality. Its enabling laws are increasingly bypassed, and the institutions of constitutional enforcement are being informally remoulded. Nowhere is this clearer than in the township where social order is increasing the *lex lokasi*, not the *lex constitutional*. That the project of constitutional transformation is increasingly detached from social reality does not mean that social change has stopped. South African society is transforming, not through legal reform as was intended, but through practised social norms.

Turning points are easy to proclaim, but hard to predict and even harder to bring about. The fundamental cause of South Africa's entropic trajectory is inequality. It is this that propels the hard scrabble to survive and the amoral scramble to get ahead. Temper inequality and you abate social cancers, whether corruption, crime, addictions, domestic violence, the *menyetla* of this book, or anything else. Yet South Africa's inequality remains entrenched after thirty years of intended transformation. Any solution to the country's unfolding crisis, however dressed up as thinking out of the box, as innovation, as a new approach, or similar consultant speak, that does not address inequality is verbal garbage.

Yet, as much as inequality of wealth and opportunity is ever present in public discourse, it remains unchallenged. Attempts to do so, such as the expropriation debate noted in Chapter 4, fizzle out inconclusively. Rather what results is more law and regulation. However, with the fundamental problem of inequality remaining, these do not change but merely regulate, indeed entrench, the *status quo*. This legal fetishism, a cycle of every more laws, assumes a capable state able to drive transformation if only given the right laws. A capable state could deliver socio-economic development, social stability, and the rule of law.[6] But we don't have one. If there was a functioning state, the looting of the Metrorail described in Chapter 10 would not have happened and the July Unrest described in Chapter 11 would not have taken place. Those proposing ever more legal regulation do not understand, or do not want to know, that this approach is ineffective, if not counterproductive, when attempted in a society that follows the *lex lokasi* and not the *lex constitutional*.

Chapter 8 focused on the opportunities presented in the township during COVID-19 lockdown prohibition. Prohibition proclamations, and the parallel ban on cigarette sales, must take the *mampara* prize for stupidity.[7] Lockdown in the township was, beyond the first few weeks, little more than the imagination of government ministers and suburban residents, illustrating yet again the extent of social distance in South Africa. All prohibition achieved was higher prices and opportunities for extortion by law enforcement officers. The lockdown is long past, but the *menyetla* of illicit alcohol sales remains given the onerous requirements to obtain a liquor licence. The *lex constitutional* is usurped, with the collusion of large companies, by *the lex lokasi*.

As described in Chapter 8, the failure of current alcohol regulation is acknowledged, but the response is more regulation. Just as the lockdown regulations were largely imaginary in the townships, so too will be the intended outcome of newly proposed regulation of alcohol distribution and sales. Instead, they will further entrench the illicit distribution systems, continue turning entrepreneurial residents into criminals, provide more opportunities for extortion, and do little to prevent alcohol abuse.

Part-time criminals secure corrupt elites

Chapter 9 highlighted the proverbial rotten apples in the health professions, skelms in white coats defrauding medial aid schemes. Chapter 8 pointed out that large brewing companies are complicit in facilitating illegal alcohol sales. We could add to this list of supposedly upright suburban citizens taking their own *menyetla*. But the bigger truth is that we are all becoming part-time criminals as the *lex lokasi* becomes the *de facto* law of the land. Once *menyetla* are widespread you have little choice but to join in or lose out. It is a form

6 The argument that developmental states, that is ones which attempt to direct as well as stimulate economic activity to achieve socially desirable goals, do not work and that the state should be small along Hayek's (2004) vision only shifts emphasis onto the second factor; providing the rule of law. For free market economic policies to succeed, proponents recognise the need for the state to ensure the rule of law (which *inter alia* provides security of ownership), necessary for free enterprise to operate.

7 Dickinson (2020b).

of moral democratisation, but one that will only exacerbate division, conflict, and social disintegration. As *menyetla* proliferate, the breakdown of collective provision and the difficulty of arresting that collapse accelerates. This is fertile ground for popularism. Popularist politics, cycles of wild promises followed by disappointment and despair that generate yet wilder promises, will accelerate the country's entropic trajectory.

The Constitution of 1996 holds us to high standards which are increasingly difficult to keep. While it remains in place, we must justify in public what we cannot maintain in private. Our shortcomings make it risky to criticise others. The boldest among us will have feet of clay. Even when we find the courage to take a stand, the Constitution's complexity makes it difficult to hold elites, local and national, public and private, to account, even as the *menyetla* they pursue are of far greater magnitude than our own.

Yet if South Africa's entropic trajectory is to be checked, looting from above and below must be arrested. But this will render little if not matched with commitment, in deeds and not words, to economic equality. For this, new social formations, disciplined and committed to collective solutions, must emerge. As yet, these lie beyond our horizon but must be built from the ground up.

GLOSSARY

Where a word is identified as a "loan word" it indicates that it is now widely used across South African language groups.

Apollo lighting: high mast lighting in townships.
Bakkie: Afrikaans loan word: pickup truck.
Blackjacks: township slang for apartheid-era township (black) police.
Black tax: requirement of employed blacks (African in particular) to provide for extended family members who are unemployed.
Black taxi: minibuses used as public transport. The industry is poorly regulated with a multitude of taxi associations in, sometimes violent, competition. The vast majority of owners, drivers, and passengers are black.
Borokgong: Sesotho: place of the bridge, at the bridge (in context, the border between South Africa and Lesotho).
Bottle store: off-licence.
Braai: barbeque.
Brown bottle beer: cheaper brands of beer typically sold in brown quart bottles.
(Ho) bua maaka: Sesotho: to tell fibs (a milder term than *ho bua leshano*: to lie).
Chafpozi: township slang: a small informal drinking establishment or other hidden location.
Cool drink: euphemism for a bribe.
De facto: Latin: in fact, actually (cf. *de jure*).
De jure: Latin: in law, in theory (cf. *de facto*).
Dikupu: Sesotho: buckets or drums (singular: *sekupu*).
Dimumu: township slang: iced pops.
Dinyatsi: Sesotho loan word: mistress/secret lover (singular: *nyatsi*).
Diza: township slang for a bribe.
Dom: Afrikaans loan word: stupid, dumb.
Dompas: Afrikaans loan word: passbook (derogatory).
Dorp: Afrikaans loan word: small town.
Folkway: transmitted norms of behaviour, shared by a social group, reproducing traditional belief and conduct.

Ghost coupons: fraudulently printed electricity coupons for pre-paid electricity meters.
Green beans: township slang for apartheid-era (black) township police.
Green bottle beer: more expensive beer (than brown bottle) sold in green bottles of various sizes.
Hlooho: Sesotho: Literally "head." In context, a stew made from the flesh of a cow's head, traditionally eaten by men, usually accompanied by pap.
Homeland: so-called "tribal areas," established under grand apartheid with the intention of creating African ethno-national states. Traditional leaders (chiefs) continue to operate in these areas in parallel to democratic governance structures in the post-apartheid period.
Imphepho: Nguni loan word: dried *Helichrysum* plants, burned as incense by *sangomas* during ritual processes of contact with ancestors and divination.
Indumba: Nguni loan word: the room used by a traditional healer. Traditionally, a low rondavel (round hut with thatched roof), but any room can be used.
Inkabi: Nguni loan word: Literally an ox, but in context a hired killer, typically recruited from rural areas.
Kaffir beer: archaic term for beer brewed from sorghum, now commonly known as *umqombothi*. The word kaffir is now pejorative.
Kitskonstables: Afrikaans: slang for apartheid-era (black) township police.
Klopjag: Afrikaans: police raid.
(Ho) koba: Sesotho: to speak indirectly or to insinuate.
Koki: a marker pen.
Kos: Afrikaans loan word: food.
Kota: township fast food; a quarter loaf of bread stuffed with chips and other fried food.
Laager: Afrikaans loan word: historically, to defensively circle ox wagons, figurately; to close ranks against others.
Leges: Latin: laws (i.e. plural of *lex*).
Lejwe: Sesotho: literally stone, used in Katlehong for the street electrical supply box.
Lekoko: Sesotho: animal hide or skin.
Leqheka: Sesotho: trick or scam.
Lex constitutional: Latin/English coined phrase: literally, constitutional law.
Lex loci: Latin: literally, local law.
Lex lokasi: Latin/township slang coined phrase: literally: the law of the township.
Lobolo: Nguni loan word: traditional "payment" made by the groom's family, denominated in cattle, to the bride's family.
(Ho) loma: Sesotho: literally to bite, in context to inform on someone.
Loose draw: township slang: a single cigarette.

Macoms: Sesotho/English: comrades, particularly between Africans in a political party context, may simply refer to ANC activists.
Maele: Sesotho: proverb or saying.
Mahae: Sesotho: rural home/place of origin.
Mahala: Nguni loan word: free (no charge or price).
Maizisitse: township slang: to hide or conceal some activity.
Makwena: fat cakes, balls of deep-fried batter, sometimes sold with fillings.
Maline: Sesotho/English: a line of rented rooms.
Malome: Sesotho: uncle, specifically your mother's brother (especially if older), responsible for, *inter alia*, leading *lobolo* negotiations.
Mampara: Nguni loan word: a stupid person.
Mangobers: those who ride the commuter trains without a ticket, fare evasion. As a verb: to *mangober.*
Mara: Afrikaans loan word: but or still (yet).
Matsoho: Sesotho: literally hands, but also labour.
Matsoho a hlatswana: Sesotho, Literally, hands wash each other, as a saying: one good turn deserves another, or help should be reciprocated.
Mekhukhu: Sesotho loan word: a shack, usually made from corrugated iron. Singular: *mokhukhu.*
Menyetla: Sesotho: an opportunity (see the Introduction). Singular: *monyetla.*
Moreki: Sesotho: the person who buys.
Morena: Sesotho: king, chief.
Mosebetsi: Sesotho: part ritual and part social gathering. Plural: *mesebetsi.*
Mosefo: township slang: something, usually money, held back in secret.
Mutatis mutandis: Latin: the same, with the necessary adjustments.
Muthi: Nguni loan word: traditional medicine, often associated with supernatural effect, including witchcraft.
Nokeng: Sesotho: at the river or place of the river.
Nyaopi: township slang/loan word: crudely refined opiate, usually smoked with cannabis.
***Nyaopi* boys**: township slang: young men using/addicted to *nyaopi*, generally derogatory.
Nyoba: Nguni loan word: euphemism for a bribe (but also sex).
(Ho) panda: township slang: to hustle.
Pap: Afrikaans loan word: porridge made from finely ground maize, may be soft or stiff, the staple starch of the township.
Pass(book): identity (ID) book or card.
Phafa: Sesotho: sjambok.
Ponto: Sesotho from English pound: a two rand coin.
Quart: a 750ml bottle of beer.
Robots: traffic lights.
Russian sausage: a cooked and smoked sausage.

Rwaza: township slang umbrella term for home brewed concoctions.
Sangoma: Nguni loan word: a traditional healer who uses divination to diagnose.
Scoop: English: a container, in context a 2-litre plastic bottle.
Seven-colour lunch: a main meal, typically Sunday lunch, with a variety of coloured food items.
Se ya voma: Nguni: we agree.
Shebeen: unlicenced drinking establishment.
Skelm: a crook or scoundrel.
Skop: sheep's head.
Sharecropping: farming another person's land in return for receiving a percentage of the crop.
Skaftin: lunch box.
Smallnyana: English/Sesotho portmanteau loan word: very small.
Snax: township slang: something nasty or bad.
***Spaza* (shop)**: a township convenience store or tuck shop selling basic items.
Spot: township slang: a small scale shebeen.
Stare decisis: Legal Latin: the rulings of higher courts bind lower courts.
Straight: A 750ml bottle of spirits.
Sub rosa: Latin: concealed or hidden.
(Ho) swanka: township slang: to show off.
Tavern: licenced township drinking establishment.
Tenderpreneur: a portmanteau of "tendering" and "entrepreneur", often used derogatorily for those securing government contracts, especially when the practice includes bribery.
Thoteng: Sesotho: velt, in context, rough land around a township.
(Ho) tjhakela: Sesotho: to visit.
Tjhotjho: euphemism for a bribe.
Tjonne: township slang: without money, broke.
Tsa bosiu: Sesotho: of the night.
(Ho) tsamaya: Sesotho: to go, travel.
(Ho) tshipa: Sesotho: to pinch or to nip. In context to bridge an electricity meter, or more broadly to describe any method where electricity is diverted past the meter.
(Ho) tshipolla: Sesotho: Reversive of *ho tshipa*, in context to reverse the bridging of an electricity meter.
(Ho) tshwara phoho: idiomatic Sesotho: to rob or mug somebody.
Tsotsis: township slang: criminals or hoodlums.
Umqombothi: Nguni loan word: sorghum beer.
Under the carpet business: a corrupt transaction or arrangement.
Vat 'n sit: Afrikaans loan phrase: cohabitation by a couple without marriage or civil union.

Wa bona! Sesotho: you see!
Waya-waya: township slang: to go on and on.
Wors: Afrikaans loan word: sausages.
Zabalaza: Nguni: the struggle.
Zol: South African slang: cannabis, can also refer to a cannabis joint.

BIBLIOGRAPHY

Abel, Richard (1995) *Politics By Other Means: Law In The Struggle Against Apartheid, 1980–1994*. Routledge.

Africa, Sandy (Chairperson), Silumko Sokupa, and Mojankunyane Gumbi (2021) *Report of the Expert Panel Into The July 2021 Civil Unrest* (29 November) https://www.thepresidency.gov.za/sites/default/files/2022-05/Report%20of%20the%20Expert%20Panel%20into%20the%20July%202021%20Civil%20Unrest.pdf [20 May 2025].

Alexander, Peter (2010) "Rebellion of the poor: South Africa's delivery protests – a preliminary analysis." *Review of African Political Economy.* Vol. 37, No. 123. Pages 25–40.

Alinsky, Saul (1989) *Rules For Radicals: A Pragmatic Primer For Realistic Radicals*. Vintage Books.

Arendse, Shaun and Executive Mukwevho (2021) "Eyewitness: community self-defence in Katlehong, Zone 3." *Marxist Workers Party* (21 July) https://marxist-workersparty.org.za/?p=3223 [21 July 2021].

Ash, Paul (2020a) "Drones join Prasa war on cable theft." *Times Live* (1 March) https://www.timeslive.co.za/sunday-times/news/2020-03-01-drones-join-prasa-war-on-cable-theft/ [10 October 2021].

—(2020b) "Cable theft and 'sabotage' cripple Prasa commuter trains." *Times Live* (16 August) https://www.timeslive.co.za/sunday-times/news/2020-08-16-cable-theft-and-sabotage-cripple-prasa-commuter-trains/ [20 October 2021].

Association of Certified Fraud Examiners SA, Health Care Forum (2018) "Medical schemes waste and abuse." *CMS News*. Issue 1, June. Pages 10–12.

Banfield, Edward (1958) *The Moral Basis Of A Backward Society*. The Free Press.

BankserveAfrica (2020) "The income of the aged in South Africa: from private pensions to government grants" (5 March) https://www.bankservafrica.com/api/public/blogblob/5e61f851714af6004249daaf [21 September 2023].

Barabino, Benedetto, Cristian Lai, and Alessandro Olivo (2020) "Fare evasion in public transport system: a review of the literature." *Public Transport.* Vol. 12. Pages 27–88.

Barron, Chris (2020) "Restoration of rail heralds 'new era.'" *Sunday Times: Business Times* (6 December) https://www.businesslive.co.za/bt/business-and-economy/2020-12-06-restoration-of-rail-heralds-new-era/ [25 October 2021].

Bartlett, John (2019) "Chile students' mass fare-dodging expands into city-wide protest." *The Guardian* (18 October) https://www.theguardian.com/world/2019/oct/18/chile-students-mass-fare-dodging-expands-into-city-wide-protest [25 October 2023].

Bateman, Chris (2015) "Medical aids often their own worst enemies with fraud." *South African Medical Journal*. Vol. 105, No. 11. Pages 887–8.

Beck, Ulrich (1992) *Risk Society: Towards A New Modernity*. SAGE.

Bekker, Simon and Richard Humphries (1985) *From Control to Confusion: The Changing Role of Administration Boards in South Africa 1971–1983*. Shuter & Schooter.

Bengu, Cebelihle (2022) "Chief Justice Zondo reveals how money lost to corruption could have benefitted the poor." *News24* (9 December) https://www.news24.com/news24/southafrica/news/chief-justice-zondo-reveals-how-money-lost-to-corruption-could-have-benefitted-the-poor-20221209 [29 December 2022].

Bolt, Maxim and Tshenolo Masha (2019) "Recognising the family house: a problem of urban custom in South African." *South African Journal Of Human Rights*. Vol. 35, No. 2. Pages 147–68.

Bond, Patrick and Peter McInnes (2007) "Decommodifying electricity in postapartheid Johannesburg." In: *Contesting Neoliberalism: Urban Frontiers*. Helga Leitner, Helga, Jamie Peck and Eric Sheppard (eds.). The Guilford Press. Pages 157–78.

Bonner, Phil and Lauren Segal (1998) *Soweto: A History*. Maskew Miller Longman.

Brederode, William (2023) "Corrupt Kusile and Medupi tender to blame for load-shedding severity – De Ruyter." *Daily Investor* (10 March) https://dailyinvestor.com/south-africa/10193/corrupt-kusile-and-medupi-tender-to-blame-for-load-shedding-severity-de-ruyter/ [21 March 2023].

Brockerhoff, Stephanie (2013) *A Review Of The Development Of Social Security Policy In South Africa*. Studies in Poverty and Inequality Institute. http://spii.org.za/wp-content/uploads/2018/02/2013-07-SPII-Working-Paper-6-Review-of-Social-Security-Policy.pdf [23 October 2023].

Broomberg, Jonathan (2018) "Fraud threatens healthcare's future." *CMS News*. Issue 1, June. Pages 19–21.

Bruce, David (2014) "Control, discipline and punish? Addressing corruption in South Africa." *SA Crime Quarterly*. No. 48. Pages 49–62.

Budlender, Geoff (2001) "South African court rules on the state's obligation to prevent mother-to-child transmission of HIV." *Law, Democracy & Development*. Vol. 5, No. 2. Pages 129–31.

Bundy, Colin (2000) "Survival and resistance: township organizations and non-violent direct action in twentieth century South Africa." In: *From Comrades To Citizens: The South African Civics Movement And The Transition To Democracy*. Adler, Glen, and Jonny Steinberg (eds.). Macmillan Press.

Burman, Sandra and Barbara Harrell-Bond (eds.) (1979) *Imposition of Law*. Academic Press.

Burns, John (1978) "'Pass' laws, aspect of apartheid blacks hate most, bring despair and pent-up fury." *New York Times* (24 May) *https://www.nytimes.com/1978/05/24/archives/pass-laws-aspect-of-apartheid-blacks-hate-most-bring-despair-and.html [29 March 2023*].

Business Day, Agency Staff (2020) "How South Africans made a plan during lockdown drinking ban." *Business Day* (31 May) https://www.businesslive.co.za/bd/national/2020-05-31-how-south-africans-made-a-plan-during-lockdown-drinking-ban/ [1 February 2022].

Business Tech, Staff Writer (2019) "Here's how many South Africans have medical aid." *Business Tech* (28 May) https://businesstech.co.za/news/lifestyle/319696/heres-how-many-south-africans-have-medical-aid/ [10 January 2022].

Buur, Lars (2008) "Democracy and its discontents: vigilantism, sovereignty and human rights in South Africa." *Review Of African Political Economy*. Vol. 35, No. 118. Pages 571–84, DOI: 10.1080/03056240802569250.

Carnie, Tony (2022) "'Mammoth effort' and R8-billion needed to clean up SA's stinking sewage and wastewater crisis." *Daily Maverick: Our Burning Planet* (7 April) https://www.dailymaverick.co.za/article/2022-04-07-mammoth-effort-and-r8-billion-needed-to-clean-up-sas-stinking-sewage-and-wastewater-crisis/ [17 April 2022].

Chabalala, Jeanette (2020) "Bodies of 3 men found on Free State farm." *News24* (11 September) https://www.news24.com/news24/southafrica/news/bodies-of-3-men-found-on-free-state-farm-20200911 [23 November 2021].

Charman, Andrew, Leif Petersen, and Thireshen Govender (2020) *Township Economy: People, Spaces And Practices*. HSRC Press.

Chaskalson, Arthur (2000) *Pharmaceutical Manufacturers Association of South Africa and Another: In re Ex Parte President of the Republic of South Africa and Others.* (CCT31/99, 25 February).

Chatterjee, Partha (2004) *The Politics of the Governed: Reflections on Political Society in Most of the World.* Columbia University Press.

—(2008) "Democracy and economic transformation in India." *Economic and Political Weekly.* Vol. 43, No. 16. Pages 55–62.

Chipkin, Ivor (2013) "Whither the state? corruption, institutions and state-building in South Africa." *Politikon*. Vol. 40, No. 2. Pages 211–31, DOI: 10.1080/02589346.2013.798457.

—and Mark Swilling (t.) (2018) *Shadow State*: *The Politics Of State Capture*. Wits University Press.

City Power (City of Johannesburg) (2021) WhatsApp message issued 4 August.

Cloete, Fanie (1995) *Local Government Transformation In South Africa*. J. L. van Schaik.

Commission for Gender Equality (2022) *Call To Action: Call To End GBVF.* https://cge.org.za/wp-content/uploads/2022/07/CGE-SAPS-REPORT.pdf [12 July 2022].

Contanze (2018) "The German kur." (19 September) https://blogs.transparent.com/german/the-german-kur/ [20 January 2022].

Coplan, David (2001) "A river runs through it: the meaning of the Lesotho-Free State border." *African Affairs*. Vol. 100. Pages 81–116.

Council for Medical Schemes (2021a) *Annual Report 2020/2021*. https://www.medicalschemes.co.za/cms-annual-report-2020-21/ [10 January 2022].

—(2021b) *Industry Report 2020*. https://www.medicalschemes.co.za/cms-annual-report-2020-21/ [10 January 2022].

—(2022) *Low-cost Benefit Option Framework Advisory Committee Report* (Draft) (May).

—(2024) *Notice: Section 59 Investigation & Final Report Re: Progress & Finalisation of Report [Joint Statement: Council for Medical Schemes & the*

Section 59 Investigation Panel]. (29 May) https://www.medicalschemes.co.za/notice-section-59-investigation-final-report/ [9 October 2024].

—(N.D.) *CMS Council*. https://www.medicalschemes.co.za/about-cms/council/ [31 October 2023].

Cummings, Scott (2018) "The social movement turn in law." *Law & Social Inquiry*. Vol. 43, Issue 2. Pages 360–416.

Daley, Suanne (1996) "15 are killed as commuters stampede in South Africa." *New York Times* (1 August) https://www.nytimes.com/1996/08/01/world/15-are-killed-as-commuters-stampede-in-south-africa.html [6 October 2021].

Damane, Aaron (2018) "More cars burnt during public protest in Katlehong." *Kathorus Mail* (27 February) https://kathorusmail.co.za/23995/more-cars-burnt-during-public-protest-in-katlehong/ [11 March 2018].

Damons, Marecia (2022) "Liquor amendment bill might be further toughened up." *GroundUp* (18 October) https://www.groundup.org.za/article/liquor-amendment-bill-might-be-further-toughened-up/ [23 May 2025].

Davenport, Rodney (1969) "African townsmen? South African Natives (Urban Areas) legislation through the years." *African Affairs*. Vol. 68, No. 271. Pages 95–109.

—(1970) "The triumph of Colonel Stallard: the transformation of the Natives (Urban Areas) Act between 1923 and 1937." *South African Historical Journal*. Vol. 2, No. 1. Pages 77–96, DOI: 10.1080/02582477008671475.

De Certeau, Michel (1988) *The Practices Of Everyday Life*. University of California Press.

defenceWeb (2021) "Unrest saw R120 million in cash stolen from ATMs and banks." (18 August) https://www.defenceweb.co.za/security/civil-security/unrest-saw-r120-million-in-cash-stolen-from-atms-and-banks/ [20 May 2025].

Deloitte (2017) "An overview of electricity consumption and pricing in South Africa." 27 February. Report prepared for Eskom Holdings SOC Ltd.

Department of Co-operative Governance and Traditional Affairs and European Commission (2009) "Township transformation timeline." https://www.sacities.net/publication/township-transformation-timeline/ [26 June 2022].

Department of Home Affairs (2019) "Updated advisory: requirements for children travelling through South African ports of entry." https://www.dha.gov.za/index.php/statements-speeches/621-updated-advisory-new-requirements-for-children-travelling-through-south-african-ports-of-entry [20 May 2025].

Department of Industry (2004) "Regulations for the registration of liquor manufacturers and distributors, and related matters arising under the Liquor Act, 2003." *Government Gazette* 26698 (17 August) http://www.thedtic.gov.za/wp-content/uploads/nla_regulations.pdf [26 January 2022].

Department of Minerals and Energy (2003) "Electricity basic services support tariff (free basic electricity) policy." *Government Gazette*. Notice 1693.

Department of Public Enterprises (2019) *Roadmap For Eskom In A Reformed Electricity Supply Industry*.

Department of Trade and Industry (2016) "Final liquor policy paper: national liquor policy review." *Government Gazette*. 30 September No. 40321.

DEPACU (Democratic Postal and Communications Union) (2017) *DEPACU Communication To Members*. 24 May.

De Ruyter, André (2023) *Truth To Power: My Three Years At Eskom*. Penguin.

De Sardan, Olivier (1999) "A moral economy of corruption in Africa?" *The Journal Of Modern African Studies*. Vol. 37, No. 1. Pages 25–52.

De Villiers, James (2019) "Here's why Prasa thinks spending R6.5 billion building walls will make it money right away." *News24* (15 October) https://web.archive.org/web/20200411051345/https://www.businessinsider.co.za/prasa-railway-lines-metrorail-cape-town-johannesburg-durban-vandalism-train-r65-billion-prasa-war-room-2019-10 [20 May 2025].

De Waal, Mandy (2012) "Metrorail unsafe, overcrowded, dangerous." *Daily Maverick* (1 June) https://www.dailymaverick.co.za/article/2012-06-01-metrorail-unsafe-overcrowded-dangerous/ [14 October 2021].

Dickinson, David (2014) *A Different Kind Of AIDS: Folk And Lay Theories In South African Townships*. Jacana/Fanele.

—(2015) "'In December we are rich, in January we are poor': consumption, saving and stealing in the kasi." In: *New South African Review*. Southall *et al.* (eds.). Wits University Press.

—(2020a) "A contested commons: Competition for public land in the Free State." *Journal Of Southern African Studies*. Vol. 46, No. 1. Pages 149–64, DOI: 10.1080/03057070.2020.1718331

—(2020b) "Alcohol and tobacco: Time for a reality check." *Mail & Guardian* (21 May) https://mg.co.za/article/2020-04-21-alcohol-and-tobacco-time-for-a-reality-check/ [31 August 2024].

—(2021a) "Communities caught between legitimate defence and mob justice." *Business Day* (26 August) https://www.businesslive.co.za/bd/opinion/2021-08-26-david-dickinson-communities-caught-between-legitimate-defence-and-mob-justice/ [4 November 2023].

— (2021b) *In Precarious Battle: Labour Broking In The South African Post Office*. UKZN Press.

—(2024) "Access to Justice Convening: 6 June 2024: Report for Wits/UJ Socio-legal Studies Network." Unpublished report.

—(2025a) "Township ghost houses created by unaffordable transfer costs." *Business Day* (6 February) https://www.businesslive.co.za/bd/opinion/2025-02-06-david-dickinson-township-ghost-houses-created-by-unaffordable-transfer-costs/ [6 February 2025].

—(2025b) "The Expropriation Act: We are focusing on the wrong questions." *GroundUp* (28 February) https://groundup.org.za/article/the-expropriation-act-we-are-focusing-on-the-wrong-questions/ [21 March 2025].

—and Louise du Plessis (2023) "The dangerous 'solution' of emergency temporary accommodation." *Maverick Citizen* (15 January) https://www.dailymaverick.co.za/article/2023-01-15-the-dangerous-solution-of-emergency-temporary-accommodation/ [15 January 2023].

—and Louise Whittaker, Geoff Bick, Daniel Benjamin, Alastair Bruyns, Natalie Kolbe, Raziya Mayet, Nhlanhla Ngiba, Derek Schraader, and Margaret van Steenderen (2008) *Natalspruit Informal Trading Area, Kathorus Townships, Ekurhuleni, Summary Report*. Wits Business School.

Dihlabeng Local Municipality (2016) *Dihlabeng Local Municipality 2016/2017 Draft Integrated Development Plan*.

Dijkstra, Lewis, Ellen Hamilton, Lall Somik, and Wahba Sameh (2020) "How do we define cities, towns, and rural areas?" World Bank Blogs. https://blogs.worldbank.org/sustainablecities/how-do-we-define-cities-towns-and-rural-areas [21 October 2023].

Ditton, Jason (1977) *Part-Time Crime: An Ethnography Of Fiddling & Pilferage*. Macmillan Press.

Dlamini, Briget and Purshottama Reddy (2018) "Theory and practice of integrated development planning: a case study of Umtshezi Local Municipality in the KwaZuluNatal province of South Africa." *African Journal Of Public Affairs*. Vol. 10, No. 1. https://hdl.handle.net/10520/EJC-e5e2c7208

Doro, Thanduxolo (2016) *Rationale For Choice Of Fuel Used By Poor Communities: A Study Of Ramaphosa Informal Settlement*. Research Report in partial fulfilment of a Masters in Health Sociology. Wits University.

Dube, Masoka (2024) "Developer must rebuild the Muldersdrift homes it destroyed." *The Citizen* (15 May)

https://www.citizen.co.za/news/south-africa/developer-must-rebuild-the-mulders-drift-homes-it-destroyed/ [18 May 2025].

Dugard, Jackie (2009) "Power to the people? A rights-based analysis of South Africa's electricity services." In: *Electric Capitalism: Recolonising Africa On The Power Grid*. David McDonald (ed.). Earthscan/HSRC Press. Pages 264–87.

—and Nompumelelo Seme (2018) *Land Reform And The Law*. https://www.wits.ac.za/news/latest-news/in-their-own-words/2018/2018-01/land-reform-and-the-law.html [28 May 2018].

Duma, Nkosikhona (2023) "Durban 'Woolies looter' will have to wait until July for sentencing." *News24* (31 May) https://www.news24.com/news24/southafrica/news/durban-woolies-looter-will-have-to-wait-until-july-for-sentencing-20230531 [31 May 2023].

Earthlife Africa/Ferrial Adam (2010) *Free Basic Electricity: A Better Life For All*. https://earthlife.org.za/wp-content/uploads/2020/11/Free-Basic-Electricity-Final-Low-res.pdf [1 November 2021].

Egan, Anthony and Alex Wafer (2004) *The Soweto Electricity Crisis Committee*. https://mediaforjustice.net/images/pdf/Egan_Wafer_SECC_Research_Report_Short.pdf [25 March 2023].

Ekurhuleni Metropolitan Municipality (2021) "Annexure D4.1: provision of free basic electricity policy (reviewed)." *2021/22 to 2023/24 Medium-term revenue and expenditure framework (MTREF) and 2021/22 reviewed integrated development plan (IDP)*. https://www.ekurhuleni.gov.za/wp-content/uploads/2022/08/Amended-Annexure-D4.1-Provision-of-free-Basic-Electricity.pdf [22 October 2023].

Eldin, Munir Fakher (2005) Review: 'The politics of the governed: reflections on popular politics in most of the world.' *Arab Studies Journal*. Vol. 13/14, No. 2/1. Pages 141–4.

Ellis, Frank (1998) "Livelihood diversification and sustainable rural livelihoods." In: *Sustainable Rural Livelihoods: What Contribution Can We Make?* Carney, D. (ed.) Department of International Development (DfID).

Ensor, Linda (2023) "Eskom says municipalities owe it R68bn and counting." *Business Day* (7 February) https://www.businesslive.co.za/bd/

national/2023-02-07-eskom-says-municipalities-owe-it-r68bn-and-counting/ [21 March 2023].
Erasmus, Des (2021) "KZN police chief Nhlanhla Mkhwanazi shoots from the hip at SAHRC hearings, says problem lies with society not policing." *Daily Maverick* (2 December) https://www.dailymaverick.co.za/article/2021-12-02-kzn-police-chief-nhlanhla-mkhwanazi-shoots-from-the-hip-at-sahrc-hearings-says-problem-lies-with-society-not-policing/ [14 December 2022].
Eskom (1997) *Eskom Submission. Truth and Reconciliation Commission: Business Sector Hearing*. October.
—(2007) *Eskom Izinyoka*. https://www.youtube.com/watch?v=n8vjq-dD0EU [2 November 2021].
—(2017) *Revenue Application FY2018/19*. Submitted to the National Energy Regulator (NERSA).
—(2021) *Integrated Report 2021: Towards A New Energy Future*.
Eskom Media Desk (2019) Media Statement. 10 July.
Evans, Ivan (1997) *Bureaucracy And Race: Native Administration In South Africa*. University of California Press.
Ewick, Patricia and Susan S. Silbey (1998) *The Common Place Of Law: Stories From Everyday Life*. University of Chicago Press.
Falk Moore, Sally (1973) "Law and social change: the semi-autonomous social field as an appropriate subject of study." *Law And Society Review*. Vol. 7. Pages 719–46.
Faull, Andrew (2013) "Policing taverns and shebeens: observation, experience and discourse." *South African Crime Quarterly*. No. 46. December.
February, Judith (2019) "State capture: an entirely new type of corruption." *Southern Africa Report*. No. 17. https://issafrica.org/research/southern-africa-report/state-capture-an-entirely-new-type-of-corruption [5 November 2023].
Felix, Jason (2021) "Govt employees who got R350 grant won't return to public service – Ayanda Dlodlo." *News24* (13 December). https://www.news24.com/news24/southafrica/news/govt-employees-who-got-r350-grant-wont-return-to-public-service-ayanda-dlodlo-20211213 [22 December 2021].
Fiil-Flynn, Maj with the Soweto Electricity Crisis Committee (2001) *The Electricity Crisis In Soweto*. Municipal Services Project: Occasional Papers Series Number 4.
Fire Ops SA (N.D.) "About Fire Ops SA." https://fireopssa.co.za/about-us/ [29 June 2023].
Flegenheimer, Matt (2014) "Fare dodging is an organised rebellion in Stockholm, and its winning." *The New York Times* (17 May) https://www.nytimes.com/2014/05/18/world/europe/fare-dodging-is-an-organized-rebellion-in-stockholm-and-its-winning.html [26 October 2021].
Gauteng Province (N.D.) "Title deeds distribution, mediation and adjudication of title deeds." *https://www.gauteng.gov.za/Services/CPM-001004* [19 April 2022].
Geffen, Nathan (2015) "Commuters must organise to improve Metrorail." *GroundUp* (19 February) https://www.groundup.org.za/article/commuters-must-organise-improve-metrorail_2695/ [14 October 2021].
Germond, Robert (1967) *Chronicles Of Basutoland*. Morija Sesuto Book Depot.

Giddens, Anthony (1999) "Risk and responsibility." *The Modern Law Review*. Vol. 62, No. 1. Pages 1–10.

Ginindza, Banele (2021) "July riots come with a R50 billion price tag for SA's economy, says Sasria." *IOL* (17 November) https://www.iol.co.za/business-report/companies/july-riots-come-with-a-r50-billion-price-tag-for-sas-economy-says-sasria-72748b8d-b7fa-42c7-92f6-216fdc6a40cf [16 April 2022].

Government of South Africa (1948) *Native Laws Commission* (Fagan Commission).

—(1998) *White Paper on Local Government*. 9 March. https://www.cogta.gov.za/cgta_2016/wp-content/uploads/2016/06/whitepaper_on_Local-Gov_1998.pdf [4 November 2023].

—(N.D.) *Regulations And Guidelines – Coronavirus COVID-19*. https://www.gov.za/covid-19/resources/regulations-and-guidelines-coronavirus-covid-19 [18 May 2023].

GroundUp, Staff Writers (2015) "Metrorail detains customers without tickets. Is it legal?" *GroundUp* (23 February) https://www.groundup.org.za/article/metrorail-detains-customers-without-tickets-it-legal_2709/ [14 October 2021].

Gumede, Bongeka (2021) "'Tooth bling' scam hits medical aids." *IOL* (15 September) https://www.iol.co.za/news/south-africa/tooth-bling-scam-hits-medical-aids-1383729 [17 January 2022].

Haffajee, Ferial with Ivor Chipkin (2022) *Days Of Zondo: The Fight For Freedom From Corruption*. Maverick 451.

Hamnett, Ian (1975) *Chieftainship And Legitimacy: An Anthropological Study Of Executive Law In Lesotho*. Routledge & Kegan Paul.

Harding, Joanne (2021) *Women's Legal Consciousness In A Poor Urban Community: Finding Order In And Around The Law*. PhD Thesis. University of Cape Town.

Hayek, Friedrich (2004) *The Road To Serfdom*. Routledge.

Herenigde Nasionale Party (Reunited National Party) (1948) *Sauer Commission Report*.

Herrick, Clare and Andrew Charman (2013) "Shebeens and crime: the multiple criminalities of South African liquor and its regulation." *South African Crime Quarterly*. No. 45. September.

Himonga, Chuma and Craig Bosch (2000) "The application of African customary law under the Constitution of South Africa: problems solved or just beginning?" *South African Law Journal*. Vol. 117, No. 306. Pages 306–41.

Hindson, Doug (1987) *Pass Controls And The Urban African Proletariat*. Raven Press.

Huddleston, Trevor (1956) *Naught For Your Comfort*. Collins.

Hunter, Qaanitah, Kaveel Singh, and Jeff Wicks (2021) *Eight Days In July: Inside The Zuma Unrest That Set South Africa Alight*. Tafelberg.

Hyslop, Jon (2005) "Political corruption: before and after apartheid." *Journal Of Southern African Studies*, Vol. 31, No. 4. Pages 773–89, DOI: 10.1080/03057070500370555.

Illidge, Myles (2022) "Post Office can't pay staff medical aid, but subsidises government grant payments." *My Broadband* (16 October) https://mybroadband.co.za/news/government/464593-post-office-cant-pay-staff-medical-aid-but-subsidises-government-grant-payments.html [14 May 2023].

Institute for Economic Justice (2021) *Introducing A Universal Basic Income Guarantee For South Africa: Towards Income Security For All.* IEJ Policy Brief. March.

IOL (2003) "Major crackdown to start on fare evaders." *IOL* (4 August) https://www.iol.co.za/news/south-africa/major-crackdown-to-start-on-fare-evaders-110826 [13 October 2021].

IOL, Staff Reporter (2016) "Metrorail to clamp down on crime this festive season." *IOL* (22 November) https://www.iol.co.za/news/metrorail-to-clamp-down-on-crime-this-festive-season-2092302 [21 December 2021].

Jansen, Jonathan (2023) *Corrupted: A study Of Chronic Dysfunction In South African Universities*. Wits University Press.

Kahn, Tamar (2022) "Stalling by medical scheme regulator 'robbing millions of private healthcare'." *Business Day* (19 May) https://www.businesslive.co.za/bd/national/health/2022-05-19-stalling-by-medical-scheme-regulator-robbing-millions-of-private-healthcare/ [14 January 2023].

—(2024a) "Scientists slam Stats SA's 2022 census as 'work of fiction'." *Business Day* (11 July) https://www.businesslive.co.za/bd/national/2024-07-11-scientists-slam-stats-sas-2022-census-as-work-of-fiction/ [2 September 2024].

—(2024b) "Medical schemes regulator moves to place MEDiPOS under provisional curatorship." *Business Day* (16 February) https://www.businesslive.co.za/bd/national/2023-02-16-medical-schemes-regulator-moves-to-place-MEDiPOS-under-provisional-curatorship/ [9 October 2024].

Kalina, Marc (2020) "Waste management in a more unequal world: centring inequality in our waste and climate change discourse." *Local Environment*. Vol. 25, No. 8. Pages 612–18.

Kane-Berman, John (1978) *Soweto: Black Revolt, White Reaction*. Raven Press.

Kendall, Francis (1991) *The Heart Of The Nation: Regional And Community Government In The New South Africa*. Amagi Books.

Khoza, Amanda (2022) "State seeks to extend R350 subsidy until basic income grant is finalised." *Business Day* (23 August) https://www.businesslive.co.za/bd/national/2022-08-23-state-seeks-to-extend-r350-subsidy-until-basic-income-grant-is-finalised/ [23 August 2022].

Kimemia, D. and A. van Niekerk (2017) "Energy poverty, shack fires and childhood burns." *South African Medical Journal*. Vol. 107, No. 4. Pages 289–291. DOI: 10.7196/samj.2017.v107i4.12436.

Kirk, David S. and Mauri Matsuda (2011) "Legal cynicism, collective efficacy and the ecology of arrest." *Criminology*. Vol. 49, No. 2. Pages 443–72.

Klare, Karl (1998) "Legal culture and transformative constitutionalism." *South African Journal Of Human Rights*. Vol. 14, No. 1. Pages 146–88.

Laganparsad, Monica, and Nomfundo Xolo (2021) "Past and present push phoenix over the edge." *New Frame*. https://allafrica.com/stories/202108010153.html [20 May 2025].

Laslett, Barbara and Rhona Rapoport (1975) "Collaborative interviewing and interactive research." *Journal of Marriage And Family*. Vol. 37, No. 4. Pages 968–77. http://www.jstor.org/stable/350846.

Lebakeng, Tshabalira (2022) "Soweto's once bustling train stations lie in ruin – it's as if they were bombed in a war." *Daily Maverick* (5 May) https://www.

dailymaverick.co.za/article/2022-05-05-sowetos-once-bustling-train-stations-lie-in-ruin-its-as-if-they-were-bombed-in-a-war/ [16 June 2023].

Ledger, Tracy (2021) *Broken Promises: Electricity Access For Low-income Households: Good Policy Intentions, Bad Trade-offs And Unintended Consequences*. Public Affairs Research Institute.

—and Mahlatse Rampedi (2020) *The End Of The Road: A Critical Review Of The Local Government Fiscal Framework.* Public Affairs Research Institute.

Levenson, Zachary (2022) *Delivery As Dispossession: Land Occupation And Eviction In The Postapartheid City.* Oxford University Press.

Legotlo, Tsholofelo and Ashley Mutezo (2018) "Understanding the types of fraud in claims to South African medical schemes." *South African Medical Journal.* Vol. 108, No. 4. Pages 299–303.

Libera, Malcolm (2024) "How much money police officers earn in South Africa." *Business Tech* (3 July) https://businesstech.co.za/news/government/780377/how-much-money-police-officers-earn-in-south-africa/ [19 May 2025].

Lipsky, Michael (1980) *Street Level Bureaucracy: Dilemmas Of The Individual In Public Service.* Russel Sage Foundation.

Luttrell, Wendy (2005) "'Good enough' methods for life-story analysis." In: *Finding Culture In Talk: A Collection Of Methods.* Naomi Quin (ed.). Palgrave Macmillan. Pages 243–68.

Mabin, Alan (1992) "Comprehensive segregation: The origins of the Group Areas Act and its planning apparatuses." *Journal Of Southern African Studies.* Vol. 18, No. 2. Pages 405–29.

Mabuza, Ernest (2022) "Court rules against SAB, says liquor ban was necessary during lockdown." *Business Day* (28 May) https://www.businesslive.co.za/bd/national/2022-05-28-court-rules-against-sab-says-liquor-ban-was-necessary-during-lockdown/ [24 May 2023].

Madubela, Anathi (2021) "Over 200 liquor stores looted in KZN and Gauteng." *News24* (14 July) https://www.news24.com/fin24/companies/over-200-liquor-stores-looted-in-kzn-and-gauteng-20210714 [18 May 2023].

Mager, Anne (1999) "The first decade of 'European beer' in apartheid South Africa: the state, the brewers and the drinking public, 1962–72." *The Journal Of African History.* Vol. 40, No. 3. Pages 365–88.

Maggott, Terri., Mbatha, S., Ceruti, C., Moyo, L., Mporo, A., Ngwane, T., Shezi, C., and Sinwell, L. (2022) *Energy Racism Report: The Electricity Crisis and the Working Class in South Africa.* Centre for Sociological Research and Practice (CSRP), University of Johannesburg.

Mahlaka Ray (2024) "Eskom wants an increase in electricity tariffs of up to 44% next year." *Daily Maverick* (20 June) https://www.dailymaverick.co.za/article/2024-06-20-eskom-wants-an-increase-in-electricity-tariffs-of-up-to-44-next-year/ [31 August 2024].

Mahlangu, Andries (2022) "Social grants the main source of income for about 25% of homes, says Stats SA." *Business Day* (23 June) https://www.businesslive.co.za/bd/economy/2022-06-23-social-grants-main-source-of-income-for-about-25-of-households-says-stats-sa/ [23 June 2022].

Maleke, Dieketseng (2022) "Supermarkets will now pay R350 grants while Sapo stops." *IOL* (11 May) https://www.iol.co.za/business-report/companies/

supermarkets-will-now-pay-r350-grants-while-sapo-stops-a5cdff72-5724-41c1-b044-8cc66597c043 [15 May 2023].

Maluleke, Risenga (2021) *General Household Survey 2020: Measuring The Progress Of Development In The Country.* Presentation. http://www.statssa.gov.za/publications/P0318/GHS%202020%20Presentation%202-Dec-21.pdf [10 January 2022].

Mandela, Nelson (1995) "Address by President Nelson Mandela at the launch of the Masakhane Campaign, Koeberg." http://www.mandela.gov.za/mandela_speeches/1995/950225_masakhane.htm [16 November 2021].

Mashego, Abram (2025) "Prasa executives accused of paying billions in dodgy tenders, R2bn to a one-day-old company." *City Press* (2 March) https://www.news24.com/citypress/news/prasa-executives-accused-of-paying-billions-in-dodgy-tenders-r2b-to-a-one-day-old-company-20250302 [9 March 2025].

Mashabela, Harry (1988) *Townships Of The PWV.* South African Institute for Race Relations.

Matshedisho, Rajohane (2009a) "'Pour me some sugar': the relations of bribery." In: *Beyond "Good Cop"/"Bad Cop": Understanding Informality And Police Corruption In South Africa*. Vigneswaran, Darshan and Julia Hornberger (eds.). Forced Migration Studies Program.

—(2009b) "Nothing succeeds like success: the manipulation of crime statistics." In: *Beyond "Good Cop"/"Bad Cop": Understanding Informality and Police Corruption in South Africa*. Vigneswaran, Darshan and Julia Hornberger (eds.). Forced Migration Studies Program.

Mathewson, James (1957) *The Establishment Of An Urban Bantu Township*. PhD thesis Potchefstroom University for Christian Higher Education (now North West University).

Mayer, Philip and Iona Mayer (1961) *Townsmen Or Tribesmen: Conservatism And The Process Of Urbanisation In A South African City.* Oxford University Press.

McGreal, Chris (2001) "Commuters' revolt: delays prompt arson at Pretoria station." *The Guardian* (21 February). https://www.theguardian.com/world/2001/feb/21/chrismcgreal [24 October 2023].

MEDiPOS (2018). *Benefit Guide 2018*. Printed copy in the author's possession.

—(2019) "Minutes of the MEDiPOS medical scheme annual general meeting held on Tuesday 25 June 2019." Printed copy in the author's possession.

—(2022) *Benefit Guide 2022.* Printed copy in the author's possession.

Mehlwana, Luvuyo (2021) "Oral health: dire shortages of dental practitioners in public sector." *Spotlight* (3 May) https://www.spotlightnsp.co.za/2021/05/03/oral-health-dire-shortage-of-dental-practitioners-in-public-sector/ [17 January 2022].

Metrorail (N.D.) *Conditions of Carriage*.

Mgidi, Emily (2021) "R100 to get into the post office!" *Daily Sun* (24 February) https://www.dailysun.co.za/News/r100-to-get-into-the-post-office-20210224 [22 December 2021].

Mkentane, Luyolo (2020) "Fikile Mbalula unveils security plan to stop theft and vandalism of Prasa assets." *Business Day* (16 September) https://www.businesslive.co.za/bd/national/2020-09-16-fikile-mbalula-unveils-security-plan-to-stop-theft-and-vandalism-of-prasa-assets/ [20 October 2021].

—(2022) "AG Tsakani Maluleke decries lack of accountability in municipal audits"

Business Day (15 June) https://www.businesslive.co.za/bd/national/2022-06-15-ag-tsakani-maluleke-decries-lack-of-accountability-in-municipal-audits/# [25 June 2022].

—(2023) "Prasa to spend R50bn over three years to improve infrastructure." *Business Day* (27 October) https://www.businesslive.co.za/bd/national/2023-10-27-prasa-to-spend-r50bn-over-three-years-to-improve-infrastructure/ [10 October 2024].

—(2024) "Capital funding shortfall rocks Prasa, Transnet and SAA." *Business Day* (23 October) https://www.businesslive.co.za/bd/national/2024-10-22-prasa-transnet-and-saa-on-road-to-recovery-says-minister/ [23 October 2024].

Mkhuseli, Sizani (2021) "Distressed Mthatha beneficiaries cough up almost a third of grant to queue outside Post Office." *Daily Maverick* (27 October) https://www.dailymaverick.co.za/article/2021-10-27-distressed-mthatha-beneficiaries-cough-up-almost-a-third-of-grant-to-queue-outside-post-office/ [22 December 2021].

Modiba, Itumeleng (2021) "Khumalo and Eden Park post offices closed." *Kathorus Mail* (26 April) https://kathorusmail.co.za/66652/khumalo-and-eden-park-post-offices-closed/ [10 May 2023].

Molosankwe, Botho (2021) "Free State cops, border post officials found guilty of demanding bribes from foreigners." *News24* (16 November) https://www.news24.com/news24/southafrica/news/free-state-cops-border-post-officials-found-guilty-of-demanding-bribes-from-foreigners-20211116 [22 October 2023].

Moolman, Mauritz (1990) *From Town To Township*. South African Institute for Race Relations.

Morris, Pauline (1981) *A History Of Black Housing In South Africa*. South Africa Foundation.

Morrison, Ella (2023) "Lawyers fed-up with shambles in Master's Offices." *GroundUp* (17 October) https://groundup.org.za/article/long-delays-in-core-legal-services-caused-by-shambolic-masters-offices/ [21 July 2024].

Mosiah, Lerato (2018) "Funding industry related fraud: killing the goose that lays the golden egg." *CMS News*. Issue 1. June. Page 15.

Mothudi, Katlego (2018) "Collaboration and analytics vital in combating medical scheme fraud." *CMS News*. Issue 1. June. Pages 13–14.

MunicipalIQ (2021) *Why Recent Civil Unrest Was (Mostly) Dissimilar To Service Delivery Protests*. https://www.municipaliq.co.za/index.php?site_page=press.php [24 June 2023].

Mvumvu, Zingisa (2020) "Former Prasa boss Lucky Montana 'faked job offer' to get a salary increase, says Popo Molefe." *Times Live* (13 March) https://www.timeslive.co.za/politics/2020-03-13-former-prasa-boss-lucky-montana-faked-job-offer-to-get-a-salary-increase-says-popo-molefe/ [15 October 2021].

Myburg, Pieter-Louis (2017) *The Republic Of Gupta*. Penguin Books.

Naidoo, Prishani and Ahmed Veriava (2009) "From local to global (and back again?): anticommodification struggles of the Soweto Electricity Crisis Committee." In: *Electric Capitalism: Recolonising Africa On The Power Grid*. David McDonald (ed.). Earthscan/HSRC Press. Pages 321–38.

News24 (2001) "Tembisa victims honoured" *News24* (31 July) https://www.news24.com/News24/Tembisa-victims-honoured-20010731 [6 October 2021].

Ngcukaitobi, Tembeka, Kerry Williams, and Adila Hassim (2021) *Section 59*

Investigation: Interim Report Summary. https://www.medicalschemes.co.za/section-59-investigation-interim-report/ [13 October 2024].

Njilo, Nonkululeko (2022) "Corruption in municipalities is overwhelming, says Shamila Batohi." *Times Live* (25 March) https://www.timeslive.co.za/politics/2022-03-25-corruption-in-municipalities-is-overwhelming-says-shamila-batohi/ [3 April 2022].

—(2024) "Fall of 'Dr' Mthimkhulu – Prasa's former head engineer sentenced to 15 years for falsifying qualifications." *Daily Maverick* (3 September) https://www.dailymaverick.co.za/article/2024-09-03-fall-of-dr-mthimkhulu-prasas-former-head-engineer-sentenced-to-15-years-for-falsifying-qualifications/ [6 October 2024].

Nkanjeni, Unathi (2022) "More people to qualify for SRD grant." *Business Day* (17 August) https://www.businesslive.co.za/bd/national/2022-08-17-more-people-to-qualify-for-srd-grant/ [17 August 2023].

Noonan, Patrick (2011) *They're Burning the Churches* (2nd edn.). Jacana.

Nye, Joseph (1967) "Corruption and political development: a cost-benefit analysis." *The American Political Science Review*. Vol. 61, No. 2. Pages 417–27.

Open Secrets (2021) "How Prasa was looted and left for scrap." *Daily Maverick* (13 April) https://www.dailymaverick.co.za/article/2021-04-13-how-prasa-was-looted-and-left-for-scrap/ [20 October 2021].

Operation Khanyisa (N.D.) https://web.archive.org/web/20130723161436/http://operationkhanyisa.co.za/blog/entry/why-no-public-outcry-about-electricity-theft [25 May 2025].

Patel, Faizel (2022) "Mbalula says vandalised Prasa rail infrastructure repairs will cost R4 billion." *Citizen* (22 March) https://www.citizen.co.za/news/south-africa/mbalula-says-vandalised-prasa-rail-infrastructure-repairs-will-cost-r4-billion/ [16 June 2023].

Pauw, B. A. (Berthold Adolf) (1963) *The Second Generation: A Study Of The Family Among Urban Bantu In East London*. Oxford University Press.

Phakathi, Bekezela (2021) "DA wants to take over running of train services in Cape Town." *Business Day* (14 October) https://www.businesslive.co.za/bd/national/2021-10-14-da-wants-to-take-over-running-of-train-services-in-cape-town/ [15 October 2021].

—(2022) "Salary scams: Fikile Mbalula exposes another layer of rot at Prasa." *Business Day* (22 March) https://www.businesslive.co.za/bd/national/2022-03-22-salary-scams-fikile-mbalula-exposes-another-layer-of-rot-at-prasa/ [27 March 2022].

Philip, Kate (2014) "A history of townships in South Africa." In: *Economics Of South African Townships*. Mahajan, Sandeep (ed.) World Bank Group.

Picard, Louis and Thomas Mogale (2015) *The Limits Of Democratic Governance In South Africa*. UCT Press.

Pieterse, Edgar (2002) *Participatory Local Governance In The Making: Opportunities Constraints And Prospects*. UCT Press.

Plaatje, Sol (2021 [1916]) *Native Life In South Africa*. Mint Editions.

Platzky, Laurine and Cherryl Walker (1985) *The Surplus People: Forced Removals In South Africa*. Raven Press.

Posel, Deborah (1997) *The Making Of Apartheid 1948–1961: Conflict And Compromise*. Clarendon.

—(2006) "Marriage at the drop of a hat: housing and partnership in South Africa's urban African township, 1920–1960s." *History Workshop Journal*. Issue 61. Pages 57–76.

Postman, Zoë (2017) "PRASA says it's on top of security problems." *GroundUp* (16 October) https://www.groundup.org.za/article/prasa-says-it-top-security-problems/ [25 October 2021].

Pospisil, Leopold (1978) *The Ethnology Of Law*. Cummings Publishing Company.

PRASA (2020) *Medium Term Expenditure Framework Corporate Plan 2020–2022*.

Public Protector (2015) *Derailed*. Report 3 of 2015/16.

—(2017) *State of Capture*. Report 6 of 2016/17.

Pauw, Jacques (2022) *Days of Zondo*. Tafelberg.

Radebe, Rapelang (2021) "7 bodies retrieved from river at Ficksburg border between SA and Lesotho." *SABC News* (3 January) https://www.sabcnews.com/sabcnews/7-bodies-retrieved-from-river-at-ficksburg-border-between-sa-and-lesotho/ [19 May 2025].

Ramaphosa, Cyril (2019) "State of the nation address by President Cyril Ramaphosa." Speech. 7 February. https://www.gov.za/news/speeches/president-cyril-ramaphosa-state-nation-address-2019-20-jun-2019 [20 May 2025].

—(2020) "President Cyril Ramaphosa: additional coronavirus COVID-19 economic and social relief measures." Speech. 21 April. https://www.gov.za/news/media-statements/president-cyril-ramaphosa-additional-coronavirus-covid-19-economic-and-social [20 May 2025].

—(2021) "President Cyril Ramaphosa: South Africa's response to coronavirus COVID-19 pandemic." Speech. 12 September. https://www.gov.za/speeches/president-cyril-ramaphosa-south-africas-response-coronavirus-covid-19-pandemic-12-sep-2021 [5 January 2022].

—(2022) "State of the nation address (SoNA)." 10 February. https://www.gov.za/speeches/president-cyril-ramaphosa-2022-state-nation-address-10-feb-2022-0000 [15 February 2022].

Rees, Rob (2020) *Workers Experience of COVID-19: A Focus On Transport And Resistance*. NALEDI.

Regter, Shimoney (2018) "Metrorail loses R175M due to fare evasions in Gauteng." *EWN* (28 May). Printed copy in author's possession.

Rispel, Laetitia, Pieter de Jager, and Sharon Fonn (2016) "Exploring corruption in the South African health sector." *Health Policy And Planning*. Vol. 31. Pages 239–49.

Rogerson, Chris and D. M. Hart (1986) "The survival of the 'informal sector:' the shebeens of black Johannesburg." *GeoJournal*. Vol. 12, No. 2. Pages 153–66.

Rueedi, Franziska (2021) *The Vaal Uprising Of 1984 & The Struggle For Freedom In South Africa*. James Currey.

Ruiters, Greg (2009) "Free basic electricity in South Africa: a strategy for helping or containing the poor?" In: *Electric Capitalism: Recolonising Africa On The Power Grid*. David McDonald (ed.). Earthscan/HSRC Press. Pages 248–63.

SABC News (2021) "Battle lines drawn between City Power and Ennerdale residents." 10 February. https://www.youtube.com/watch?v=EXSphho8XSI [4 October 2021].

Saferspaces (2022) *Toxic Masculinity And Violence In South Africa*. https://www.saferspaces.org.za/understand/entry/toxic-masculinity-and-violence-in-south-africa [12 July 2022].

Sanders, Peter (1975) *Moshoeshoe: Chief Of The Sotho*. Heinemann.

SAPO employees (2021a) WhatsApp group conversation 24 February.

—(2021b) WhatsApp group conversation 20 February.

Savage, Michael (1986) "The imposition of pass laws on the African population in South Africa 1916–1984." *African Affairs*. Vol. 85, Issue 339. Pages 181–205, DOI: 10.1093/oxfordjournals.afraf.a097774

SCOPA (Standing Committee on Public Accounts) (2021) *PRASA Annual Report, Deviations, Expansions & SIU Investigations: Meeting Summary*. 2 March. https://pmg.org.za/committee-meeting/32420/ [15 October 2021].

Seleka, Ntwaagae (2021a) "Zandspruit mob justice: magistrate denies 9 of 14 accused bail, says murders were gruesome." *News24* (14 September) https://www.news24.com/news24/zandspruit-mob-justice-magistrate-denies-9-of-14-accused-bail-says-murders-were-gruesome-20210914 [20 October 2024]

—(2021b) "'Brutal vigilantism' prevalent in Zandspruit, court hears." *News24* (14 September) https://www.news24.com/news24/SouthAfrica/News/brutal-vigilantism-prevalent-in-zandspruit-court-hears-20210914 [27 April 2022].

Simmel, Georg (1906) "The sociology of secrecy and of secret societies." *The American Journal Of Sociology*. Vol. 11, No. 4. Pages 441–98.

Smith, Thomas (2004) "Electricity theft: a comparative analysis." *Energy Policy*. Vol. 32. Pages 2067–76, DOI: 10.10160/S0301-4215(03)00182-4.

Spink, Kathryn (1991) *Black Sash: The Beginning Of A Bridge In South Africa*. Methuen.

State vs Ndebele and Another. South Gauteng High Court. Case No: SS16/2010. Date of Judgement: 21 February 2011.

Statista (2019a) "Market share of beer producers in South Africa in 2018." https://www.statista.com/statistics/1026129/beer-market-share-south-africa/ [28 January 2022].

—(2019b) "Share of individuals who are members of medical aid schemes in South Africa from 2018 to 2019, by population group." https://www.statista.com/statistics/1115752/share-of-medical-aid-scheme-members-in-south-africa-by-population-group/ [10 January 2022].

Stats South Africa (2018) *Victims Of Crime Survey (2017/2018)*. http://www.statssa.gov.za/publications/P0341/presentation.pdf [12 July 2022].

—(2019) *General Household Survey 2018*. Statistical Release: P0318. https://www.statssa.gov.za/publications/P0318/P03182018.pdf [10 January 2022].

—(2020a) *Crimes Against Women In South Africa, An Analysis Of The Phenomenon Of GBV And Femicide*. https://www.parliament.gov.za/storage/app/media/1_Stock/Events_Institutional/2020/womens_charter_2020/docs/30-07-2020/A_Statistical_Overview_R_Maluleke.pdf [11 July 2022].

—(2020b) *General Household Survey 2019*. Statistical Release: P0318. *https://www.statssa.gov.za/publications/P0318/P03182019.pdf* [4 November 2023].

—(2022) *Quarterly Labour Force Survey, Q3: 2021*. Statistical Release P0211.

Steyn, Lisa (2020) "Of pineapples and potatoes: prices flex amid the pandemic." *Business Day* (27 April) https://www.businesslive.co.za/bd/

national/2020-04-27-of-pineapples-and-potatoes-prices-flex-amid-the-pandemic/ [28 January 2022].

Theunissen, Garth and Katharine Child (2021) "Medical aid schemes blame laws for barring cheaper health cover." *Business Day* (3 October) https://www.businesslive.co.za/bd/companies/healthcare/2021-10-03-medical-aid-schemes-blame-laws-for-barring-cheaper-health-cover/ [3 October 2023].

Thomas, Kim (2018) *The Rule Of The Gun: Hits And Assassinations In South Africa, January 2000 To December 2017* https://globalinitiative.net/analysis/the-rule-of-the-gun-hits-and-assassinations-in-south-africa-2000-2017/ [21 October 2023].

Thompson, Edward (E. P.) (1993) *Customs In Common: Studies In Traditional Popular Culture*. The New Press.

Times Live (2020) "1,718 schools vandalised during COVID-19 lockdown: Angie Motshekga." *Times Live* (6 July) https://www.timeslive.co.za/news/south-africa/2020-07-06-1718-schools-vandalised-during-covid-19-lockdown-angie-motshekga/ [20 October 2021].

—(2021) "Woman farm owner bust 'soliciting cash' for stolen vehicles to cross to Lesotho." *Sowetan Live* (21 May) https://www.sowetanlive.co.za/news/south-africa/2021-05-21-woman-farm-owner-bust-soliciting-cash-for-stolen-vehicles-to-cross-to-lesotho/ [22 May 2022].

Transvaal Local Government (1922) *Transvaal Local Government Commission (Stallard Commission)*.

Tshwane, Tebogo (2021) "Off the rails: Prasa bungles multimillion-rand plan to hire thousands of volunteers as 'guards.'" *Daily Maverick* (7 August) https://www.dailymaverick.co.za/article/2021-07-08-off-the-rails-prasa-bungles-multimillion-rand-plan-to-hire-thousands-of-volunteers-as-guards/ [20 October 2021].

Union Official A (2021) Telephone conversation 11 March.

Union Official B (2021) Telephone conversation 3 March.

—(2023) Telephone conversation 10 May.

Van der Merwe, Marelise (2018) "Electricity theft causes power cuts – Eskom." *News24: Business* (3 July) https://www.news24.com/fin24/economy/eskom/electricity-theft-causes-power-cuts-eskom-20180703 [2 November 2021].

Van Heusden, Peter (2009) "Discipline and the new 'logic of delivery': prepaid electricity in South Africa and beyond." In: *Electric Capitalism: Recolonising Africa On The Power Grid*. David McDonald (ed.). Earthscan/HSRC Press. Pages 229–47.

Vigneswaran, Darshan and Julia Hornberger (eds.) (2009) *Beyond "Good Cop"/"Bad Cop": Understanding Informality And Police Corruption In South Africa*. Forced Migration Studies Program.

Von Holdt, Karl (2019) *The Political Economy Of Corruption: Elite-formation, Factions And Violence*. SWOP Working Paper 10.

—, Malose Langa, Sepetla Molapo, Nomfundo Mogapi, Kindiza Ngubeni, Jacob Dlamini, and Adele Kirsten (2011) *Insurgent Citizenship, Collective Violence And The Struggle For A Place In The New South Africa*. CSVR/SWOP. https://www.csvr.org.za/docs/thesmokethatcalls.pdf [29 June 2023].

Van Onselen, Charles (1996) *The Seed Is Mine: The Life Of Kas Maine, A South African Sharecropper 1894–1985*. James Currey.

Von Schnitzler, Antina (2016) *Democracy's Infrastructure: Techno-Politics & Protest After Apartheid.* Princetown University Press.

Washinyira, Tariro (2021) "Commuters wary of trains as service resumes." *GroundUp* (18 February) https://www.groundup.org.za/article/commuters-wary-trains-service-resumes/ [20 October 2021].

—(2023) "PRASA's decision to cancel railway security contracts 'reckless and irresponsible' says SCOPA chair." *GroundUp* (21 April) https://www.groundup.org.za/article/prasas-decision-to-cancel-railway-security-contract-was-reckless-and-irresponsible-says-scopa-chair/ [1 November 2023].

WHO (2018) *Global Status Report On Alcohol And Health 2018.*

Wikipedia (N.D.a) *Tenderpreneur* page [25 September 2023]

—(N.D.b) *Farebox Recovery Ratio* page [24 October 2023].

World Bank Group (2014) *Economics Of South African Townships: Special Focus On Diepsloot.* Sandeep Mahajan (ed.). DOI: 10.1596/978-1-4648-0301-7

Yelland, Chris and Yolandi Groenewad (2017) "Eskom is set to make massive loss, report shows." *EE Publishers and Fin24* (16 November) https://www.news24.com/fin24/economy/eskom/eskom-is-set-to-make-massive-loss-report-shows-20171116 [8 November 2021].

Zondo, Raymond (2022) *Judicial Commission Of Inquiry Into Allegations of State Capture, Corruption And Fraud In The Public Sector Including Organs Of State* ("Zondo Commission"). Four Reports, 12 Volumes. https://www.statecapture.org.za/site/information/reports [4 November 2023].

Zulu, Lindiwe (2021) "Minister Lindiwe Zulu: re-introduction of special COVID-19 SRD grant." Speech. 4 August. https://www.gov.za/speeches/minister-lindiwe-zulu-re-introduction-special-covid-19-srd-grant-4-aug-2021-0000 [10 January 2022].

#UniteBehind (N.D.) "Get our trains back on track." https://unitebehind.org.za/campaigns/fix-our-trains/ [26 October 2021].

Legislation

Bantu (Urban Areas) Consolidation Act 25 of 1945

Black Local Authorities Act 102 of 1982

Constitution of the Republic Of South Africa Act 200 of 1993 (Interim Constitution)

Constitution of the Republic Of South Africa Act 108 of 1996 (Final Constitution)

Conversion of Certain Rights Into Leasehold Or Ownership Act 81 of 1988

Electricity Basic Services Support Tariff (Free Basic Electricity) Policy Government Notice 1693 of 2003

Electricity Pricing Policy Government Notice 1398 of 2008

Electricity Regulation Act 4 of 2006

Employment Equity Act 55 of 1998

Extension Of Security Of Tenure Act 62 of 1997

Gauteng Liquor Act 2 of 2003

Government Regulation 1036 of 1968. Regulations Governing the Control and Supervision of an Urban Black Residential Area and Relevant Matters. Drawn up in terms of the *Bantu (Urban Areas) Consolidation Act* 25 of 1945

Labour Relations Act 66 of 1995

Legal Succession to the South Africa Transport Services Act 9 of 1989
Liquor Act 27 of 1989
Liquor Act 59 of 2003
Local Government: Municipal Systems Act 32 of 2000
Local Government Transition Act 209 of 1993
Medical Schemes Act 131 of 1998
Municipal Finance Management Act 56 of 2003
Natal Province Act No. 23 of 1908
Native Beer Act Natal Province Act 23 of 1908
Native Land Act 27 of 1913
Natives (Prohibition of Interdicts) Act 64 of 1956
Prevention and Combatting Of Corrupt Activities Act 12 of 2004
Prevention and Combatting Of Trafficking in Persons Act 7 of 2013
Prevention Of Illegal Eviction From And Unlawful Occupation of Land Act 19 of 1998
Prevention Of Illegal Squatting Act 52 of 1951
Slums Act 53 of 1934
Tobacco Products Control Amendments Act 63 of 2008
Trust Property Control Act 57 of 1988
Upgrading of Tenure Rights Act (ULTRA) Act 112 of 1991
Urban Areas Act 21 of 1923

INDEX

Printed and bound by CPI Group (UK) Ltd, Croydon, CR0 4YY

13/09/2026

14961005-0005